TEACHER'S EDITION

My Little Island

3

ALWAYS LEARNING

PEARSON

My Little Island 3
Teacher's Edition

Pearson Education, 10 Bank Street, White Plains, NY 10606 USA

Staff credits: The people who made up the ***My Little Island*** team, representing editorial, production, design, manufacturing, and marketing, are Rhea Banker, Carol Brown, Tracey Munz Cataldo, Dave Dickey, Gina DiLillo, Christine Edmonds, Nancy Flaggman, Yoko Mia Hirano, Caroline Kasterine, Ed Lamprich, Theodore Lane, Christopher Leonowicz, Emily Lippincott, Maria Pia Marrella, Kate McLoughlin, Linda Moser, Leslie Patterson, Pamela Pia, Nicole Santos, Donna Schaffer, Mairead Stack, Kenneth Volcjak, and Lauren Weidenman.
Text design: Tracey Munz Cataldo
Text composition: TSI Graphics
Text font: Fiendstar Bold

Illustrations: Abraham Balcázar, José Luis Briseño
Photos: All photos are used under license from Shutterstock.com except for the following. Page 15 (top middle right) iStockphoto.com, (bottom left) Bildagentur Zoonar GmbH/Shutterstock, (bottom middle left) Robin Nelson/PhotoEdit, (bottom middle right) iStockphoto.com; p. 25 (top middle left) NASA.gov, (bottom middle right) iStockphoto.com; p. 32 (left) Anderson Ross/Blend Images/Getty Images, (right) Tudor Photography. Pearson Education Ltd; p. 35 (top right) iStockphoto.com, (bottom left) iStockphoto.com, (bottom middle right) iStockphoto.com, (bottom right) iStockphoto.com; p. 42 (left) Photodisc/Photolibrary; p. 52 (right) Picture Partners/Alamy; p. 82 (right) iStockphoto.com; p. 92 (left) Corbis/Photolibrary, (right) Charlie Loram/Photolibrary.

www.pearsonelt.com

ISBN–10: 0-13-279545-0
ISBN–13: 978-0-13-279545-6

Printed in the United States of America
4 18

Contents

Program and Philosophy

My Little Island is a three-level program for teaching English to 3 to 5-year-old children whose first language is not English. It is based on four over-arching beliefs:

Sammy the Squirrel

1. Realities of the child's world must be at the core of the program and the basis for materials chosen.
2. A learner who is engaged will learn better.
3. Each child is unique in personality, interests, and learning styles and will benefit from materials that reflect this.
4. Successful learning only occurs when skills presented build on each other and are reviewed meaningfully.

This unique and engaging program takes children on an exciting fantasy-island adventure with characters their own age, introducing two new characters at each level. Each level has nine units. After an introductory or review welcome unit, there are eight thematic units, which are recycled and build on each other at each level of the program. In this level's welcome unit, children meet Lou and Sue, and learn some questions to ask new friends and some actions to use. Children also are reacquainted with Sammy the Squirrel, the program's mascot, who appears throughout the program and supports children as they learn (when he isn't getting into mischief!). The welcome unit also reviews target language and vocabulary from the previous levels.

The program is designed to help children learn to communicate in English through a four-skills-based approach that builds increasing language proficiency through prereading/reading, prewriting/writing, listening, and speaking lessons and activities. Children begin the program looking at and listening to picture stories. By this third book, children are comfortable reading along with stories that have simple text. At this level, children trace letters in words, preparing them for writing words. Listening and speaking skills, which are critical for language learning, are developed throughout the program, with more emphasis at this level.

The program uses a natural approach to teaching language through TPR® (Total Physical Response). Associating gestures with vocabulary and language structures builds a positive attitude and confidence, while at the same time, helps children attach meaning to the language they are learning. The opening lesson in each unit shows characters engaged in activities and includes a song about what they are doing, along with suggested actions for children to do. Lessons build, using a kinesthetic approach. Still, throughout the program, children learn English through a wide range of activity types to accommodate all learning styles. And learners get to experience all mediums. Children do traditional activities in their books and workbooks. They participate in class activities and projects, as well as engage with the program's digital tools as they interact with their classmates on the interactive whiteboard (ActiveTeach) and the CD-ROM.

My Little Island equips young learners for the technological, global world of the 21st century not only by teaching them English and digital literacy, but also by fostering critical skills to help them become successful, contributing members of society. Skills most helpful for the future include: *flexibility, adaptability to constant change, critical and analytical thinking, communication, collaboration, creativity,* and *problem solving*. By nurturing these critical skills and abilities in children, the program ensures that children develop into more autonomous primary-age learners and beyond.

By addressing these preprimary objectives and developing skills and strategies for communicating in a global community, *My Little Island* prepares children to meet expectations of the Starter level of **CYLET (Cambridge Young Learners English Tests)** and ensures that they will continue to be successful and enjoy their learning experiences in English.

JOIN US AT THE GREAT TEACHERS PRIMARY PLACE!

Find inspiring ideas for your primary classroom, discover new techniques and solutions that work, connect with other primary teachers, and share your own stories and creativity.

The Great Teachers Primary Place is the place to go for free classroom resources and countless activities for primary teachers everywhere.

Go to www.pearsonlongman.com/primaryplace and register for membership.

Members of The Great Teachers Primary Place will receive exclusive access to:

- ✓ free articles on current trends in the primary classroom!
- ✓ free reproducible activity sheets to download and use in your classroom!
- ✓ free Teacher Primary Packs filled with posters, story cards, and games to use in your classroom!
- ✓ exclusive access to professional development via print materials and web conferences!

Components

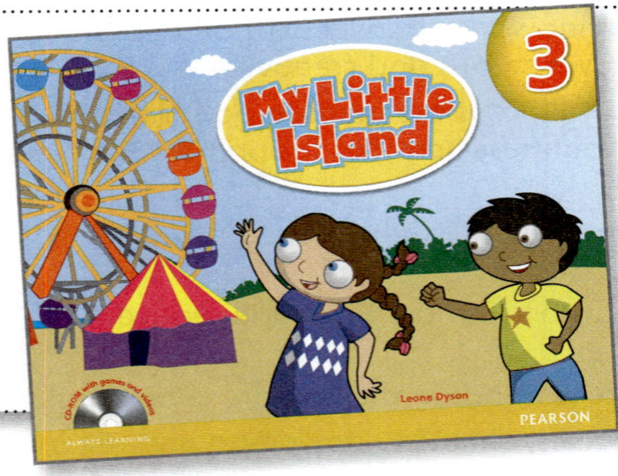

STUDENT BOOK WITH CD-ROM

A welcome unit opens the Student Book and serves as a review of the program's first two books. Eight thematic units follow, and include presentation and practice of the new lexical sets of vocabulary and language structures. Vocabulary builds throughout the program, from basic greetings, classroom objects, and the family, to words used to talk about community workers and places, school activities, and feelings. Children listen to and read along with stories that include target language; sing songs and say chants; match and draw; and play games, collaborate, and communicate with partners, in small groups, and with the whole class.

The first lesson presents the unit's target vocabulary in a scene, along with a thematic song accompanied by meaningful gestures and actions.

The vocabulary lesson presents target vocabulary with photographs. There are eight new words per unit.

Next, children listen to, act out, and read along with a story that has simple text and presents new language structures.

Stories are included on the Class Audio CDs, the CD-ROM, and ActiveTeach.

This lesson develops listening skills. Children listen to and follow directions for an activity that develops target vocabulary and language.

This lesson develops speaking skills. Children ask and answer questions using a conversation model right on the page. An Extra Practice icon directs children to a practice lesson at the back of the book.

The unit's phonics lesson helps children recognize sound-symbol relationships between sounds and letters as children learn how to read simple words in English.

The next lesson helps children develop skill in numeracy and math concepts. In this example, children trace and count different classroom objects.

This lesson prompts children to choose the right course of action in a given situation as it helps them develop good values.

The unit's review lesson includes a sticker activity for children to check their comprehension of vocabulary and language, and a cross-curricular project.

TEACHER'S EDITION WITH ACTIVETEACH

The interleaved Teacher's Edition has full-size Student Book pages right beside the teaching lessons. Simple four-step lesson plans include Getting Ready activities, a Working in the Book section, Consolidating activities, and an Optional: Using Digital Components section. Icons signal when to use components. A two-page Unit Overview maps each unit's content and objectives. It also provides bulletin-board ideas and story summaries, and shows how curriculum and home-school connections are made.

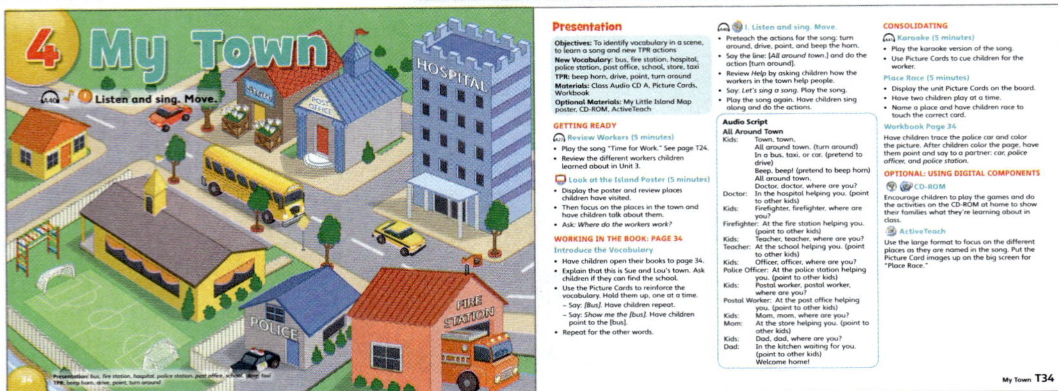

AUDIO PROGRAM

Class Audio CDs contain all of the level's songs, chants, stories, and listening comprehension activities. The Teacher's Edition indicates when and how to use these. Audio icons with track numbers on the Student Book pages also provide cues for which songs, chants, and listening exercises to use with the activities.

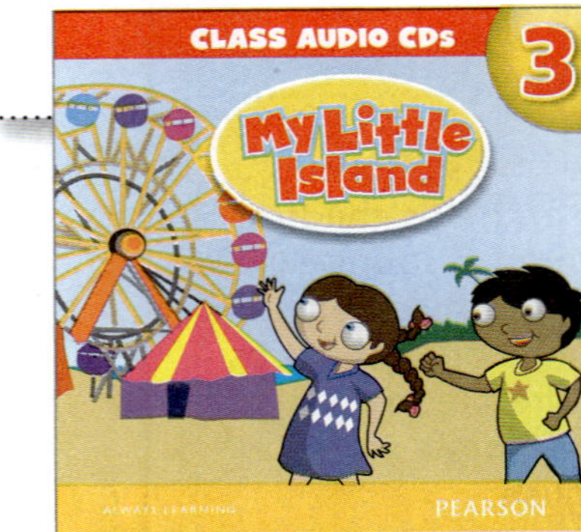

WORKBOOK WITH AUDIO CD

The Workbook provides practice and reinforcement of Student Book lessons. Children practice developing fine motor skills as they trace, match, and color theme-related pictures. The level's characters, Lou and Sue, and the program's mascot, Sammy the Squirrel, appear throughout for continuity and fun. An Audio CD with songs and chants is included. Annotated pages, with answers, can be found in the Teacher's Edition.

POSTERS

Three colorful posters motivate children as they continue their island adventure to learn English. The *My Little Island* map gives children a bird's-eye view of the island. *Meet Your New Friends!* introduces each Student Book's main characters. *Shapes and Colors All Around* presents a reference for important concepts.

PICTURE CARDS

Sixty-four colorful photographs of the target vocabulary appear on Picture Cards for presentation, review, and games. These also appear in ActiveTeach and the CD-ROM. An index of the cards is available on page TI26 of this book.

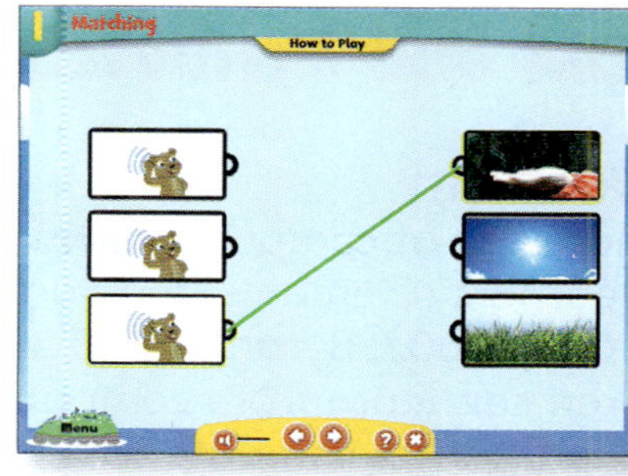

CD-ROM

The CD-ROM features program stories, as well as matching, sorting, concentration, and multiple-choice games and activities. An animation rewards children at the end of each activity. Stories are also accessible word-by-word. Live-action videos are included, and scripts are available on pages TI27–TI30 of this book.

ACTIVETEACH

Student Book pages can be projected onto the big screen, using this interactive whiteboard program with tools. Audio for songs, chants, directions, listening activities, videos, and Picture Cards is included.

WEBSITE

The companion website has complete product information, component descriptions, a sample unit, scope and sequences, letters home, the theme song, and videos. The link is: www.pearsonelt.com/mylittleisland.

BIG BOOK

The *My Little Island Big Book* engages children in a hands-on shared reading experience. Children will feel at ease and comfortable as their teacher turns the pages and models reading the selections aloud, encouraging them to join in when they are comfortable. The large, over-sized pages allow children to easily point to words and to picture details.

Digital Tools: CD-ROM and ActiveTeach

YOUNG LEARNERS AND TECHNOLOGY

Research shows that appropriate use of computer technology in education is beneficial for learners (Clements and Sarama, 2003; Waxman, Connell, and Gray, 2002; Byram and Bingham, 2001). Broadly speaking, children can learn *from* computers and *with* computers. Children learn *from* computers when the computer assumes the role of a tutor, with the goal of importing and increasing basic knowledge and skills. Children learn *with* computers when the computers serve as a facilitating tool, with the goal of developing critical thinking skills, research skills, and the creative imagination (Ringstaff and Kelley, 2002).

Computer activities should be age-appropriate and foster instruction in ways that increase learning, motivation, personal productivity, and creativity. For example, Perry (2009) noted that "Children three to five years old are natural 'manipulators' of the world—they learn through controlling the movement and interactions between objects in their world—dolls, blocks, toy cars, and their own bodies." Children are naturally curious and willing to interact with computers, and they enjoy their ability to control the type, pace, and repetition of an activity. In some cases, children have even managed to learn how to use a computer with no instruction at all, through their own curiosity, fearlessness, and persistence (Mitra, 1999).

References

Byram, E., and Bingham, M. (2001). "Factors Influencing the Effective Use of Technology for Teaching and Learning: Lessons Learned from SEIR-TEC Intensive Site Schools, 2nd Edition." Greensboro: NC: SERVE.

Clements, D.H., and Sarama, J. (2003). "Strip Mining for Gold: Research and Policy in Educational Technology—A Response to 'Fool's Gold.'" *Educational Technology Review*, 11 (1), 7-69.

Kneas, K. M., and Perry, B. D. (2009). "Using Technology in the Early Childhood Classroom." *Early Childhood Today.* (Retrieved November 5, 2009, from the World Wide Web.) Scholastic.

Mitra, S. (1999). "Hole in the wall—can kids learn computer literacy by themselves?" Generation YES Blog. (Retrieved November 5, 2009, from the World Wide Web.)

Ringstaff C., and Kelley, L. (2002). "The Learning Return on Our Educational Technology Investment." San Francisco, CA: WestEd.

Waxman, H.C., Connell, M. L., and Gray, J. (2002). "A Quantitative Synthesis of Recent Research on the Effects of Teaching and Learning with Technology on Student Outcomes." Naperville, IL: North Central Regional Educational Laboratory.

TECHNOLOGY IN MY LITTLE ISLAND

Children in the *My Little Island* program become familiar with digitized learning through ActiveTeach and the CD-ROMs. These components prepare them for more intensive digitized and computer- and game-based programs like *Our Discovery Island*. The CD-ROM offers a variety of fun-filled games for each thematic unit, with each level's games increasing in difficulty. At the end of each unit, children also play "Look and Find"—a Quest-like activity in which children must find unit-related items in scenes. Children can bring the CD-ROM home and share what they are learning with caregivers and even play the games and view the program's videos together.

ActiveTeach provides access to the entire *My Little Island* Student Book and allows teachers to project pages up on the big screen, using interactive tools like a pen, highlighter, and eraser, so that all children become involved with a page at the same time. Teachers can demonstrate how to do activities, highlight target vocabulary and language, show children how to trace, and focus their attention on story characters and lesson features. In addition, the Picture Card images, the songs and chants, and the unit videos make this an invaluable teaching aid.

Program Highlights

CROSS-CURRICULAR CONNECTIONS

Research shows language programs that help young learners to make curriculum connections among school subjects have more successful learning outcomes. *My Little Island* offers integrated, level-appropriate curriculum connections in every unit through engaging activities. Colorful icons help teachers find these activities easily.

Art

A wide range of art activities helps young children develop fine motor skills, recognize and reproduce patterns, learn about colors, and create pictures that have meaning for them. In addition, the art program develops visual literacy through illustrations that help young learners construct meaning and develop related language and communication skills.

Health and Safety

Health and safety activities guide children to make healthy choices and be safe in their everyday lives.

Math

Math lessons help children develop basic math concepts and skill in numeracy. Games on the CD-ROM and other activities also help young children develop basic understandings in math.

Music and Movement

Each unit opens with a song, accompanied by TPR. Other songs, as well as chants, appear throughout the units and provide opportunities for children to move and gesture along with the music.

Science

Simple science activities engage children in the fascinating world of science and provide opportunities for children to communicate about it.

Social Studies

As young children find out about the culture on the island, they are reminded of the social structures that make up their own world, such as family, school, and friends, as well as town and country life.

Each unit has a culminating cross-curricular project.

HOME-SCHOOL CONNECTIONS AND VALUES

Support from family and others at home is very important to a child's total learning experience. Research shows that language acquisition is enhanced through parental interest, involvement, and support. *My Little Island* encourages strong home-school connections. A general letter about the program, as well as a letter for each unit—each of which includes activities and tips—serves to involve families. Unit projects can be taken home and shared. Children should be encouraged to take home the CD-ROM and the Songs and Chants CD to reinforce what they are learning (and singing about) in class. Children are encouraged to share the program's songs, chants, and stories at home.

Each thematic unit includes a values lesson, with a short, catchy chant. Children look at two photographs in their Student Book and choose the right thing to do in a given situation. These values lessons encourage young children to think about themselves and how they interact with their family members, friends, and others.

TEACHING LITERACY

Phonics

Young children in the *My Little Island* program are probably just beginning to discover sound-symbol relationships in their first language. Since sounds in English may have multiple spellings and a child's first language may be more straightforward, the *My Little Island* program takes a gradual approach to phonics, beginning with phonemic awareness (becoming aware of the sounds in words) and gradually introducing sound-symbol correspondences.

At this level, a phonics lesson is included in each thematic unit. The program has already introduced children to sound-symbol correspondences for various consonant letters so children should understand that letters stand for sounds. At this level, children review sound-symbol correspondences for consonant letters and sounds, learn new ones, and go on to learn vowel letters and short vowel sounds.

The program guides children from receptive language development to language production as they move from phonemic awareness to reading and writing simple words. The program also presents common words that do not follow spelling rules (sight words) in environmental print throughout the program.

Prewriting

My Little Island reinforces the development of prewriting skills as an important part of a child's early learning development. In preparing for primary school, children need to develop the cognitive and physical skills they need for writing as well as the necessary skills for reading. The program helps children develop gross motor skills through movement, songs with accompanying actions, and games; and fine motor skills, as well as eye-hand coordination, through a variety of activities. The Student Book and Workbook offer a wide range of opportunities to develop these skills through activities such as: coloring, painting, drawing, connecting dots, tracing, matching, manipulating cutouts and stickers, and making unit projects.

Prereading

Before children read the printed word, they learn basic literacy concepts, such as left-to-right directionality and holding a book in the appropriate orientation. Literacy activities appear throughout the program's Teacher's Edition, providing teachers with suggestions for developing young children's reading skills. Children progress from looking at and listening to picture stories without words to experiencing stories with words, continuing and more developed at this level.

ASSESSMENT

As children enjoy their learning experiences in *My Little Island*, it is important to assess their progress at regular intervals. The review at the end of each unit provides opportunities to review and evaluate what children have understood and retained. The review lesson is also a great way to help children recall songs, stories, concepts, and vocabulary that they particularly like or remember and to stimulate class discussions. The culminating unit project serves as another demonstration of what children have learned. Children build self-esteem as their efforts are rewarded with *Good job!* stickers and as they are praised and commended for their achievements, finishing the unit on a happy, positive note.

My Little Island endorses portfolios as an excellent way to keep track of children's progress. Portfolios for *My Little Island* should include samples of children's work collected throughout the year and notes that include children's own reflections and opinions about what they are learning. Children can decorate their portfolios and should be encouraged to take pride in them as they share them with one another at school. Children's portfolios can also be shown to parents and family during meetings to highlight progress or sent home at the completion of units as well as at the end of the term.

Informal assessment is ongoing. Watching and listening to children as they do their work and learn English, recording progress and problems, checking comprehension, and having informal conversations to keep track of how a child is doing are all important. Encouraging children to check one another's work also helps in this process.

Scope and Sequence

My Little Island 3

Unit	New Vocabulary	New Structures	TPR Actions	Reviewed Language (vocabulary and structures)	Values	Cross-Curricular Project	Phonics Lesson & Prewriting/ Writing	Math
1 Welcome	friend(s), Lou, Sue	*How old are you? / I'm [6].*	give five, hold up fingers, jump, wave	*It's a [rectangle]. It's [red]. The [puppet] is [red]. The [chair] is in the [living room]. I like/don't like [yogurt]. Can you see [the sun]? / Yes. What color is it? / It's [yellow].* animals, classroom objects, colors, family members, foods, numbers, parts of the body			Phonics: initial letters and sounds Prewriting/Writing: tracing letters: *b, d, f, g, k, l, m, n, p, s, t*	Counting 1–6
2 At School	classroom, computer room, music room, play, playground, read, sing, use the computer	*Where do you [read]? / In the [classroom].*	flap arms, hold up fingers, jump, kick, march, point, question action, read, use a computer, write, write letters in the air	classroom items; car, hen	Follow rules.	Social Studies: Poster about school	Phonics: initial *c, h,* and *j* Prewriting/Writing: directionality, letter tracing, letters in contexts, tracing a short sentence	Counting 1–10
3 Workers	artist, astronaut, dentist, doctor, firefighter, nurse, police officer, vet, worker(s)	*I want to be a [police officer]. What do you want to be? / I want to be a [doctor].*	flap arms, hold up fingers, kick, march, march in place, point, write, write letters in the air	*It's [Sammy]! I'm [Sue].* 1–10; animals; red	Stay safe.	Safety: Poster about safety (preventing fires)	Phonics: initial *q, r* and *v* Prewriting/Writing: directionality, letter tracing, letters in contexts, tracing a short sentence	Counting 1–12
4 My Town	bus, fire station, hospital, police station, post office, school, store, taxi	*Where does [your dad] work? / [He] works at the [fire station]. Where does [he] work? / [He] works at a [hospital].*	beep horn, drive, flap arms, hold up fingers, kick, march, point, tap knees, turn around, write, write letters in the air	1–12; aunt, box, teacher, uncle, windy, yellow	Ask for help.	Math: Building made out of shapes	Phonics: initial *w* and *y*, and medial/ final *x* sounds Prewriting/Writing: directionality, letter tracing, letters in contexts, tracing a short sentence	Counting 1–14

Unit	New Vocabulary	New Structures	TPR Actions	Reviewed Language (vocabulary and structures)	Values	Cross-Curricular Project	Phonics Lesson & Prewriting/ Writing	Math
5 Clothes	dress, jacket, pants, shirt, shoes, skirt, socks, sweater	*What [are you] wearing? / [I'm] wearing a [dress]. What [is Grandpa] wearing? / [He's] wearing a [shirt] and [pants].*	brush teeth, flap arms, hold up fingers, hold up 8 fingers, kick, march, point, punch the air, stretch, tap knees, touch clothes, write, write *e* in the air	*How's the weather? / It's [sunny].* 8, 1–14; colors, shapes; bed, hen, pen	Take care of your clothes.	Art: Design your own T-shirt	Phonics: short *e* Prewriting/Writing: directionality, letter tracing, letters in contexts, tracing part of a sentence	Counting 1–16
6 Feelings	excited, happy, hungry, mad, sad, scared, thirsty, tired	*How do you feel? / I'm [excited]. How does [Lou] feel? / He's [excited].*	brush teeth, cry, cup mouth, drink, eat, flap arms, hold up fingers, jump, kick, march, point, put on mask, question action, shiver, tap knees, write, write *a* in the air, yawn	1–16; food; cat, dad, grandma, grandpa, hand, mom	Don't fight.	Social Studies: Poster about feelings	Phonics: short *a* Prewriting/Writing: directionality, letter tracing, letters in contexts, tracing a short sentence	Counting 1–18
7 Healthy Food	banana, carrot, fork, lettuce, mango, orange, plate, tomato	*What do you want, [Lou]? / I want [an orange] and [a banana], please.*	brush teeth, flap arms, hold up fingers, jump, kick, look action, march, point, pretend to eat, rub tummy, tap knees, write, write *o* in the air	1–4, 1–18; colors, family members; box, bread, cheese, cookie, doll, hot, salad	Eat healthy food.	Health: Food rainbow	Phonics: short *o* Prewriting/Writing: directionality, letter tracing, letters in contexts, tracing a short sentence	Counting 1–20
8 The Zoo	bat, bear, elephant, lion, monkey, penguin, sea lion, zebra	*What's that? / It's a [small] [bat].*	clap, eat, flap arms, look, make claws, roar, scratch, waddle, write *u* in the air	bus, cup, mouse, sun	Include everyone.	Art: Elephant mask	Phonics: short *u* Prewriting/Writing: directionality, letter tracing, letters in contexts, tracing a short sentence	Simple addition
9 Places	apartment, building, field, forest, mountain, river, street, traffic light	*Where do [bears] live? / [They] live in the [country]. [Bears] live in the [city], too.*	point to floor, point to self, trace smile, write *i* in the air	bird(s), cars, ducks, fish, goats, house, milk, mouse, tree(s)	Take care of our world.	Social Studies: Recycling poster	Phonics: short *i* Prewriting/Writing: directionality, letter tracing, letters in contexts, tracing a short sentence	Simple subtraction

Time Guidelines

My Little Island is flexibly designed to suit individual teacher's specific classroom needs and scheduling requirements. It is estimated that teaching materials for the Student Book and related practice in the Workbook may take up to 30–60 minutes of classroom time. By using the digital components, the optional activities in the Teacher's Edition, as well as other program resources, teachers can plan to add 15–30 minutes a lesson. For classes meeting three to five hours a week, this means covering approximately two to three Student Book pages and other component segments per week. This adds up to about one unit per month. Below is a chart with recommendations for pacing one thematic unit, along with optional program suggestions.

The actual time it may take for teachers to cover a Student Book unit depends on many factors, such as: how much time is needed for review or for presentation of new material, how many optional components are used, and how many times features are revisited. Approximate time frames are given for optional activities. The degree to which teachers integrate the digital components, the posters, the Picture Cards, and so on, will also affect planning. Additionally, the makeup and needs of any given class, as well as how well the children cooperate as a group and how engaged and well-behaved they are, are all factors for teachers to consider in planning time.

PLANNING MODEL: LEVEL 3, UNIT 2 IN MONTH 2

Week	Day	Student Book	Workbook	Other Components: add 15–30 minutes
1	Day 1	Song and vocabulary presentation	Two activities practicing vocabulary	Class Audio CD, CD-ROM, Picture Cards, ActiveTeach
	Days 2–3	Story (two pages) with new structure presentation	Two activities supporting story	Class Audio CD, CD-ROM, Picture Cards, ActiveTeach
2	Day 4	Listening/speaking practice	Two activities supporting speaking*	Class Audio CD, CD-ROM, Picture Cards, ActiveTeach
3	Day 5	Phonics	Activity supporting phonics	Class Audio CD, CD-ROM, Picture Cards, ActiveTeach
	Day 6	Math introduced with chant	Activity supporting math	Class Audio CD, CD-ROM, Picture Cards, ActiveTeach
4	Day 7	Values activity and chant	Activity supporting values	Class Audio CD, CD-ROM, Picture Cards, ActiveTeach
	Day 8	Review/Assessment, project and sticker activity	Activity for review/personalization	Class Audio CD, CD-ROM, Picture Cards, ActiveTeach
	Anytime	Optional lessons for extra practice with speaking and for holidays in back section		Class Audio CD, Picture Cards, ActiveTeach

*Note that there are ten Workbook pages for each ten-page Student Book unit. While generally there is one Workbook page for each Student Book page, there is one exception: For the listening/speaking lessons, there are two practice pages in the Workbook for the speaking lesson in the Student Book (instead of one for listening and one for speaking).

Map

KIMMY'S HOUSE
BILLY'S HOUSE
Store
POST OFFICE
HOSPITAL
SUE'S HOME
ZOO
BATS
LOU'S HOUSE
TIMMY'S HOUSE
POLICE
FIRE STATION
LILLY'S HOUSE

1 Welcome

Unit Overview

Objectives

- ✓ To meet characters
- ✓ To learn greetings
- ✓ To sing songs and chant
- ✓ To do basic TPR movements
- ✓ To practice fine and gross motor skills
- ✓ To review language structures: *It's a [rectangle]., It's [red]., The [puppet] is [red]., The [chair] is in the [living room]., I like / don't like [yogurt]., Can you see [the sun]?,* and *What color is it? / It's [yellow].*
- ✓ To learn and practice new language structures: *How old are you? / I'm [6].*
- ✓ To practice new language by listening and speaking
- ✓ To review colors, numbers, shapes, and other vocabulary from Level 2
- ✓ To review phonics: the sounds that *b, d, f, g, k, l, m, n, p, s,* and *t* stand for at the beginning of words
- ✓ To count 1–6

Vocabulary

New: friend(s), Lou, Sue

Review: 1–6, animals, classroom objects, colors, family members, foods, numbers, parts of the body

Materials

Student Book pages 4–13; Workbook pages 4–13; Class Audio CD A: Tracks 3–13; Program Posters: My Little Island Map, Shapes and Colors All Around, Meet Your New Friends!; stickers (back of Student Book and shown on page T108)

Optional: CD-ROM, ActiveTeach, Sammy the Squirrel puppet

Songs and Chants

- ✓ Hello Song (Class Audio CD A: Tracks 3, 4)
- ✓ Good-bye Song (Class Audio CD A: Tracks 5, 6)
- ✓ Old Friends, New Friends (Class Audio CD A: Tracks 7, 8)

Home-School Connections

Copy the General Letter Home on page T125 for children to bring home to introduce the third level of *My Little Island* to their families. The Unit 1 Letter Home is available online at www.pearsonelt.com/mylittleisland.

SKILLS

Cross-Curricular Connections

- remember patterns, recognize numbers and shapes
- sing, chant, and move to music

Preschool Learning Outcomes

✓ Understand new language structures.

✓ Recognize and produce the sounds that *p, t, m, s, d, l, b, k, n, f,* and *g* stand for at the beginning of words.

✓ Write the letters *b, d, g, k, l, m, n, p, s,* and *t*.

✓ Sing songs and say chants with TPR.

✓ Join in games and interact.

✓ Talk about self and surroundings.

✓ Develop a positive attitude toward the English language.

✓ Understand the directionality of print.

Digital Practice

- Have children use the CD-ROM for vocabulary practice or review.
- Use ActiveTeach to go over Student Book pages together as a class.

LEARN BY DOING

TPR

✓ give [someone] five, hold up fingers to count, jump, wave

Phonics

✓ Recognize and produce the sounds that *b, d, f, g, k, l, m, n, p, s,* and *t* stand for at the beginning of words.

✓ Write the letters *b, d, f, g, k, l, m, n, p, s,* and *t*.

✓ Complete Student Book page 13 with children.

✓ Have children listen to the audio.

✓ Have children sing songs and say chants.

Prereading and Prewriting

✓ Talk about the characters. Practice fine motor skills.

✓ Draw, color, and trace.

BULLETIN BOARD DISPLAY

We Know English!

✓ Create a bulletin board celebrating what children know in English.

Materials

- photocopies of teacher-made "I know . . ." index cards
- teacher-made name labels
- markers, crayons
- pushpins

Directions

1. Make and copy index cards with *I know. . . .*
2. Use a black marker to make name labels for each child.
3. Have children use markers or crayons to decorate their name labels.
4. Arrange the name labels on the bulletin board.
5. As you post the name labels, ask individuals to tell you one thing they know in English. Accept all answers.
6. Use the information to complete an "I know . . ." card for each child.
7. Post an "I know . . ." card by each child's name.

1 Welcome

A7 1 **Listen and sing. Move.**

Presentation: *friend(s), How old are you? I'm [6].* **Review:** numbers **TPR:** give five, hold up fingers, jump, wave

Presentation

Objectives: To introduce the book and the new characters, to learn and practice greetings, to sing a song, to review numbers

New Vocabulary: *friend(s)*

New Structure: *How old are you? / I'm [6].*

TPR: give five, hold up fingers, jump, wave

Materials: Class Audio CD A, Workbook

Optional Materials: My Little Island Map poster, Meet Your New Friends! Poster, Sammy the Squirrel puppet, CD-ROM, ActiveTeach, ball

GETTING READY

Look at the My Little Island Map Poster (5 minutes)

- Display the My Little Island Map. Ask children if they remember any of the places. Have volunteers tell about their favorite ones.
- Invite children to guess where they will visit next.

Meet Your New Friends! (5 minutes)

- Display the Meet Your New Friends! poster.
- Ask children to point to and name the friends they know from Level 1 (Kimmy and Timmy) and Level 2 (Lilly and Billy).
- Point to Lou and say: *This is Lou! Hello, Lou!*
- Wave *hello*. Invite children to wave and say *hello*.
- Follow a similar procedure for Sue.
- Then point to Sammy on the poster and say: *Hi, Sammy!*
- Have Sammy the puppet respond: *Hi, Teacher! Hello, class!*

A3 Play the "Hello Song" (5 minutes)

Teach children the "Hello Song," using the Sammy the Squirrel puppet. Consider starting every class with this song.

Audio Script

Hello Song

Teacher: Hello. Hello, (wave, wave) children.
Are you ready to play?
Hello. Hello, (wave, wave) children.
Let's learn English today.
Children: Hello. Hello, (wave, wave) teacher.
We're ready to play.
Hello. Hello, (wave, wave) teacher.
We speak English—HOORAY!

WORKING IN THE BOOK: PAGE 4

A7 1. Listen and sing. Move.

- Talk about what's happening in the illustration.
- Point out that it's Sue's birthday, and her family is having a party for her. Review family words.
- Tell children that Sue is 6 years old.
- Ask a few children: *How old are you?*
- Help them answer: *I'm [five].*
- Review these actions: *hold up [five] fingers, jump, wave.*
- Demonstrate with a volunteer how to give someone a high five.
- Play the audio. Sing along and do the TPR actions.
- Play the audio again and invite children to do the actions with you.
- Encourage children to sing along when they are ready. Pause and cue them to answer the question with their age.

Audio Script

Old Friends, New Friends

Old friends, new friends,
Jump and jive. (jump)
Find a friend
And give him five. (give high five to classmate)

Hello, hello. (wave)
I'm five years old. (hold up 5 fingers)
How old are you?

Hello, hello. (wave)
I'm six years old. (hold up 6 fingers)
It's my birthday!
Want to play?

Hello, hello. (wave)
How old are you?
I'm ________ (pause for age)
How about you?

Old friends, new friends,
Jump and jive. (jump)
Find a friend
And give her five. (give high five to classmate)

CONSOLIDATING

Circle Game (5 minutes)

- Have children sit in a circle.
- Pass a ball to the child on your right. Ask: *How old are you?* Cue the answer: *I'm [six].*
- Continue in this way around the circle.

Workbook Page 4

Have children trace *6*, draw six candles, and color. Have partners count the candles.

OPTIONAL: USING DIGITAL COMPONENTS

CD-ROM

Have children take home the CD-ROM to introduce their families to the new characters.

ActiveTeach

Use ActiveTeach to review with the whole class.

Review

Objectives: To review classroom objects, colors, numbers; *It's a [rectangle]. / It's [red].*

Materials: Class Audio CD A, Workbook

Optional Materials: Sammy the Squirrel puppet, Shapes and Colors All Around poster, CD-ROM, ActiveTeach, different colored shape cutouts

GETTING READY

Ask and Answer with TPR (10 minutes)

- Use the Sammy puppet to demonstrate how to play the game.
- Ask Sammy: *How old are you?*
- Have Sammy answer: *I'm [five].*
- Ask Sammy to name an action. Have Sammy say: *Hop!*
- Then do the action by hopping five times.
- Have Sammy play the game with children around the room.
- Use actions from the song "Old Friends, New Friends" (give high five, hold up [four] fingers, jump, wave).

Shapes and Colors All Around Poster (10 minutes)

- Display the poster.
- Invite individual children to point to a color or shape on the poster and say: *It's [red]* or *It's a [square].*
- Then invite volunteers to find classroom objects that are the same color or shape.

WORKING IN THE BOOK: PAGE 5

2. Color and say.

- Have children turn to page 5.
- Name each color in the border and have children repeat after you.
- Point out Sammy and explain that he's at a place called a factory that makes shapes.
- Have children point to the shapes and name them.
- Say: *Color the shapes.*
- Have children color in the shapes.
- Have them take turns describing the shapes: *It's a [rectangle]. It's [red].*

CONSOLIDATING

Shape and Color Patterns (10 minutes)

- Use colored construction paper to make cutouts of different shapes.
- Arrange children in small groups.
- Give a set of cutouts to each group.
- Name a pattern: [*circle, circle, square, star*] or [*blue, red, red, purple*]
- Help group members work together to create the pattern using their cutouts.
- Then invite volunteers to dictate patterns to their groups.

A5 Good-bye Song (5 minutes)

- Teach children the "Good-bye Song."
- Consider ending every class with this song.

Audio Script

Good-bye Song

Good-bye, children. (clap, clap, wave)
Good-bye. Good-bye.
Have a nice day!
Good-bye, teacher. (clap, clap, wave)
Good-bye. Good-bye.
Have a nice day!
Good-bye! Good-bye! Good-bye! (wave)

Workbook Page 5

Have children count the shapes and write how many of each shape there are. Then have children color the page and practice saying with a partner: *It's a [square].* and *[Five] [squares].*

OPTIONAL: USING DIGITAL COMPONENTS

CD-ROM

Have children take their CD-ROMs home to share the games, activities, and Picture Cards with their families.

ActiveTeach

Use ActiveTeach to focus on the different colored rectangles in the border. Invite volunteers to use the pen feature to follow the directions by coloring in the shapes.

REVIEW

2 Color and say.

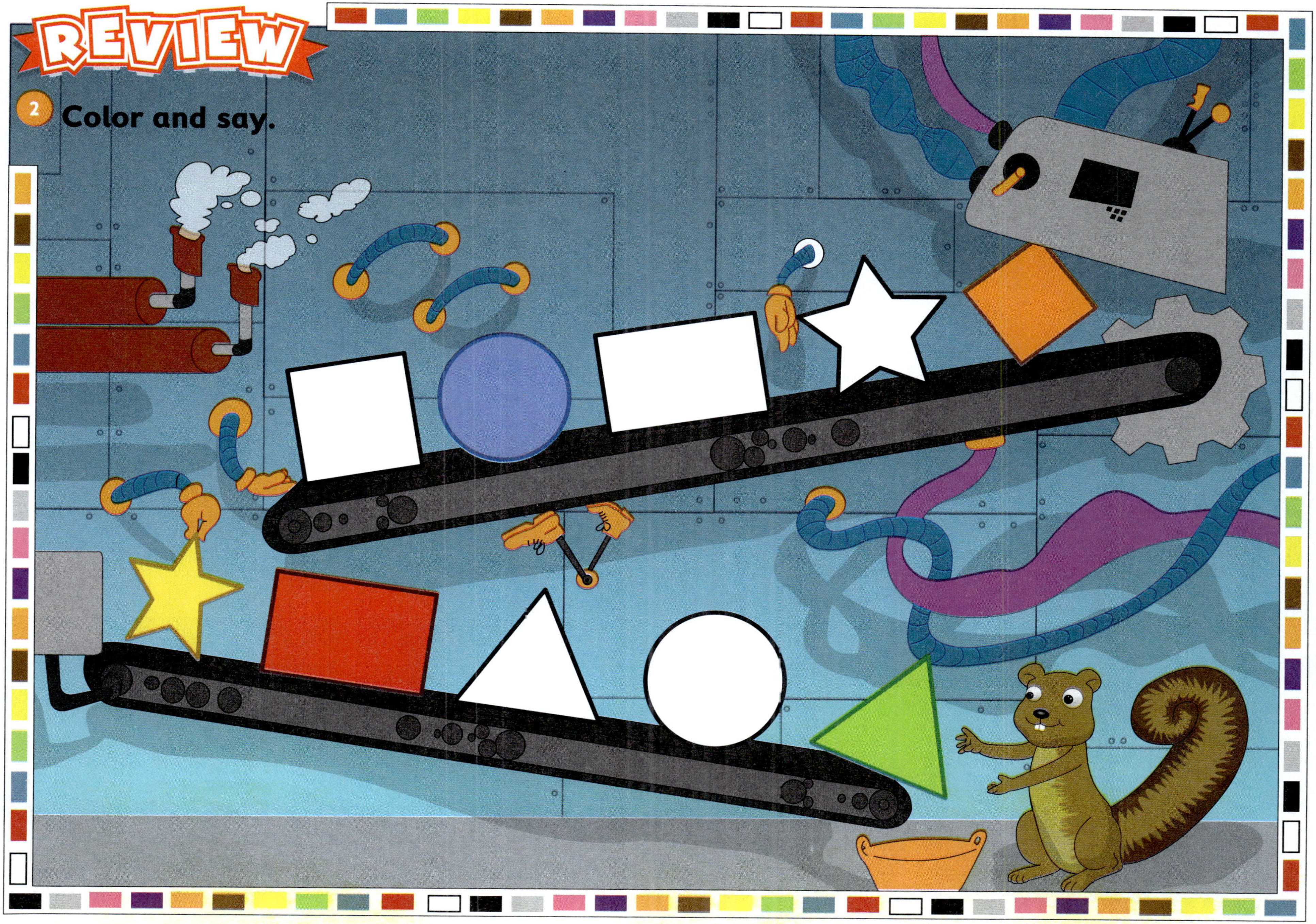

Review: *It's a [rectangle]. It's [red].*

REVIEW

3 **Trace. Count and match. Say.**

Review: classroom objects, numbers, colors **Math:** counting *1–6*

Review

Objectives: To review classroom objects, numbers 1–6, and colors

Materials: Workbook

Optional Materials: Sammy the Squirrel puppet; CD-ROM; ActiveTeach; classroom items, box

GETTING READY

Steal the Bacon (10 minutes)

- Divide the class into groups of five.
- Have two groups face each other with classroom items on the floor between them: backpack, notebook, crayon, pair of safety scissors, marker, pen.
- Assign each child in each group a number from 1 to 6.
- Say a number and a classroom item: *Four. Get the backpack!*
- Cue the two children assigned a 4 to grab the backpack. Give a point to the child who gets it first.
- Continue until you have called out all the numbers and everyone has had a turn.

Count How Many (5 minutes)

- Call out three names. Tell those children to stand up.
- Ask Sammy: *How many?*
- Have Sammy point and count: *One, two, three. Three children.*
- Continue in this way a few times.
- Then invite volunteers to call out names and ask how many.

WORKING IN THE BOOK: PAGE 6

3. Trace. Count and match. Say.

- Have children turn to page 6.
- Explain that Lou is in a store looking at school supplies.
- Point to each item and say: *What's this? It's a [computer].*
- Point to the numbers. Have children say the numbers with you.
- Have children trace the numbers.
- Tell children to count each group of items and draw a line to the number that tells how many.
- Do the first item with children.

CONSOLIDATING

Touch and Guess (5 minutes)

- Blindfold a volunteer.
- Help him or her touch one of the following items that you have arranged close by: backpack, book, chair, computer, crayon, markers, notebook, pen, pencil, scissors, table.
- Have the volunteer guess: *It's a [notebook].*
- Cue the class to call out "yes" if the guess is correct and "no" if not.

How Many? Box (5 minutes)

- Have children cover their eyes.
- Place two crayons in a box.
- Say: *Open your eyes.*
- Shake the box so children can hear the two crayons moving around.
- Ask: *How many?*
- Take the crayons out and count them to confirm children's guesses.
- Repeat the activity with different numbers of crayons.

Workbook Page 6

Have children draw the missing items in Picture B to make the two pictures match. Then have children color the page and practice the language with a partner.

OPTIONAL: USING DIGITAL COMPONENTS

CD-ROM

Have children take the CD-ROM home to show their families the words and numbers they are reviewing in class.

ActiveTeach

Use ActiveTeach to model the exercise beforehand or to confirm answers at the end. Invite volunteers to use the pen to trace the numbers on the page and to match the groups of items with the numbers.

Review

Objectives: To review *The [puppet] is [red].*
Materials: Class Audio CD A, Workbook
Optional Materials: Sammy the Squirrel puppet; CD-ROM; ActiveTeach; toys, school supplies, crayons or colored paper, slips of paper

GETTING READY

Sort and Review (5 minutes)

- Gather together toys such as a car, bicycle, boat, doll, teddy bear, Sammy puppet, train, kite, and ball.
- Also gather some school supplies.
- Display the toys and supplies.
- Tell children that they are going to help you sort the things into two groups: toys and school supplies.
- As you pick up each item, say: *This is a [puppet]. It's a [toy].* Have children repeat.

Group Chain (10 minutes)

- Use crayons or colored paper to review colors.
- Explain that children will march around the room as you play music and that when the music stops, everyone should freeze and stop marching.
- Call out a command: *Touch green!*
- Everyone has to touch something green or touch someone who is touching something green.
- The goal of the game is to have everyone be connected in each round.

WORKING IN THE BOOK: PAGE 7

A9 4. Listen and color. Say.

- Have children turn to page 7.
- Point to each toy and ask: *What's this?*
- Elicit the response: *It's a [car].*
- Explain that children will listen to sentences and color toys based on what they hear.
- Play the audio. Have children color.

Audio Script

The puppet is red.
The car is blue.
The boat is yellow.
The bike is pink.
The kite is orange.

- Finally, invite volunteers to share their work. Have them point and say: *The [puppet] is [red].*

CONSOLIDATING

I Spy (10 minutes)

- Model the game with Sammy.
- Place toys and school supplies of different colors around the room beforehand.
- Point to your eye and say: *I spy with my little eye something [blue]. Sammy, look around.*
- Have Sammy look around and guess: *The notebook? [No.] The car? [No.] The ball? [Yes!]*
- Have Sammy lead the game and children guess.
- To have children lead the game, ask the child leader to whisper the item to you beforehand so you can help as needed.

Group Charades (10 minutes)

- Write toy vocabulary words four or five times each, on slips of paper, one word per slip. Make enough so that everyone gets one.
- Hand out the slips of paper.
- Have children walk around and get in groups based on their words. (All the "trains" get together, and so on.)
- Have the children in each group work together to create a simple charade for playing with their toy.
- Have children perform for the class and have classmates guess the toy.

Workbook Page 7

Have children match the toys to the gray shapes and color the picture. Then have partners take turns pointing to a toy and naming it.

OPTIONAL: USING DIGITAL COMPONENTS

CD-ROM

Have children play the games on the CD-ROM to review toys and colors and to share what they've learned with their families.

ActiveTeach

Use ActiveTeach to point to the different toys. Invite volunteers to use the marker tool to color the toys and then identify them.

REVIEW

A9 **4** **Listen and color. Say.**

Review: *The [puppet] is [red].*

REVIEW

A10 5 **Listen and write.**

Review

Objectives: To review family members and numbers
Writing: numbers 1–7
Materials: Class Audio CD A, Workbook
Optional Materials: CD-ROM; ActiveTeach; paper plates, markers

GETTING READY

Share What You Know (5 minutes)

- Gather photos of family members that children bring from home.
- Display the photos and ask children to name the different family members: *This is [dad].*

Prepare for the Exercise (10 minutes)

- Model writing the numbers 1–7 on the board, and have children practice on scrap paper.
- Gather seven paper plates, and give one to each of seven volunteers.
- Have the volunteers stand in a line facing the class.
- Gesture to the first volunteer with a plate. Say: *This is my [dad]. He's number 1.*
- Hand a marker to the child and ask him or her to write the number *1* on the plate.
- Continue until all the plates are numbered.
- Repeat the activity with another set of plates and seven more volunteers until every child has participated.

WORKING IN THE BOOK: PAGE 8

A10 5. Listen and write.

- Have children turn to page 8.
- Ask them to talk about the picture.
- Explain that Sue's family is cooking out at Sue's grandpa's house.
- Point to the family members and ask children to guess who each one is.
- Have children listen to the audio and write numbers on the plates based on what they hear.
- Point to Sue as the first line plays. Model writing the number 1 on Sue's plate.
- Have children continue on their own.

Audio Script

I'm Sue. I'm number 1.
This is my family.
This is my mom. She's number 2.
This is my dad. He's number 3.
This is my grandma. She's number 4.
This is my uncle. He's number 5.
This is my aunt. She's number 6.
This is my cousin. He's number 7.

CONSOLIDATING

Get in Order (5 minutes)

- Reuse the numbered plates from Getting Ready.
- Gather seven volunteers in a group.
- Give each one a numbered plate.
- Mix children up so that the numbers are not in order.
- Have the group form a line in number order without talking. Explain that they can help each other get in order by showing their cards, holding up fingers, and gesturing.

Workbook Page 8

Have children match the family members' faces to their bodies and draw the faces. After children color the page, have partners take turns pointing to and naming the family members.

OPTIONAL: USING DIGITAL COMPONENTS

CD-ROM

Have children play the games on the CD-ROM with family members to reinforce class work and help get families involved.

ActiveTeach

Use the pen tool to write the numbers on the plates, or invite volunteers to write them.

Review

Objectives: To review *The [chair] is in the [living room].*

Materials: Class Audio CD A, Workbook

Optional Materials: Sammy the Squirrel puppet, CD-ROM, ActiveTeach, blank outlines of a five-room house

GETTING READY

Share What You Know (5 minutes)

- On the board draw the outline of a large house with five empty rooms.
- Explain that you will draw items in each room and have children name the room.
- Begin to draw items inside the bedroom, such as a bed, a window, and so on.
- When children name the correct room, label it *bedroom* and continue to the next room.
- Once all the rooms are labeled, invite children to name the furniture they know for each room.
- Elicit words from Level 1 (*table, chair, bed, clock, door, lamp, toy box, window*), Level 2 (rooms), and any other words children know.

Charades (10 minutes)

- Brainstorm some activities people do in each room in a house.
- Pretend to brush your teeth.
- Ask Sammy: *Where am I?*
- Have Sammy guess: *The kitchen?*
- Say: *No, no, Sammy. Guess again!*
- Have Sammy guess: *The bathroom?*
- Say: *Very good, Sammy! I'm in the bathroom.*
- Invite a volunteer to mime an action.
- Have children guess where he or she is and continue with other actions.

WORKING IN THE BOOK: PAGE 9

A11 6. Listen, say, and match.

- Have children turn to page 9. Say: *This is a house. What do you see?*
- Elicit names of rooms, furniture, and colors.
- Encourage children to use complete sentences: *I see the living room. This is the bedroom. The sofa is in the living room. I see four chairs in the dining room. The bed is orange.*
- Point to the example item and the line to the living room. Say: *The chair is in the living room.*
- Tell children to listen and draw lines from the other furniture to the rooms.

Audio Script

The chair is in the living room.
The table is in the kitchen.
The clock is in the dining room.
The toy box is in the bedroom.
The window is in the bathroom.

CONSOLIDATING

Move and Say TPR (10 minutes)

- As a class, practice an action for each word:
  - bed (sleep action)
  - chair (sit action)
  - clock (clock action)
  - door (turn a door knob)
  - window (open a window)
- Label different parts of the classroom as a bathroom, a bedroom, a dining room, a kitchen, and a living room.
- Say: *The bed is in the bedroom.*
- Lead a volunteer to the "bedroom" as you repeat: *The bed is in the bedroom.*
- Once in the "bedroom," have the child do the action that goes with "bed."
- Continue in this way.

Say and Draw (10 minutes)

- Provide blank outlines of a five-room house.
- Have children work in pairs.
- C1 says: *The [chair] is in the [living room]* and C2 draws the [chair].
- Have children continue in this way and then switch roles.

Workbook Page 9

Have children draw the pieces of furniture in the rooms. After children color the page, have partners point to and name the rooms.

OPTIONAL: USING DIGITAL COMPONENTS

CD-ROM

Invite children to play the games on the CD-ROM with their families to show them what they are reviewing in class.

ActiveTeach

Use ActiveTeach to model drawing lines from the pieces of furniture to the rooms and to check completed pages together.

REVIEW

A11 **6 Listen, say, and match.**

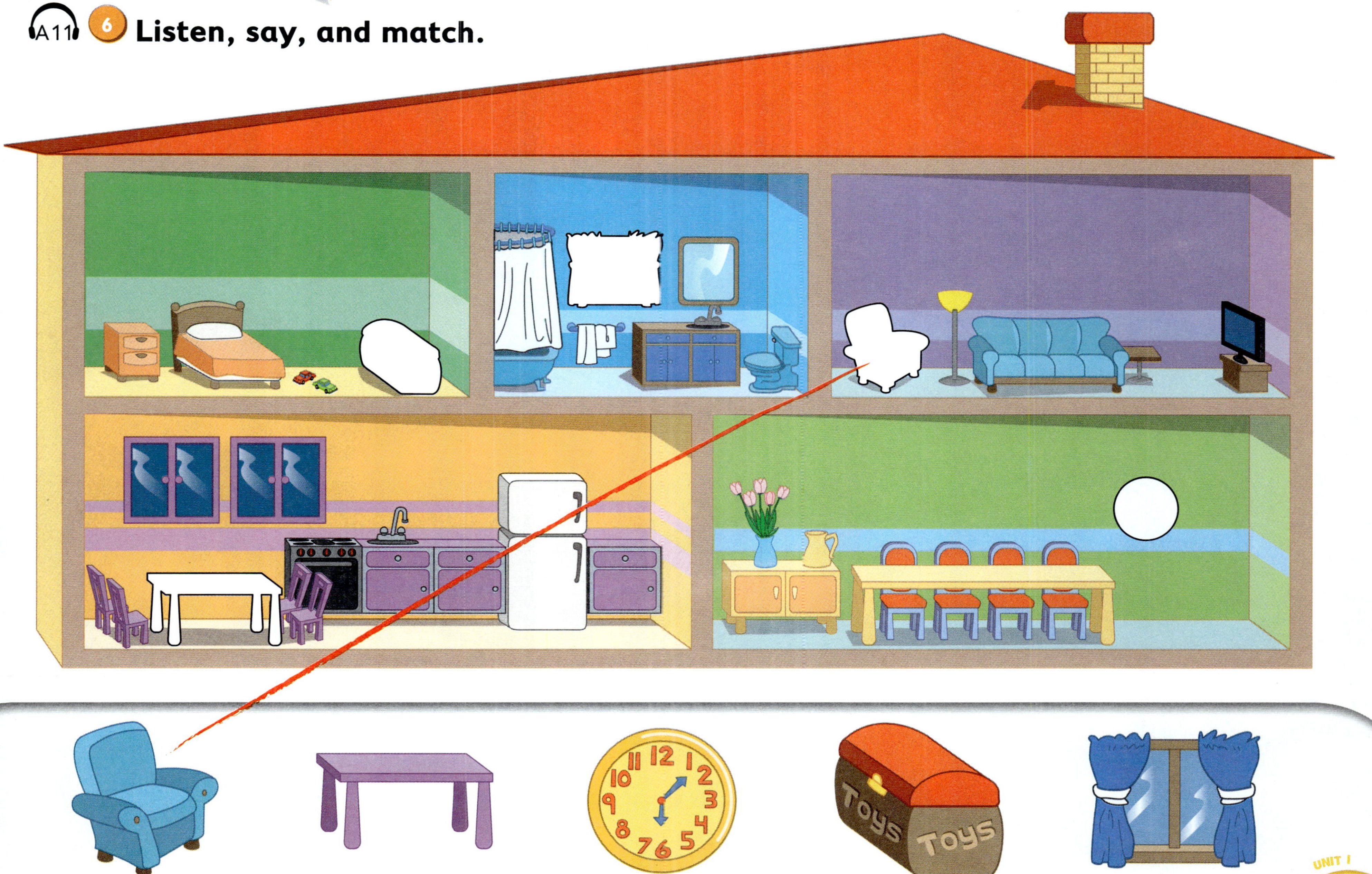

Review: *The [chair] is in the [living room].*

REVIEW

7 **Color and say.**

Review: foods, colors, *I like/don't like [yogurt].*

Review

Objectives: To review colors and foods, and *I like / don't like [yogurt].*

Materials: Workbook

Optional Materials: Sammy the Squirrel puppet; CD-ROM; ActiveTeach; photos or drawings of food, a bag

GETTING READY

Share What You Know (5 minutes)

- Gather photos or drawings of food from Level 1 (cake, cheese, juice, milk, water, yogurt) and Level 2 (apples, bread, chicken, cookies, pasta, salad).
- Hold one up and ask: *What's this?*
- Elicit: *It's [cake].*
- Ask individuals: *Do you like [cake]?*
- Elicit: *Yes, I do* or *No, I don't.*

Ask and Answer (5 minutes)

- Place the food pictures in a bag.
- Invite a volunteer to pick one.
- C1 asks C2: *Do you like [bread]?*
- C2 answers: *Yes, I do.* or *No, I don't.*
- Then C2 picks another food picture and asks C3.
- Continue this way.

WORKING IN THE BOOK: PAGE 10

7. Color and say.

- Have children turn to page 10.
- Invite them to guess where Lou is. (He's in the kitchen.)
- Point to each food item and ask: *What's this?*
- Invite volunteers to answer.
- Have children color the food items.
- Invite them to share their work: *This is [cheese]. It's [yellow]. I [like / don't like] [cheese].*

CONSOLIDATING

Guessing Game (5 minutes)

- Tell children that Sammy is going to guess whether each child likes a certain food.
- Call on the first child. Say: *Ella—bread.*
- Sammy says either *yes* or *no.*
- Then the child says to confirm: *I like bread* or *I don't like bread.*
- If Sammy guessed correctly, have children clap and if incorrectly, have them stamp their feet.
- When children understand the game, invite volunteers to guess what foods their classmates like and don't like.

Memory Chain (10 minutes)

- Have children stand in a circle.
- Begin the chain. Say: *I like apples.*
- The next child builds on your sentence: *I like apples and juice.*
- The next child builds further: *I like apples and juice and bread.*
- Continue until someone makes a mistake.

Make a Home Connection!

Help children create simple three-column "Like / Don't Like" charts to fill out with their families. Have children make several charts for different foods (leave space at the top for children to draw a food). Column 1 is for the family member's name, Column 2 has a smiley face, and Column 3 has a frowning face. Have children share their charts in class. Have them vote on the most popular family foods.

Workbook Page 10

Have children match the food items and color the page. Have partners take turns pointing to and naming each food.

OPTIONAL: USING DIGITAL COMPONENTS

CD-ROM

Encourage children to have older family members play each type of game with them at least once to be sure they know how to play each one.

ActiveTeach

Use ActiveTeach to demonstrate coloring the different foods. Invite volunteers to model how to use the marker tool.

Review

Objectives: To review animals and parts of the body
Materials: Workbook
Optional Materials: CD-ROM, ActiveTeach

GETTING READY

I Tricked You! (10 minutes)

- Review parts of the body from Level 1 (ears, eyes, face, hair, mouth, nose) and Level 2 (arms, body, feet, hands, head, legs).
- Review these actions: Open / Close your eyes. Open / Close your mouth. Point to your [nose]. Wiggle your [ears]. Shake your [head]. Tap your [leg].
- Do each action and say the words. Have children do the action and repeat.
- Explain that you are going to play a trick: that you will say one thing, but do something else.
- Tell children they have to do what you *say*, not what you *do*.
- Model with a volunteer. Wiggle your ears but say: *Point to your nose.*
- If the volunteer wiggles his or her ears, say: *No, I tricked you!*
- If the volunteer points to his or her nose, say: *Good job!*

Review Animals (5 minutes)

- Review the animals children learned in Level 1 (bird, cat, dog, fish, mouse, turtle) and Level 2 (cow, duck, goat, hen, horse, sheep).
- For each one, say the animal's name and then pretend to move like the animal and / or make the animal sound.
- If necessary, remind children of the English words for the different sounds animals make. (bird: *tweet*; cat: *meow*; cow: *moo*; dog: *woof*; duck: *quack*; frog: *ribbit*; goat: *maah*; hen: *cluck*; horse: *neigh*; mouse: *squeak*; sheep: *baah*)
- Then name an animal and invite children to do the movement and / or say the sound.

WORKING IN THE BOOK: PAGE 11

8. Say and match.

- Have children turn to page 11.
- Point to each animal on the right. Ask: *What is it?*
- Elicit: *It's a [goat].*
- Have children look at the parts of the animals' bodies on the left.
- Tell children they will draw a line from each part of the body to the animal it goes with.
- Point out that the first one is done as an example.
- Encourage children to share their work and say: *I see [eyes]. It's a [frog].*
- Check to be sure children match the goat with its legs, the bird with its feet, the mouse with its ears, and the dog with its nose.

CONSOLIDATING

Move Like an Animal (10 minutes)

- Lead the class in chanting: *Move like an animal, move like an animal, move like an animal, 1 – 2 – 3!*
- Name an animal. Then lead in chanting: *Move like a [fish], move like a [fish], move like a [fish], 1 – 2 – 3!* Everyone moves like a [fish].
- Repeat for other animals.

Draw and Guess (5 minutes)

- Play a drawing game on the board.
- Invite a volunteer to name a part of the body.
- Make a drawing of it for one specific animal. For example, draw one cow leg.
- Ask children to guess the animal.
- Keep adding to your picture until children can guess the correct animal.

Workbook Page 11

Have children trace the different parts of the animals' bodies. Then have children color the page. Finally, have children work with a partner to name the animals and the parts of the body.

OPTIONAL: USING DIGITAL COMPONENTS

CD-ROM

Have children take the CD-ROM home to play the games with their families.

ActiveTeach

Use ActiveTeach to help children focus on the part of each animal's body. For example, use the pen tool to trace the outline of the dog's eyes.

REVIEW

8 **Say and match.**

I see eyes! It's a frog.

1 

2 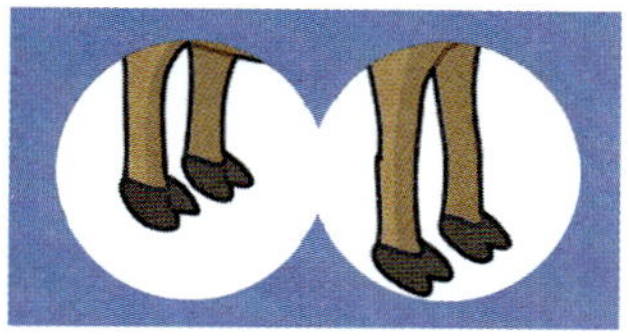

3 

4 

5 

REVIEW

A12 9 **Listen, say, and color.**

Review: *Can you see [the sun]? Yes. What color is it? It's [yellow].*

Review

Objectives: To review *Can you see [the sun]? / Yes. / What color is it? / It's [yellow].*
Materials: Class Audio CD A, Workbook
Optional Materials: CD-ROM, ActiveTeach

GETTING READY

Review Weather with TPR (10 minutes)

- Teach a physical response for each kind of weather. (Sunny: shade your eyes; hot: fan yourself; cold: shiver; snowy: flutter your fingers downward like snowflakes; windy: fly a kite; rainy: open an umbrella.)
- Say the word, do the action, and have children repeat.
- Say: *Show me [hot].*
- Have children do the action and say: *[Hot].*
- Finally, point to a window and ask: *How's the weather today?*

Review Nature Words (5 minutes)

- Review the backyard words children learned in Level 1 (flower, grass, nest, rain, sun, tree).
- Draw a large square on the board. Say: *This is my backyard.*
- Ask children to name things they might see in a backyard.
- As they name each item, draw it in the square.

WORKING IN THE BOOK: PAGE 12

A12 9. Listen, say, and color.

- Have children open to page 12.
- Tell children they will listen and color the pictures based on what they hear.
- Do the first one (the sun) as a group.
- To save time, children can make a colored dot on each picture as they hear it on the audio and then color it in afterwards.

Audio Script

Can you see the sun? / Yes.
What color is it? / It's yellow.
Can you see the nest in the tree? / Yes.
What color is it? / It's brown.
Can you see the rock? / Yes.
What color is it? / It's gray.
Can you see the grass? / Yes.
What color is it? / It's green.
Can you see a flower? / Yes.
What color is it? / It's pink.
Can you see one more flower? / Yes.
What color is it? / It's blue.

- Finally, invite partners to talk about the scene, using the audio as a model.
- Check that children colored the nest brown, the rock gray, the grass green, and one flower pink and one blue.

CONSOLIDATING

Imaginary Walk (5 minutes)

- Pretend to go on a walk.
- As you describe what you see or hear, encourage children to do the actions with you:
  - We're on a walk in a forest! (March in place.)
  - It's sunny and hot. (Pretend to be hot and fan yourself.)
  - Listen to the birds. (Place your hand to your ear; then make tweeting sounds.)
  - Look at the flower! (Bend down and pretend to smell a flower).
  - Oh, no, it's windy. (Blow air out of your mouth to make a wind sound.)

Can You Find It? (5 minutes)

- Play a search-and-find game in the classroom.
- Explain that you're thinking of [a table] and have children guess which [table] it is.
- Ask a volunteer: *Can you see [a table]?*
- Elicit: *Yes, I can.*
- Ask: *What color is it?*
- Have the volunteer point to the object and answer: *It's [blue].*
- If he or she is correct, say: *Yes, that's it!* If not, say: *No, try again.*

Workbook Page 12

Have children connect the dots and color the picture. Then have partners ask and answer: *How's the weather? It's cloudy and windy.*

OPTIONAL: USING DIGITAL COMPONENTS

CD-ROM

Because the games on the CD-ROM repeat the same formats, once a child learns how to play a game type, he or she can teach family members how to play other examples of the same game type.

ActiveTeach

Help the class use the large digital format to review the nature and weather words and use the pen tool to circle and then color the items.

Review

Objectives: To review sound-symbol correspondences for *b /b/, d /d/, f /f/, g /g/, k /k/, l /l/, m /m/, n /n/, p /p/, s /s/, t /t/*
Prewriting: trace initial letters *b, d, f, g, k, l, m, n, p, s, t*
Materials: Class Audio CD A, Workbook
Optional Materials: CD-ROM, ActiveTeach

GETTING READY

Review Sounds (10 minutes)

- Write these letters on the board: *b, d, f, g, k, l, m, n, p, s, t.*
- Draw a simple picture beneath each letter as a cue for a word that starts with the sound the letter represents. (Draw a bird under *b*, for example.)
- Point to and say each letter, the initial sound it represents, and the word. For example: *B. /b/. Bird.*
- Have children repeat.
- Invite children to say other words that begin with each sound/letter.
- Leave the letters and drawings on the board for reference.

Practice Letter Formation (10 minutes)

- On the board, trace over each letter again.
- Use the following words to reinforce how to make the letters:
  - P: Down, around.
  - S: Curve and curve.
  - B: Down, around, around.
  - F: Down, straight across, straight across.
- After you trace over each letter, have children air write the letter and repeat the words to tell how they are making the letter.

WORKING IN THE BOOK: PAGE 13

A13 10. Listen and trace. Say.

- Have children open to page 13.
- Tell children they will listen and trace letters.
- Play the audio. Pause after each letter to give children time to trace it.

Audio Script

P sounds like puh	puh	pencil
T sounds like tuh	tuh	table
M sounds like muh	muh	marker
S sounds like suh	suh	sun
D sounds like duh	duh	duck
L sounds like luh	luh	lamp
B sounds like buh	buh	bird
K sounds like kuh	kuh	kite
N sounds like nuh	nuh	nose
F sounds like fuh	fuh	fish
G sounds like guh	guh	goat

- After children complete the page, invite volunteers to point and say: *[P]. [P] sounds like [/p/]. [Pencil].*

CONSOLIDATING

Choose It (5 minutes)

- Display two known objects (or pictures) that begin with different sounds / letters that children know.
- Choose one and say the letter and sound it begins with.
- Have children choose the object (or picture) with that initial letter / sound.

Find Your Partner (5 minutes)

- Whisper a different familiar letter or a word that begins with that letter in each child's ear.
- Use each letter only once and only one word that begins with that letter / sound.
- At your signal, children walk around the room and find their partner. For example, the child who is "b" partners with the child who is "bird."
- Use this pair activity throughout the year.

Workbook Page 13

Have children trace each letter and match it to the item that begins with the letter. Then have children color the page and practice saying the letter sounds and words with a partner.

OPTIONAL: USING DIGITAL COMPONENTS

CD-ROM

Have children review Unit 1 by playing the games on the CD-ROM with their families.

ActiveTeach

Use the large digital format to model tracing the letters. Say: *Down, around, curve*, and so on, as children trace.

REVIEW

A13 **10** **Listen and trace. Say.**

p  t  m 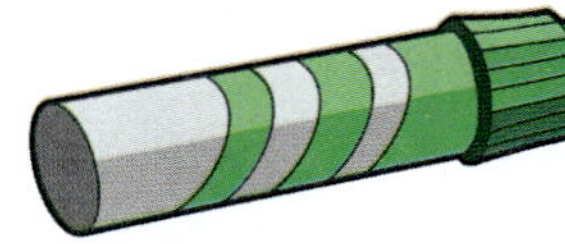

s  d  l 

b  k  n 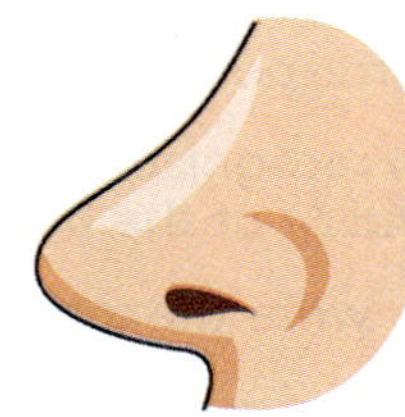

f  g 

2 At School

Unit Overview

Objectives

- ✓ To learn school vocabulary
- ✓ To sing songs and chant
- ✓ To do new TPR movements
- ✓ To practice fine and gross motor skills
- ✓ To understand and role-play a story
- ✓ To learn and practice new language structures: *Where do you [read]? / In the [classroom].*
- ✓ To practice sound-symbol correspondences: *c* /k/, *h* /h/, *j* /ĵ/
- ✓ To recognize and produce /k/, /h/ and /ĵ/ at the beginning of words
- ✓ To write the letters *c*, *h*, and *j*
- ✓ To review and count 1–10
- ✓ To learn how to write the numbers 7–10
- ✓ To learn the value of following rules
- ✓ To practice writing a short sentence
- ✓ To practice new language by listening and speaking
- ✓ To learn and review unit vocabulary and language structures

Vocabulary

New: classroom, computer room, music room, play, playground, read, sing, use the computer

Review: numbers 1–10; classroom items; car, hen

Home-School Connections

Copy the Letter Home for children to bring home to share what they'll be learning in Unit 2 of *My Little Island*. The Letter Home is available online at www.pearsonelt.com/mylittleisland.

Values

Follow rules.

Materials

Student Book pages 14–23; Workbook Pages 14–23; Picture Cards 1–8; Class Audio CD A: Tracks 14–26; Program Posters: Meet Your New Friends!, My Little Island Map, Shapes and Colors All Around; stickers (back of Student Book and shown on page T108)

Optional: CD-ROM, ActiveTeach, Big Book, Sammy the Squirrel Puppet

Songs and Chants

- ✓ What Do You Do at School? (Class Audio CD A: Tracks 14, 15)
- ✓ *C, H, J* Cheer (Class Audio CD A: Tracks 19, 20)
- ✓ Count to 10 Chant (Class Audio CD A: Tracks 22, 23)
- ✓ Follow Rules Chant (Class Audio CD A: Tracks 24, 25)

Story

"My School": Sue shows her grandma around her school. Her grandma asks where Sue reads, sings, and plays. Sue shows her the classroom, the music room, and the computer room!

Language Structures: *Where do you [read]? / In the [classroom].*

SKILLS

Cross-Curricular Connections

- count to 10, write numbers 7–10
- learn the value of following rules
- sing, chant, and move to music
- make a poster of places at school

Preschool Learning Outcomes

✓ Recognize intonation in questions.
✓ Use short answers to questions.
✓ Understand new language structures.
✓ Recognize and produce the sounds that initial *c*, *h*, and *j* stand for.
✓ Write the letters *c*, *h*, and *j* in words.
✓ Listen to and follow a story with words.
✓ Make predictions, using pictures.
✓ Sing songs and say chants with TPR.
✓ Join in games and interact.
✓ Talk about self and surroundings.
✓ Develop a positive attitude toward the English language.

Digital Practice

- Have children use the CD-ROM for vocabulary practice in class or at home.
- Use ActiveTeach to go over Student Book pages together as a class.

LEARN BY DOING

TPR

✓ flap arms, hold up fingers, jump, kick, march, point, question action, read, use a computer, write, write letters in the air, hold up fingers to count

Phonics

✓ Recognize sound-symbol correspondences: initial *c* /k/, *h* /h/, and *j* /ĵ/.
✓ Write the letters *c*, *h*, and *j*.
✓ Complete Phonics page 20.
✓ Listen to the audio.
✓ Sing songs and say chants.

Prereading and Prewriting

✓ Follow a four-page story.
✓ Talk about the characters.
✓ Act out the story to show comprehension.
✓ Practice fine motor skills.
✓ Trace letters and a short sentence.

BULLETIN BOARD DISPLAY

School Match-Up

✓ Create an interactive bulletin board to use throughout the unit.

Materials

- photos or drawings of children doing things in school
- photos or drawings of places in your school
- colored string
- push pins
- teacher-made labels

Directions

1. If you have access to a camera and photo printing, take photographs for this project. If not, use teacher- and child-made drawings.
2. Divide the board into two columns.
3. In the first column, display pictures of children engaged in activities from this unit (play, point, read, sing, use the computer).
4. In the second column, display pictures of the target places (classroom, computer room, music room, playground).
5. To the right of each activity, use a push pin to attach a piece of colored string.
6. Show children how to use the string to match each activity in Column 1 with a place in Column 2.

2 At School

A14 1 **Listen and sing. Move.**

Presentation: *classroom, computer room, music room, play, playground, read, sing, use the computer* **TPR:** jump, point, question action, read, use a computer

Presentation

Objectives: To identify classroom vocabulary in scenes, to learn a song and new TPR actions

New Vocabulary: classroom, computer room, music room, play, playground, read, sing, use the computer

TPR: jump, point, question action, read, use a computer

Materials: Class Audio CD A, Picture Cards, Workbook

Optional Materials: My Little Island Map poster, Sammy the Squirrel puppet, CD-ROM, ActiveTeach, ball

GETTING READY

Look at the Island Map Poster (5 minutes)

- Show the island map and ask children to name the places they've already visited.
- Explain that children will visit the school.

Review Classroom Vocabulary (5 minutes)

- Explain that you will toss a ball to one child at a time who should point to and name a classroom object: *I see [a book]* and then toss the ball back to you.
- Elicit or help children with words from Level 1 (*book, chair, crayon, pencil, table, teacher*) and Level 2 (*backpack, computer, markers, notebook, pen, scissors*).

WORKING IN THE BOOK: PAGE 14

Present Vocabulary and TPR

- Have children talk about the pictures on page 14.
- Use the unit Picture Cards to reinforce the vocabulary. Say: *[Classroom]* and have children repeat.

  Say: *[Find the classroom]* and have children point to the picture of it in their books.
- Follow a similar procedure for the playground, the computer room, and the music room.
- Use TPR actions to clarify meaning.

A14 1. Listen and sing. Move.

- Tell children to listen to a song to find out what Sue and Lou do at school.
- Play the audio. Use the Picture Cards and do the actions to clarify meaning.
- Play the audio again. Invite children to do the actions with you and sing along when ready.

Audio Script

What Do You Do at School?

Hello to you! (point to other kids)
What do you do?
What do you do at school? (question action)

I read, read, read (pretend to read, open hands)
As a rule / In the classroom / At my school.

Hello to you! (point to other kids)
What do you do?
What do you do at school? (question action)

I play, play, play (jump up and down)
As a rule / On the playground / At my school.

Hello to you! (point to other kids)
What do you do?
What do you do at school? (question action)

I use the computer (pretend to type)
As a rule / In the computer room / At my school.

Hello to you! (point to other kids)
What do you do?
What do you do at school? (question action)

I sing, sing, sing
As a rule / In the music room / At my school.

Hello to you! (point to other kids)
What do you do?
What do you do at school? (question action)

CONSOLIDATING

Charades (10 minutes)

- Display the Picture Cards for reference.
- Play a game of charades.
- Pretend to do an action and have children guess the word.
- Reinforce the vocabulary: *Yes, I [play] on the [playground].*
- Invite children to act out for the class as well.

A15 Karaoke (5 minutes)

- Play the karaoke version of the song.
- Hold up Picture Cards to cue children for each verse.
- Encourage everyone to sing the chorus together.

Workbook Page 14

Have children match each place at school with a picture of a child and write the number in the box. Then have children color the page and work with a partner to name each place and activity.

OPTIONAL: USING DIGITAL COMPONENTS

CD-ROM

Have children play the games and do the activities on the CD-ROM at home to show their families what they're learning about in class.

ActiveTeach

Reinforce vocabulary using the Picture Card images on ActiveTeach.

Vocabulary

Objective: To practice new words
New Vocabulary: classroom, computer room, music room, play, playground, read, sing, use the computer
Writing: numbers 1–8
Materials: Class Audio CD A, Workbook
Optional Materials: Picture Cards, Sammy the Squirrel puppet, CD-ROM, ActiveTeach

GETTING READY

A14 Review the Song (10 minutes)

- Say: *Let's sing the song again.*
- Sing and act out "What Do You Do at School?" with children.
- Arrange the class in two groups.
- Have one group sing and act out the chorus and questions and the other sing and act out the answers.
- Play and sing the song once more.

Prepare for the Exercise (5 minutes)

- Display the Picture Cards on the board.
- Write the vocabulary word or words under each one.
- Draw a simple box next to each word to look like Student Book page 15.
- Demonstrate with Sammy or a prepared volunteer.
- Have Sammy say: *Number one. Read.*
- Model searching for the *read* Picture Card.
- Then write the number 1 in the box next to the word.
- Do a few more, and then invite volunteers to finish.
- At the end, lead the class in saying each number and word in order, for example: *1 – read, 2 – play*, and so on.

WORKING IN THE BOOK: PAGE 15

A16 2. Listen. Find and number. Say.

- Have children open their books to page 15.
- Explain that children need to listen and write numbers.
- Point out that the first one is done as an example.
- Play the first part of the audio track. Pause after each item to allow children time to find and write.

Audio Script

1. read
2. play
3. sing
4. use the computer
5. classroom
6. playground
7. music room
8. computer room

- For additional practice, say each vocabulary word aloud and have children clap twice, pause, clap once, pause, clap twice again, and repeat the word.

CONSOLIDATING

Going on a School Walk (10 minutes)

- Display the classroom Picture Cards around the room.
- Lead the class on a "walk around school."
- For each card and "room" say: *I [sing] in the [music room]*. Pretend to sing.
- Have the class follow you.
- For fun, model some silly actions along with the others from Levels 1 and 2: *I [write] in the [classroom]; I [wiggle] in the [music room].*

Match and Say (5 minutes)

- Display the Picture Cards on the board in two rows.
- Put the rooms in one row and the actions in the other.
- Invite children to come to the board and draw lines from an action to a room and say: *I [use the computer] in the [computer room].*

Workbook Page 15

Have children match each place at school with a child doing an activity there. Then have children color the page. Finally, have partners take turns naming each activity and the place at school where children do it.

OPTIONAL: USING DIGITAL COMPONENTS

CD-ROM

Have children practice the new vocabulary using the games on the CD-ROM.

ActiveTeach

Use the large digital format to model numbering the boxes on the Student Book page. For additional vocabulary practice, use the Picture Cards on ActiveTeach.

VOCABULARY

A16 **2** **Listen. Find and number. Say.**

classroom

playground

read 1

play

music room

computer room

sing

use the computer

Story

Objectives: To read and understand a story, to use and understand speech bubbles, to learn a new language structure, to listen to and recognize the intonation in a sentence, to role-play

New Structures: *Where do you [read]? In the [classroom].*

Materials: Class Audio CD A, Workbook

Optional Materials: Picture Cards, Sammy the Squirrel puppet, CD-ROM, ActiveTeach

GETTING READY

Story Concepts (5 minutes)

- Tell children you are going to help them read a story.
- Encourage children to share what they know about reading stories in books.
- Review literacy concepts using either the Student Book or another book. Make it fun by using Sammy the Squirrel.
  - Have Sammy pretend to read a book upside down; shake your head and say: *No, no, Sammy*. Model turning the book right-side up.
  - Have Sammy read the last page first; say: *No, no, Sammy.* Model starting from the first page and moving forward.
  - Have him flip through the pages randomly; say: *No, no, Sammy.* Model turning the pages one by one in order.
- Focus on speech bubbles.
  - On the board draw a simple face.
  - Draw a speech bubble next to the face and in it, write: *Hello*.
  - Explain that the tail of the speech bubble points to the character who's talking and that the words in the bubble show what the character is saying.

Introduce the Story (5 minutes)

- Hold up Student Book page 16.
- Focus on the first page of "My School." Ask children to talk about what they see.
- Explain that it's Family Day at Sue's school and Grandma is at school with her.
- Talk about special days at school. Does your school have a day when family comes to school? Ask children who in their family has come to school and who they would like to come. (Use TPR and gestures as needed.)
- Take a picture walk through the rest of the story.
- Have children predict what will happen. Revisit predictions later.

WORKING IN THE BOOK: PAGES 16–17

A17 3. Look and listen. Act it out.

- Have children open to page 16.
- Play the audio and pause at each story page to make sure children are on the right page and understand what's happening.
- If needed, help them understand that Sue's grandma is surprised when Sue says she plays in the computer room.
- Play the story audio again. Point to each speech bubble as the words are spoken.
- Encourage children to speak along with the characters.
- Invite volunteers to act out the story with the audio.

Audio Script

My School

Page 1	Sue:	This is my school!
	Grandma:	I like it! Where do you read?
Page 2	Sue:	In the classroom.
	Grandma:	How nice. Where do you sing?
Page 3	Sue:	In the music room.
	Grandma:	How nice. Where do you play?
Page 4	Sue:	In the computer room.
	Grandma:	Oh. You play computer games!

Look at New Language

- Point out the language structure Grandma uses to ask about Sue's school: *Where do you [read]?*
- Focus on Sue's answers: *In the [classroom].*
- Practice with Sammy. Show him a Picture Card and ask: *Where do you [read]?*
- Have Sammy answer: *In the [classroom].*
- Invite children to practice the exchange with Sammy, and then in pairs.

A17 ### Listen to the Intonation

- Play the story audio. Point out how the rise and fall of the speaker's voice differs in questions and answers.
- Have children repeat each question and answer, copying the intonation.

CONSOLIDATING

Role-Play (10 minutes)

- Have pairs of children act out the story.
- First, play the audio and have pairs of children pantomime.
- Then invite volunteers to act out the dialogue without the audio.

Make a Home Connection!

Have a family day for your class. Invite children to show their parents around the school and use the new structures they've learned to answer questions about the rooms at school.

Workbook Page 16

Have children trace the path from place to place in school. Have partners take turns asking and answering questions from the story: *Where do you [read]? In the [classroom].* Finally, have children color the page.

Workbook Page 17

Tell children to circle things that *don't* belong in a music room (duck, doll, toy box, and cat). Then have children color the page. Finally, have partners practice asking and answering: *Where do you [sing]? In the [music room].*

OPTIONAL: USING DIGITAL COMPONENTS

CD-ROM

Have children review the story on their CD-ROM at home. Encourage them to use the Story Time feature and do word-by-word reading with family members.

ActiveTeach

Use the large digital format to focus on the speech bubbles. Point to a character and then drag the pointer under each word she speaks as it plays on the audio.

LISTENING

A18 **4 Listen and match. Write.**

1

2

3

4

1

Practice: *Where do you [read]? In the [classroom].*

Listening

Objectives: To practice listening comprehension, to practice new unit vocabulary and structures

Materials: Class Audio CD A

Optional Materials: Picture Cards, Sammy the Squirrel puppet, CD-ROM, ActiveTeach

GETTING READY

A17 Revisit the Story (10 minutes)

- Reread "At School" together.
- Play the audio and have children read along.

Prepare for the Exercise (5 minutes)

- Choose four volunteers.
- Draw four faces in a row on the board. If possible, make the faces resemble the volunteers.
- Write a number *1–4* by each face, as on Student Book page 18.
- Beneath the faces, display the school-room Picture Cards and draw four simple write-in boxes under the cards.
- Have Sammy point to the first face and number and ask the first volunteer: *Number one: Where do you [use the computer]?*
- Cue the child to answer: *In the [computer room].*
- Point to the *1* next to the face, and write the number in the box under the [computer room] and continue.

WORKING IN THE BOOK: PAGE 18

A18 4. Listen and match. Write.

- Have children open to page 18.
- Explain that they will listen to the children pictured on the page answer questions, and will number the pictures of places in school based on their answers.
- Play the audio. Point out that the first item is done as an example.

Audio Script

1. Where do you read?
   In the classroom.
2. Where do you play?
   On the playground.
3. Where do you sing?
   In the music room.
4. Where do you use the computer?
   In the computer room.

CONSOLIDATING

Matching Card Game (5 minutes)

- Make two stacks of unit Picture Cards: Stack A includes vocabulary for actions: *play, read, sing, use a computer*. Stack B includes room vocabulary: *classroom, computer room, music room, playground*.
- Shuffle the cards in each stack.
- Have a volunteer pick a card from Stack A and ask: *Where do you [read]?*
- Have another volunteer pick a card from Stack B and answer: *In the [classroom].*
- If the cards match (for example, *read* and *classroom*), cue the class to say: *It's a match!*
- If the cards don't match (for example, *read* and *playground*), cue the class to say: *No way! Where do you [read]?* Then cue the two volunteers to answer.

Chant and Move TPR (10 minutes)

- Review school and playground actions children have learned.
- For each one, say the word, do the action, and have children repeat: climb, color, cut, dance, draw, jump, listen, look, paint, run, sing, sit down, speak, stand up, type, walk, write.
- Then teach children a simple chant:

  I [climb, climb, climb] in the [playground]. (pretend to climb)

  Where do I [climb]? (clap, clap)

  In the [playground]!
- Lead children in saying the chant and doing the actions.

OPTIONAL: USING DIGITAL COMPONENTS

CD-ROM

Have children use the CD-ROM at home to show their families what they're learning about places at school and activities.

ActiveTeach

Use the large digital format to model numbering the pictures. Invite volunteers to write the numbers using the pen tool.

Speaking

Objectives: To practice speaking, to practice new unit vocabulary and structures

Materials: Workbook

Optional Materials: Picture Cards, Sammy the Squirrel puppet, CD-ROM, ActiveTeach, Class Audio CD, teacher-made survey

GETTING READY

Pass the Card (10 minutes)

- Have children sit in a circle. Play some music.
- Have children pass around the Picture Cards of places at school while the music plays.
- Stop the music. Ask: *Where do you [play]?*
- Tell children to check their cards and cue the child with the [playground] card to say: *In the [playground].*
- Continue for the other three places.

A18 Practice Intonation (5 minutes)

- Prepare for the speaking practice by focusing on intonation.
- Play the audio for Exercise 4 on Student Book page 18. Tell children to focus on the different intonation for the questions and the answers.
- Pause the audio after children listen to a question or answer and have them repeat, copying the speakers' intonations.

WORKING IN THE BOOK: PAGE 19

5. Ask and answer. Circle.

- Have children open to page 19.
- Focus on the first item, which is done as an example.
- Call attention to the boy and girl with the speech bubbles at the bottom of the page.
- Point to and read the speech bubbles: *Where do you read? In the classroom.*
- Tell children they will work in pairs, using the speech bubble text as a model.
- Tell them to ask and answer questions about what the other two children on the page are doing and then circle one of the three places on the right. Remind them to follow the example.

CONSOLIDATING

Make an Activities Survey (10 minutes)

- Ask: *Where do you read in school?* Elicit: *In the classroom.*
- Then ask: *Where do you read at home?* Elicit: *In [my bedroom].*
- Repeat with a few more examples of activities people do at home, such as eat and sleep.
- Create a generic survey in the form of a grid with the actions listed down the side and the rooms listed across the top. Make photocopies for children to take home.
- Include a picture clue by each word.
- Point to the first action. Ask: *Where do you [eat]?*
- Elicit responses from a few children. Write their names in the boxes under the rooms. For example, if Martha eats in the kitchen, write "Martha" in the box under kitchen.
- Continue with the other actions.
- Encourage children to take the survey home, do it with family members, and then share results with the class.

Mixed-Up Sentences (5 minutes)

- Invite four volunteers to stand.
- Whisper a different word into each child's ear: *Where, do, you, [play].*
- Have them stand in a line but not in sentence order and say their words, for example: *you, [play], Where, do.*
- Invite another volunteer to arrange them in the correct order.
- Have children say their words in order to make a question. Invite the class to answer it.
- Repeat with the other questions and answers.

Extra Practice: Student Book page 94 and T94

For extra practice speaking, have students turn to page 94 in the back of their books. For teacher support, turn to page T94 in this book.

Workbook Page 18

Have children work with a partner to complete this page. Tell one child to spin a pencil and ask a question prompted by the picture, such as this: *Where do you use the [computer]?* Have the other child answer appropriately: *In the [computer room].* Have children color the page.

Workbook Page 19

Have children circle the pictures to show where they do each activity. Have partners share their work by asking and answering questions: *Where do you [sing]? In the [music room].* Finally, invite children to color the page.

OPTIONAL: USING DIGITAL COMPONENTS

CD-ROM

Have children use the CD-ROM at home. Have them mimic the audio to practice speaking skills.

ActiveTeach

Use the large digital format to model circling the correct pictures on the page.

SPEAKING

EXTRA PRACTICE
Page 94

5 **Ask and answer. Circle.**

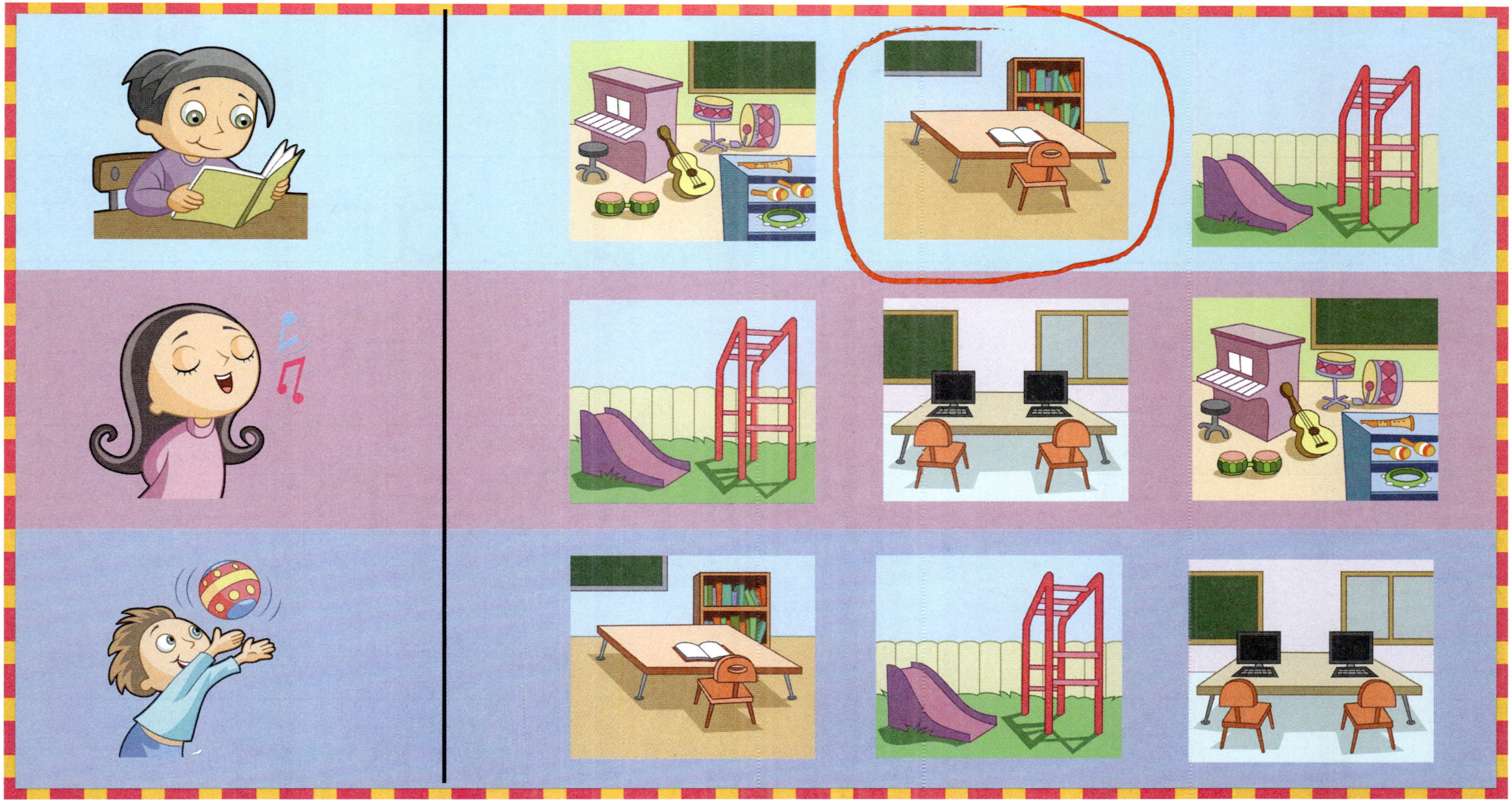

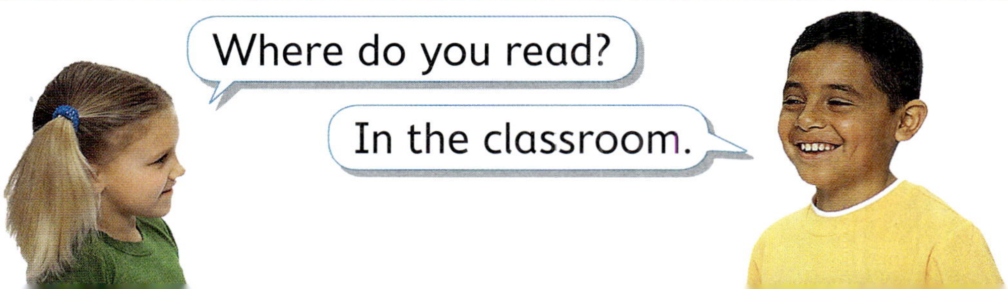

Practice: *Where do you [read]? In the [classroom].*

PHONICS

A19 A21 6 **Listen. Trace, write, and say.**

c c

car

h h

hen

j j

jump

Phonics: initial *c, h, j* **Prewriting/Writing:** directionality, letter tracing, letters in contexts
Review: *car, hen* **TPR:** write letters in the air

Phonics

Objectives: To learn the sounds that *c*, *h*, and *j* stand for at the beginning of words, to understand sound-symbol correspondences, to recognize left-to-right directionality, to trace and write letters in contexts

New Sounds and Letters: *c* /k/, *h* /h/, *j* /j/

Review: car, hen

TPR: write *c* in the air

Materials: Class Audio CD A, Workbook

Optional Materials: Picture Cards, CD-ROM, ActiveTeach

GETTING READY

Introduce the Letters (10 minutes)

- Write the entire alphabet on the board.
- Circle the letter *c*.
- Say: *This is* c. *C stands for* cuh *in words like* car *and* cat. Remind children that *k* stands for the same sound in words like *kite*.
- Write the letters *c-a-r* on the board.
- Underline the *c*. Say: *Cuh*.
- Run your finger under the word as you slowly say: *Car*.
- Repeat for *h* in *hello* and *hen*; *j* in *juice* and *jump*.

WORKING IN THE BOOK: PAGE 20

A19 A21 ### 6. Listen. Trace, write, and say.

- Show children the picture of Sue cheering.
- Jump up and down and pretend to be a cheerleader as you say: *Give me a c!*
- Explain that when a cheerleader says *Give me a c!*, the fans yell out: C!
- Play the chant and do the actions.
- Play it again and have children respond. Encourage them to repeat the fans' lines.

Audio Script

***C, H, J* Cheer**

Sue: Give me a *c!*
Fans: *C!*
Sue: What does *c* sound like?
Fans: Cuh!
Sue: Give me a *c* word!
Fans: Cuh . . . *car!*
Sue: Show me a *c!* (write *c* in the air)
Let's hear it for *c!*
Fans: Hooray!

Sue: Give me an *h!*
Fans: *H!*
Sue: What does *h* sound like?
Fans: Huh!
Sue: Give me an *h* word!
Fans: Huh . . . *hen!*
Sue: Show me an *h!* (write *h* in the air)
Let's hear it for *h!*
Fans: Hooray!

Sue: Give me a *j!*
Fans: *J!*
Sue: What does *j* sound like?
Fans: Juh!
Sue: Give me a *j* word!
Fans: Juh . . . *jump!*
Sue: Show me a *j!* (write *j* in the air)
Let's hear it for *j!*
Fans: Hooray!

- Focus children on the page again.
- Point to the *c* on the left. Model tracing the letter with your finger. Then have children trace it and then write it several times.
- Then point to the word *car* on the right. Say: *Cuh. Car.*
- Model tracing the *c* at the beginning of the word. Then have children trace it.
- Repeat for the other letters and words.
- Finally, have children take turns pointing to and reading the letters and words.
- For additional practice, have children listen to Class Audio CD A: Track 21.
  - Play the audio, pausing after each word to allow children to listen to the initial sound and then say the letter that stands for the sound.
  - Say: *That's good!* when children say the correct letter.

Audio Script

Now listen and say the letters.
car, cat, hen, horse, jump, juice

CONSOLIDATING

Body Letters (5 minutes)

- Help children create shapes with their bodies for *c*, *j*, and *h*.
- For a *c*, have children sit on the floor with their legs curved up and their arms curved over. For a *j*, have children stand up straight with hand cupped over head (for the dot) and one leg up, bent at the knee.
- For an *h*, have children work with a partner with one child standing up straight and the other in front, arching over with hands and feet on the floor.

Workbook Page 20

Have children trace the letters and words and color the pictures. Then have partners point to the letters and pictures and name them.

OPTIONAL: USING DIGITAL COMPONENTS

CD-ROM

Have children play the games and do the activities on the CD-ROM at home to show what they are learning in the unit.

ActiveTeach

Demonstrate tracing the letters on the big screen. Invite volunteers to write the letters.

Math

Objectives: To count items 1–10, to write numbers 7–10

Review: numbers 1–10, classroom items

TPR: flap arms, hold up fingers, kick, march, write

Materials: Class Audio CD A, Workbook

Optional Materials: CD-ROM; ActiveTeach; classroom objects, teacher-made number and dot cards (save to use later)

GETTING READY

Review Numbers (10 minutes)

- Review numbers 1–10 by counting real objects in the classroom.
- Hold up or point to one item. Say: *One. One [book].* Have children repeat.
- Write the number on the board. Draw one circle under it to show how many.
- Repeat with 2–10, using other items.
- Identify groups of items or children and ask: *How many?*

Air Numbers (5 minutes)

- Have children take turns writing numbers *1–10* in the air.
- Each time, invite the class to guess which number the child is writing.

WORKING IN THE BOOK: PAGE 21

A22 7. Listen, say, and trace. Count and write.

- Play the chant and act it out.
- Play it again and invite children to chant and do the actions with you.

Audio Script

Count to 10 Chant

1, 2, 3, (hold up fingers for counting)
Buzz like a bee. (flap arms and buzz)
4, 5, 6, (hold up fingers for counting)
Do high kicks. (kick)
7, 8, 9, (hold up fingers for counting)
March in a line. (march in place)
10! 10! 10!
Write with a pen. (pretend to write)

- Have children look at page 21. Count 1–10 and point to the numbers 7–10 on the top right as you say each one.
- Ask children to point and repeat after you and then trace each number in their books.
- Next, explain that Lou is counting the classroom objects on the table.
- Say: *Let's count crayons with Lou. 1, 2, 3, 4, 5, 6, 7.*
- Point to the picture of the crayon on the notebook. Say: *See 7. 7 crayons. I write 7.* (Trace the 7 with your fingers.)
- Have individuals or groups count the other items on the table and write the number of each next to its picture.

CONSOLIDATING

A23 How Many Voices? (5 minutes)

- Play the karaoke version of the chant.
- Have children count while you chant the rest.
- Have a few volunteers put their heads down so they can't see.
- Quietly, choose a small group to chant. Don't let the volunteers know how many children you picked.
- Play the karaoke chant and have the small group chant.
- When you're finished, ask the volunteers to guess how many children chanted.

Group Concentration (10 minutes)

- Prepare twenty playing cards.
- Write one number from *1–10* on ten cards.
- Draw one to ten dots on the other ten cards.
- Divide the class into two groups. Shuffle each set of cards.
- Give the number cards to one group and the dot cards to the other.
- Tell children not to show their cards to anyone.
- Have the two groups face each other.
- Invite two volunteers to play.
- Player 1 names one child from each group. The two children show their cards to the player.
- If the cards match, the player keeps them. If not, the children return to their groups.
- Repeat with Player 2. Continue several times and then with other volunteers. The player with the most pairs at the end wins.

Workbook Page 21

Have children trace the numbers, count the items, and then match each group of items to a number. After children color the page, have partners count and name the items, for example: *1, 2, 3, 4. Four pencils.*

OPTIONAL: USING DIGITAL COMPONENTS

CD-ROM

Have children play the games on the CD-ROM to practice and review numbers.

ActiveTeach

Invite volunteers to use the pen tool to count each group of items and write the numbers.

MATH

A22 7 **Listen, say, and trace. Count and write.**

7 8 9 10

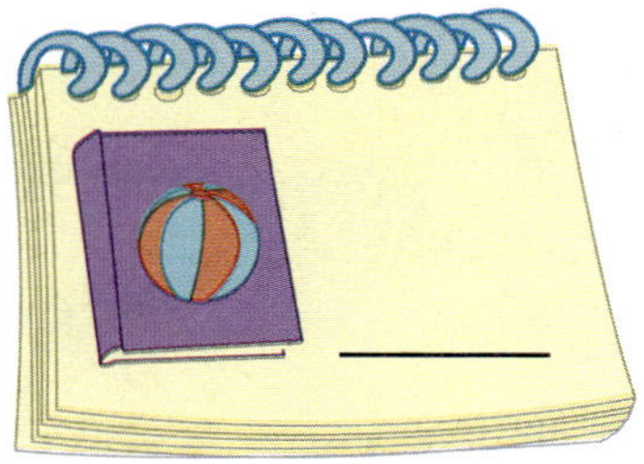

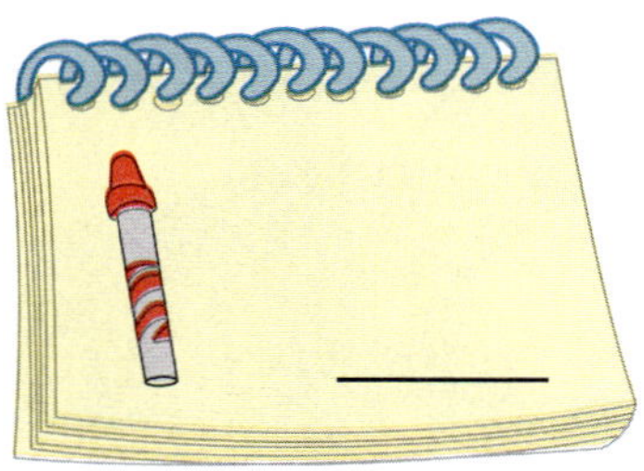

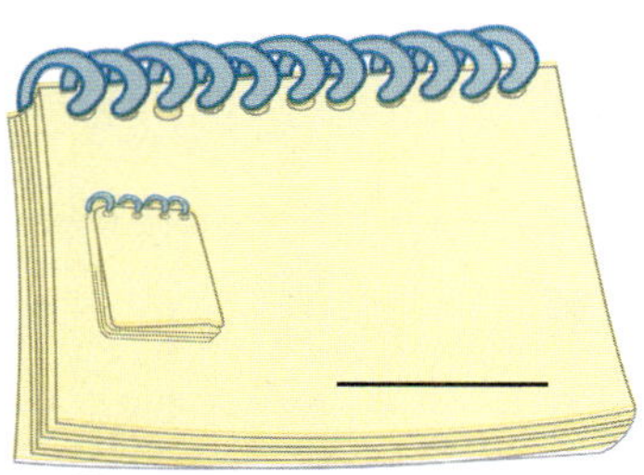

VALUES Follow rules.

A24 8 **Listen and say. Draw and trace.**

Follow rules.

Values: Follow rules. **Prewriting:** tracing a short sentence

Values

Objective: To learn about the value of putting things away
New Values Language: Follow rules.
Prewriting: tracing a short sentence
Materials: Class Audio CD A, Workbook
Optional Materials: Sammy the Squirrel puppet, CD-ROM, ActiveTeach, poster board

GETTING READY

Introduce Following Rules (5 minutes)

- Tell children that a rule is something they must do, such as use the crosswalk to cross the street.
- Talk to them about why rules are important.
- Introduce ideas about safety, fairness, and group harmony.
- Help children think of some rules that might make your class safer, fairer, or happier.
- Revisit some of the values that children learned in Levels 1 and 2: ask nicely, say *sorry*, help others, put away your toys, cover your nose and mouth, share, be nice to animals, play safely, put things away, help your family, be careful, wash your hands, eat properly, do your chores, dress for the weather.
- Ask if any of those values make good classroom rules. Note these to refer to later.

Role Play: Sammy (5 minutes)

- Do a few simple role plays with the Sammy puppet, such as having him cough with or without covering his mouth.
- Each time, name a rule.
- If Sammy doesn't follow the rule, say: *Sammy, [cover your mouth]. Follow rules.*
- If Sammy follows the rule, say: *Good job! You follow rules, Sammy.*

WORKING IN THE BOOK: PAGE 22

A24 8. Listen and say. Draw and trace.

- Have children open their books to page 22.
- Play the dialogue on the first part of the audio and ask children to look at the photos as they listen.
- Have volunteers repeat the dialogue with you.

Audio Script

Teacher: Are you finished playing?
Boys: Yes, we are.
Teacher: Remember to clean up. That's a school rule.
Boys: Okay.
Teacher: Share toys. That's a school rule, too.

- Then play the chant on the second part of the audio. Have children listen and then chant along with the audio when they are ready.

Audio Script

Follow Rules Chant
Clean up. Listen now.
Follow school rules.
Play nicely. Listen now.
Follow school rules.

- Talk about each photo with the class and have children discuss whether the children in each photo are following rules or not.
- Now point to the faces below each photo. Tell children to draw a smile on the face below the photo where children are following rules and a frown under the photo where children are *not* following rules.
- Finally, have children read and trace the sentence: *Follow rules.*

Talk about it!

- Call attention to "Talk about it!"
- Share something people can do to help them follow rules (make a list of classroom rules, for example). Invite children to talk about ways they can follow rules.

CONSOLIDATING

Class Rules (10 minutes)

- On a large piece of poster board, make a list of class rules.
- Invite children to name rules they think are important.
- Draw a picture cue next to each rule.
- Refer to these throughout the year.

Role Play: Children (10 minutes)

- Invite pairs or small groups to role-play.
- Refer to your class rules beforehand.
- Have each group pick one rule. Then ask them to act out following the rule or not following it.
- If they do not follow the rule, cue the class to call out: *Follow the rules!*
- If they do follow it, cue the class to call out: *Good job! You follow rules.*

Workbook Page 22

Have children color the page and say chorally: *Follow rules.*

OPTIONAL: USING DIGITAL COMPONENTS

CD-ROM

Have children play the games and do the activities on the CD-ROM at home to show their families the values they're learning in class.

ActiveTeach

Focus on the two pictures. Use the pointer to highlight details that illustrate who is following rules and who isn't. Confirm which face should be smiling and which, frowning.

Review / Assessment

Objectives: To review and assess new unit vocabulary and structures

Review: *Where do you [read]? In the [classroom].*

Materials: Class Audio CD A, Workbook, stickers (in the back of the Student Book and shown on page T108)

Optional Materials: Picture Cards; CD-ROM; ActiveTeach; poster board, drawing paper, crayons or markers

GETTING READY

A Sing and Move (10 minutes)

- Invite children to sing and move to the various songs and chants from the unit.
- Invite children to tell which song or chant they like best.

Play a Review Game (5 minutes)

- Divide the class into two teams.
- Display the Picture Cards on the board.
- Point to an action card and gesture to Group 1.
- Elicit from Group 1: *Where do you [play]?*
- Invite one volunteer from Group 2 to point to the card that answers the question.
- Have Group 2 answer together: *In the [playground].*

WORKING IN THE BOOK: PAGE 23

9. Stick and say.

- Distribute the stickers (but not the reward sticker).
- Have children open to page 23.
- Help children notice the sticker outlines in their books and then stick the correct ones in place. Begin with item 1 and say: *Find the [music room] sticker.*
- Have children hold up that sticker.
- Say: *Stick the sticker.*
- Have children stick the sticker and say: *The [music room].*
- Repeat with the other stickers (classroom, computer room, playground).

A26 10. Listen and circle.

- Explain that you will play the audio and that children will listen and circle the answer to each question.
- Confirm the answers with the class.

Audio Script

1. Where do you use the computer?
2. Where do you read?
3. Where do you sing?
4. Where do you play?

I Can! Use the Reward Sticker

- Help children talk about what they have learned in this unit. Encourage them to use positive language:
  - I can ask and answer: *Where do you [read]? In the [classroom].*
  - I can count to ten. I can write the numbers *1–10*, too.
- Distribute the reward stickers.
- Show children where to stick the stickers (on the Unit 2 Good Job! placeholder).

CONSOLIDATING

Congratulations Chant (5 minutes)

- Ask children to each choose one thing they learned in the unit (a vocabulary word, a structure, a number, a letter).
- Have children stand in a circle.
- Have each child chant to tell what he or she learned while the class claps.
- For example:
  - C1: *I know* (clap, clap) *[music room].* (clap, clap)
  - C2: *I can* (clap, clap) *[write the number 7].* (clap, clap)
- End by congratulating the class!

Social Studies Project: Our School Poster

- Have children work in groups of four.
- Have each child in a group draw a different place at school.
- Brainstorm details for the places, such as furniture, artwork, and children doing specific activities.
- Attach drawings of four different places to one poster. Label or have a child label the poster: *OUR SCHOOL.*

Workbook Page 23

Have children draw their favorite place at school. Then have them color the page. Finally, ask partners to share their work and say: *Where do you [play]? On the [playground].*

OPTIONAL: USING DIGITAL COMPONENTS

CD-ROM

Have children play the games and do the activities on the CD-ROM at home to show their families what they're learning about in class.

ActiveTeach

Use ActiveTeach to check answers as a class.

REVIEW I can!

9 **Stick and say.** A26 **10** **Listen and circle.**

1

2

3

4

Project

3 Workers

Unit Overview

Objectives

- To learn vocabulary for workers
- To sing songs and chant
- To do new TPR movements
- To practice fine and gross motor skills
- To understand and role-play a story
- To learn and practice new language structures: *What do you want to be? I want to be a [police officer].*
- To practice sound-symbol correspondences: *q* /kw/, *r* /r/, and *v* /v/
- To recognize and produce the sounds that *q*, *r*, and *v* stand for at the beginning of words
- To write the letters *q*, *r*, and *v*
- To learn how to count to 12
- To learn how to write numbers 11 and 12
- To learn the value of staying safe
- To practice writing a short sentence
- To practice new language by listening and speaking
- To learn and review unit vocabulary and language structures

Vocabulary

New: artist, astronaut, dentist, doctor, firefighter, nurse, police officer, vet, worker(s); numbers 11, 12

Review: numbers 1–10; animals; red

Home-School Connections

Copy the Letter Home for children to bring home to share what they'll be learning in Unit 3 of *My Little Island*. The Letter Home is available online at www.pearsonelt.com/mylittleisland.

Values

Stay safe.

Materials

Student Book pages 24–33; Workbook Pages 24–33; Picture Cards 9–16; Class Audio CD A: Tracks 27–39; Program Posters: Meet Your New Friends!; My Little Island Map, Shapes and Colors All Around; stickers (back of Student Book and shown on page T108)

Optional: CD-ROM, ActiveTeach, Big Book, Sammy the Squirrel Puppet

Songs and Chants

- Time for Work (Class Audio CD A: Tracks 27, 28)
- *Q, R, V* Cheer (Class Audio CD A: Tracks 32, 33)
- Count to 12 Chant (Class Audio CD A: Tracks 35, 36)
- Stay Safe Chant (Class Audio CD A: Tracks 37, 38)

Story

"Let's Go": Sue and Lou tell each other what they want to be when they grow up. When Sammy gets hurt, Sue decides she wants to be a vet instead.

Language Structure: *I want to be a [police officer].*

SKILLS

Cross-Curricular Connections

count to 12, write numbers 9–12

learn the value of staying safe

sing, chant, and move to music

make a poster about safety (preventing fires)

Preschool Learning Outcomes

✓ Recognize intonation in questions.

✓ Use short answers to questions.

✓ Understand new language structures.

✓ Recognize and produce the sounds that initial *q*, *r*, and *v* stand for.

✓ Write the letters *q*, *r*, and *v* in words.

✓ Listen to and follow a story with words.

✓ Make predictions based on pictures.

✓ Sing songs and say chants with TPR.

✓ Join in games and interact.

✓ Talk about self and surroundings.

✓ Develop a positive attitude toward the English language.

Digital Practice

Have children use the CD-ROM for vocabulary practice in class or at home.

Use ActiveTeach to go over Student Book pages together as a class.

LEARN BY DOING

TPR

✓ flap arms, hold up fingers to count, kick, march, march in place, point, write, write letters in the air

Phonics

✓ Recognize sound-symbol correspondences: *q* /kw/, *r* /r/, *v* /v/.

✓ Write the letters *q*, *r*, and *v*.

✓ Complete page 30.

✓ Listen to the audio.

✓ Sing songs and say chants.

Prereading and Prewriting

✓ Follow a four-page story.

✓ Talk about the characters.

✓ Act out the story to show comprehension.

✓ Practice fine-motor skills.

✓ Trace letters and a short sentence.

BULLETIN BOARD DISPLAY

What Do You Want to Be?

✓ Create a thematic bulletin board.

Materials

- photos or drawings of workers in and outside the community
- teacher-made labels for workers
- teacher-made or child-made name tags

Directions

1. Divide the bulletin board into eight sections, one for each worker.
2. Label each section with a teacher-made label (*artist*, *astronaut*, etc.).
3. Within each section, display photos or child-made drawings of the worker.
4. If possible, take photos of workers in your community to add to the display.
5. Write each child's name or have the child write it on a name tag.
6. Have children tape their name tag in one worker's section on the board and say: *I want to be a/an [artist].*

3 Workers

A27 1 **Listen and sing. Move.**

Presentation: *artist, astronaut, dentist, doctor, firefighter, nurse, police officer, vet, worker(s)* **TPR:** march in place

Presentation

Objectives: To identify vocabulary in a scene, to learn a song and do actions

New Vocabulary: artist, astronaut, dentist, doctor, firefighter, nurse, police officer, vet, worker(s)

TPR: march in place

Materials: Class Audio CD A, Picture Cards, Workbook

Optional Materials: My Little Island Map poster, CD-ROM, ActiveTeach

GETTING READY

Share What You Know (5 minutes)

- Gesture to yourself. Say: *I'm a teacher.*
- Show photos or other pictures of people doing other work.
- Explain that these are all workers.
- Invite children to talk about the work people do: What do their parents do? What do they want to do when they grow up?

Look at the Island Poster (5 minutes)

- Display the My Little Island Map poster.
- Ask children to talk about the places they have visited on the island.
- Then show the pictures of different workers. Ask children where on the island these people might work.

WORKING IN THE BOOK: PAGE 24

Introduce the Vocabulary

- Have children open to page 24.
- Explain that Sue, Lou, and their friends are playing dress up and that they are dressed as different workers.
- Use the Picture Cards to teach the vocabulary. Hold up a picture.
- Say: *Artist.* Have children repeat.
- Say: *Show me the artist in your book.* Have children point to the child dressed as an artist.
- Repeat with the other words.

A27 1. Listen and sing. Move.

- Display the picture cards.
- Say: *Let's sing a song.* Play the song.
- Have children point to the Picture Cards as workers are named in the song.
- Play the song again. Invite children to sing along when they are ready.

Audio Script

Time for Work

Work, work, work. (march in place as though going off to work)
It's time to go to work.
The doctor, the firefighter,
The nurse, the police officer.
Work, work, work. (march in place as though going off to work)
It's time to go to work.

Work, work, work. (march in place as though going off to work)
It's time to go to work.
The dentist, the vet,
The astronaut, the artist.
Work, work, work. (march in place as though going off to work)
It's time to go to work.

CONSOLIDATING

A28 Karaoke (5 minutes)

- Display the Picture Cards on the board.
- Play the karaoke version of the song and have children sing along and do the actions.
- Point to the unit Picture Cards to cue children for different workers.

Let's Move (10 minutes)

- Brainstorm a simple action for each worker such as:
  - *artist*: paint on an easel;
  - *astronaut*: float as if in space;
  - *dentist*: open mouth wide and pretend to polish teeth;
  - *doctor*: hand to wrist as if taking pulse;
  - *firefighter*: pretend to hold a hose and move it as if putting out a fire;
  - *nurse*: finger to arm as if giving a shot;
  - *police officer*: one hand up to signal stop, the other beckoning for cars to move;
  - *vet*: cradle an imaginary cat or dog in one arm and pet it with the other hand.
- Discuss when and why each worker does each action.

Workbook Page 24

Have children connect the dots to complete the picture. Have them color the picture and say: *Firefighter.*

OPTIONAL: USING DIGITAL COMPONENTS

CD-ROM

Have children play the games and do the activities on the CD-ROM at home to show their families what they're learning about in class.

ActiveTeach

Use the large digital format to focus on the different workers as they are named in song.

Vocabulary

Objective: To practice new words
New Vocabulary: artist, astronaut, dentist, doctor, firefighter, nurse, police officer, vet
Writing: numbers 1–8
Materials: Class Audio CD A, Workbook
Optional Materials: Picture Cards, CD-ROM, ActiveTeach

GETTING READY

A27 Review the Song (10 minutes)

- Revisit the gestures for the workers from Consolidating activity Let's Move on page T24.
- Play "Time for Work."
- Encourage children to do the gestures for each worker.

Thumbs-Up or Thumbs-Down (10 minutes)

- Ask a volunteer to be your helper.
- Display the unit Picture Cards for reference.
- Explain that the helper will name a worker and you will do an action for that worker (paint a picture, direct traffic, and so on).
- Tell children that if you do the correct action, the helper will give a thumbs-up and if not, he or she will give a thumbs-down.
- Continue in this way but invite the class to join in.

WORKING IN THE BOOK: PAGE 25

A29 2. Listen. Find and number. Say.

- Have children look at the pictures on page 25.
- Tell them to listen to the audio and find and number the pictures of the workers.
- Play the audio and have children write the numbers.

Audio Script

1. nurse
2. artist
3. police officer
4. doctor
5. firefighter
6. astronaut
7. vet
8. dentist

- Check children's work as a class. Have volunteers point and say: *[1] [nurse].* Continue with the rest of the pictures.
- For additional practice, say each vocabulary word aloud and have children clap twice, pause, clap twice again, pause, clap once, and repeat the word.

CONSOLIDATING

Who's Missing? (10 minutes)

- Display the Picture Cards on the board in a row.
- Lead the class in chorally reciting the words in order.
- Have children put their heads on their desks.
- Take away a card.
- Have children look up. Challenge them to name the missing card.
- Repeat several times.
- For a challenge, mix up the order first, and then take away a card.

Who Am I? (5 minutes)

- Have the class stand in a circle.
- Explain that you will go first.
- Hold a unit Picture Card of a worker over your head facing toward the group. Hold the card so you cannot see what it is.
- Explain that you are going to guess what card you are holding. Ask the class to give you hints by doing gestures for the worker on the card.
- After you guess correctly, invite other children to take turns holding a card and guessing.

Workbook Page 25

Have children match the objects with the workers. After children color the page, have partners point and name each worker: *artist, dentist, doctor, police officer, teacher.*

OPTIONAL: USING DIGITAL COMPONENTS

CD-ROM

Have children play the games on the CD-ROM with their families to show the words they know for different workers.

ActiveTeach

Use the large digital format to model numbering the boxes on the Student Book page. For additional vocabulary practice, use the Picture Card images.

VOCABULARY

A29 **2** **Listen. Find and number. Say.**

doctor

astronaut

vet

nurse

firefighter

artist

police officer

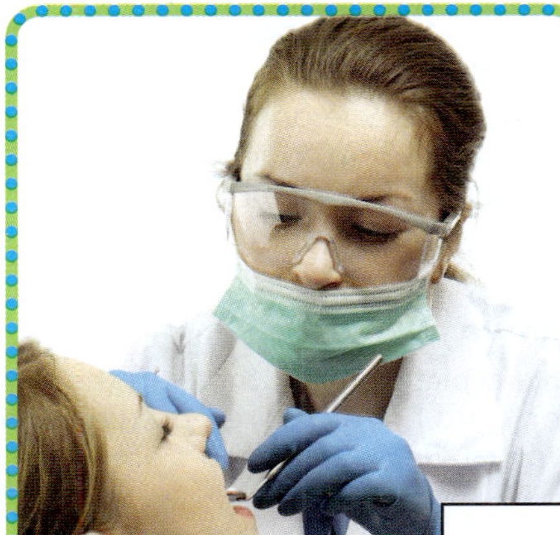

dentist

Practice: *doctor, astronaut, vet, nurse, firefighter, artist, police officer, dentist* **Writing:** *1–8*

Story

Objectives: To read and understand a story, to identify and understand speech bubbles, to learn a new language structure, to listen and identify intonation, to role-play, to practice new vocabulary

New Structure: *I want to be a [police officer].*

Review: *It's Sammy!*

Materials: Class Audio CD A, Workbook

Optional Materials: Picture Cards, Sammy the Squirrel puppet, CD-ROM, ActiveTeach, ball

GETTING READY

Peek-a-Boo Picture Cards (5 minutes)

- Hide the unit Picture Cards in a bag.
- Slowly pull one card out of the bag.
- Have children try to name the worker before they see the whole picture of it.
- Repeat with the others.

Introduce the Story (5 minutes)

- Hold up Student Book page 26.
- Focus on the first page of "Let's Go." Ask children to talk about the picture.
- Explain that Sue and Lou are playing dress-up. Ask children to name each worker.
- Tell children that Sue wants to be a police officer and Lou wants to be a firefighter.
- Invite a few children to tell you what they want to be.
- Take a picture walk through the rest of the story and have children predict what will happen. Revisit children's predictions later.

WORKING IN THE BOOK: PAGES 26 AND 27

A30 3. Look and listen. Act it out.

- Have children open their books to page 26.
- Play the audio, pausing at each story page to make sure children are on the right one and are following what's happening.
- Have children talk about what each character wants to be.
- Ask children why Sue says she wants to be a vet. Help them understand that Sammy is hurt and she wants to help him.
- Play the story audio again. Point to each speech bubble as the words are spoken.
- Encourage children to speak along with the characters.
- Invite volunteers to act out the story with the audio.

Audio Script

Let's Go

Page 1	Sue:	I want to be a police officer.
	Lou:	I want to be a firefighter.
Page 2	Sue:	I want to be an artist.
	Lou:	You are an artist!
Page 3	Sue:	What's that?
	Lou:	It's Sammy!
Page 4	Sue:	Oh! Now I want to be a vet.
	Lou:	Let's go!

Look at New Language

- Point out the new language the characters use to talk about the worker they want to be: *I want to be a [vet].*
- Then ask Sammy: *What do you want to be?*
- Have Sammy answer: *I want to be a / an [astronaut].*
- Invite volunteers to say what they want to be.

A30 Listen to Intonation and Tone of Voice

- Have children close their eyes and listen while you play the story audio.
- Point out the intonation and tone of voice used for the statements, exclamations, and questions: *I want to be an artist. / You are an artist! / What's that? / It's Sammy!*
- Pause after each statement, exclamation, and question on the audio and have children mimic the intonation and tone of voice.

CONSOLIDATING

Role-Play (10 minutes)

- Have pairs of children act out the story.
- First, play the audio and have pairs of children pantomime along with the story.
- Then invite volunteers to act the story out without the audio.

Toss and Say (5 minutes)

- Have children stand in a circle.
- Hold a ball and say: *I want to be a vet.*
- Do the gesture for vet (see page T24).
- Toss the ball to C1. Cue C1 to say: *I want to be a / n [artist]* and do the gesture.
- Have C1 toss the ball to C2, and so on.

Workbook Page 26

Have children circle the correct pictures to show what Sue wants to be. After children color the page, have partners take turns pretending to be Sue and saying: *I want to be a police officer. I want to be an artist.* and *I want to be a vet.*

Workbook Page 27

Have children trace the fire truck and color the page. Then have partners take turns pretending to be Lou and saying: *I want to be a firefighter.*

OPTIONAL: USING DIGITAL COMPONENTS

CD-ROM

Have children review the story on their CD-ROM at home. Encourage them to use the Story Time feature and do word-by-word reading with family members.

ActiveTeach

Use the large digital format to focus on the speech bubbles. Play the audio and point to a character. Then drag the pointer under each word the character speaks as it plays on the audio.

LISTENING

A31 4 **Listen and circle.**

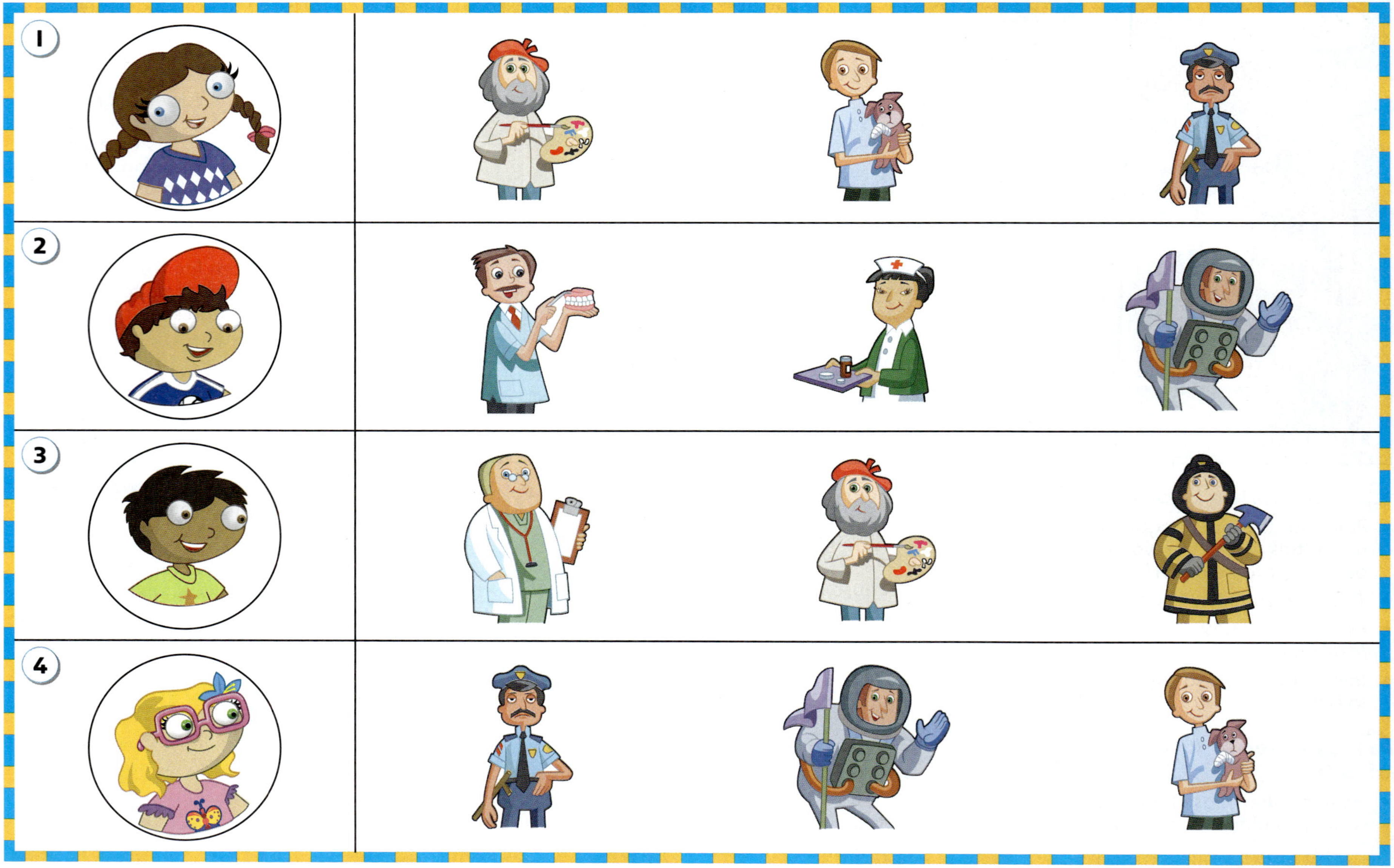

Practice: *I want to be a [vet].* **Review:** *I'm [Sue].*

Listening

Objectives: To practice listening comprehension, to practice new unit vocabulary and structures

Review: *I'm [Sue].*

Materials: Class Audio CD A

Optional Materials: Picture Cards, Sammy the Squirrel puppet, CD-ROM, ActiveTeach

GETTING READY

A30 Revisit the Story (10 minutes)

- Challenge children to retell "Let's Go."
- Then reread the story together.
- Play the audio and have children read along.
- Invite volunteers to act out the story.

Prepare for the Exercise (5 minutes)

- On the board display three Picture Cards of workers in a row.
- Have Sammy say: *I'm Sammy. I want to be a [firefighter].*
- Circle the [firefighter] card and continue.
- Switch the cards and invite volunteers to stand and say: *I'm [Miranda]. I want to be a [vet].*
- Each time, invite another volunteer to circle the correct card.

WORKING IN THE BOOK: PAGE 28

A31 4. Listen and circle.

- Have children open their books to page 28.
- Point to each numbered character on the left. Ask: *Who's number [1]? [Sue.]*
- If needed, identify Billy and Lilly from Level 2.
- Explain that you will play the audio. Children will listen for the number and then circle the worker each character wants to be.
- Do the first one together with the class.

Audio Script

1. I'm Sue. I want to be a vet.
2. I'm Billy. I want to be a dentist.
3. I'm Lou. I want to be a firefighter.
4. I'm Lilly. I want to be an astronaut.

CONSOLIDATING

Review and Apply Structure (5 minutes)

- Review the language structure from Level 2, Unit 3: *Who's [she]? [She's] my [grandma].*
- Remind children that they used this structure to talk about family members, but now they will use it to talk about workers.
- Practice with Sammy. Hold up the *artist* Picture Card. Ask: *Who's she?* Have Sammy answer: *She's an artist.*
- Then divide the class into two groups.
- Hold up a card. Have Group A ask: *Who's [she]?*
- Have Group B answer: *[She's] an [artist].*

Move Like an Astronaut (10 minutes)

- Ask children if they've ever seen a movie or TV program with an astronaut in outer space.
- Explain that astronauts in space float because there isn't any gravity to hold them down.
- Use TPR and prior knowledge to help children understand the concept of gravity:
  - A balloon floats in the air.
  - Gravity on Earth holds us to the ground (walk normally).
  - Lack of gravity in outer space makes an astronaut float (point to the sky and pretend to float).
- Have children take turns moving like an astronaut.
- Name an action: *[Dance]* and lead the class in doing the action like an astronaut in outer space would do it.

OPTIONAL: USING DIGITAL COMPONENTS

CD-ROM

Have children play the games on the CD-ROM at home to show their families the different workers they know.

ActiveTeach

Use the large digital format to model circling the pictures. Invite volunteers to circle the answers using the pen tool. For additional practice, repeat the exercise, using different workers. For example, say that Sue wants to be a [police officer], and so on. Have volunteers circle the new answers on the screen.

Speaking

Objectives: To practice speaking, to practice new unit vocabulary and structures

Materials: Workbook

Optional Materials: Picture Cards; Sammy the Squirrel puppet; CD-ROM; ActiveTeach; drawing supplies, slips of paper

GETTING READY

Practice the Dialogue (5 minutes)

- Ask Sammy: *Sammy, what do you want to be?*
- Have Sammy respond: *I want to be a [nurse]. Teacher, what do you want to be?*
- Answer with: *I want to be an [astronaut].*
- Then invite partners to ask and answer.

Find Your Partner (5 minutes)

- Prepare enough slips of paper for everyone in the class. Write a worker on each one.
- Hand out the papers. Make sure everyone knows what his or her worker is and doesn't tell anyone else.
- At your signal, have children walk around the room and ask each other: *What do you want to be?*
- Have children answer with the worker on their slips of paper.
- When a child finds someone who is the same worker, the two stay together as partners for the next activity.

WORKING IN THE BOOK: PAGE 29

5. Choose and draw. Ask and answer.

- Call children's attention to the three pictures of workers on page 29. Explain that pictures 1–3 show workers (a doctor, an artist, an astronaut) and picture 4 gives no clues to who the worker is.
- Ask: *What do you want to be?*
- Point out the face that has been drawn for the first item, the doctor. Tell each child to choose one of the other two workers shown and draw his or her own face on that picture or fill in the blank face on picture 4 if they want to be a different worker.
- If a child fills in the face on picture 4, tell him or her to draw details (such as clothing or tools) that will identify the worker.
- Have partners ask and answer questions about the pictures they have drawn and the workers they want to be.

CONSOLIDATING

Chain Game (10 minutes)

- Have children stand in a circle.
- Cue C1 to say: *I want to be a [vet].*
- Cue C2 to say: *[C1] wants to be a [vet]. I want to be a [nurse].*
- Have C3 continue the chain, and so on.
- Tell children to give hints to their classmates to help them. For example, if C3 forgets what C1 wants to be, C1 can do the gesture for [vet] provided on page T24.

Worker Drawing (10 minutes)

- Distribute drawing supplies.
- Ask children to draw pictures of themselves as workers.
- Brainstorm details to help identify each worker. For example, an astronaut might have a spaceship, and a vet, an animal.
- When children finish, have them share their drawings with the class, one at a time.
- Each time, have the class ask: *What do you want to be?* and the child show his or her drawing and answer: *I want to be a [nurse].*

Extra Practice: Student Book page 95 and T95

For extra practice speaking, have students turn to page 95 in the back of their books. For teacher support, turn to page T95 in this book.

Big Book Talk (10 minutes)

- Use the Big Book to get children talking.
- Read the "The Bus Ride" to children a few times and then encourage them to "read" along with you.
- Help children talk about why everyone got off the bus. Invite them to tell the story in their own words.

Workbook Page 28

Have children trace the police officer's outline. Once children have colored the page, have them tell a partner: *I want to be a police officer.*

Workbook Page 29

Have children trace the pictures and color the page. Then have them practice these structures with a partner: *What do you want to be? I want to be a [doctor].*

OPTIONAL: USING DIGITAL COMPONENTS

CD-ROM

Have children use the CD-ROM at home to practice speaking skills. Explain that they can copy intonation from the audio.

ActiveTeach

Use the large digital format to model drawing faces on the workers.

SPEAKING

EXTRA PRACTICE Page 95

5 **Choose and draw. Ask and answer.**

1

2

3

4

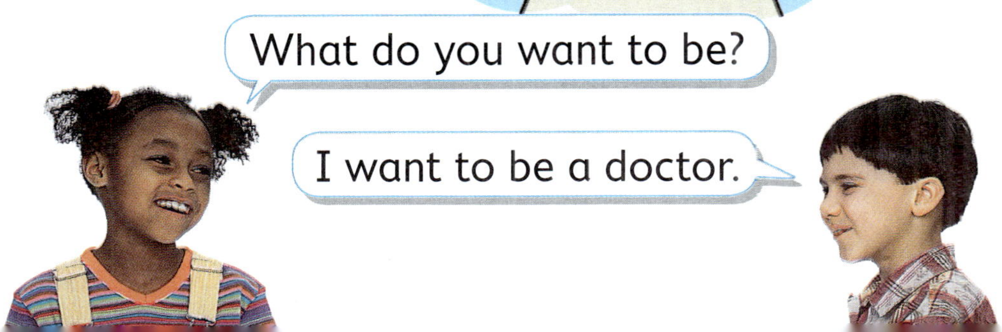

Practice: *What do you want to be? I want to be a [doctor].*

PHONICS

A32 A34 6 **Listen. Trace, write, and say.**

q q

queen

r r

red

v v

vet

Phonics: initial *q*, *r*, *v* **Prewriting/Writing:** directionality, letter tracing, letters in contexts **Review:** *red* **TPR:** write letters in the air

Phonics

Objectives: To learn the sounds that *q*, *r*, and *v* stand for at the beginning of words, to understand sound-symbol correspondences, to recognize left-to-right directionality, to trace and write letters in word contexts

New Sounds and Letters: *q* /kw/, *r* /r/, *v* /v/

Review: red

TPR: write a *q* in the air

Materials: Class Audio CD A, Workbook

Optional Materials: Picture Cards, CD-ROM, ActiveTeach, pencils with erasers

GETTING READY

Review the Letters (5 minutes)

- On the board, write the letters *c*, *h*, and *j*.
- Say the letter names and sounds and have children repeat.
- Ask volunteers for words and names that begin with the *c* /k/, *h*, and *j*.

Introduce the Letters (5 minutes)

- Write the letter *q* on the board.
- Say: *This is* q. *Q stands for /kw/ in words like* queen *and* quiet.
- Write the letters *q-u-e-e-n and* underline the *q*. Say: /kw/.
- Underline the *u*. Explain that *q* and *u* are friends and go together.
- Run your finger under the word as you slowly say: *queen*.
- Repeat with the other letters (*r* for *red*; *v* for *vet*).

WORKING IN THE BOOK: PAGE 30

A32 A34 6. Listen. Trace, write, and say.

- Have children open to page 30.
- Remind them that when a cheerleader says: *Give me a* q!, the fans should yell out: *q!*
- Play the chant and do the actions.
- Play it again and elicit children's responses. Encourage them to repeat the fans' lines.

Audio Script

***Q, R, V* Cheer**

Sue: Give me a *q!*
Fans: *Q!*
Sue: What does *q* sound like?
Fans: Kwuh!
Sue: Give me a *q* word!
Fans: Kwuh . . . *queen!*
Sue: Show me a *q!* (write *q* in the air) Let's hear it for *q!*
Fans: Hooray!

Sue: Give me an *r!*
Fans: *R*!
Sue: What does r sound like?
Fans: Ruh!
Sue: Give me an *r* word!
Fans: Rrrr . . . red!
Sue: Show me an *r*! (write *r* in the air) Let's hear it for *r*!
Fans: Hooray!

Sue: Give me a *v*!
Fans: *V*!
Sue: What does *v* sound like?
Fans: Vuh!
Sue: Give me a *v* word!
Fans: Vvvv . . . vet!
Sue: Show me a *v*! (write *v* in the air) Let's hear it for *v*!
Fans: Hooray!

- Point to the *q* on the left. Model tracing the letter and have children trace.
- Then point to the word *queen*. Point and say: /kw/ and *queen*.
- Model tracing the *q* at the beginning of the word. Then have children trace it.
- Repeat for the other letters and words.
- Finally, have children take turns pointing to and reading the words and letters.
- For additional practice, have children listen to Class Audio CD A: Track 34.
  – Play the audio, pausing after each word to allow children time to say the initial sound.

Audio Script

Now listen and say the letters.

queen, quack, red, run, vet, van

CONSOLIDATING

"Hand" Writing (10 minutes)

- Use a pencil eraser to write a letter of the alphabet on a volunteer's hand. Model proper pencil grip.
- Have the volunteer guess the letter.
- Continue with other volunteers and familiar letters.
- Have partners practice "hand" writing.

Workbook Page 30

Have children trace the letters and words and color the pictures. Then have partners share their work by pointing to the letters and pictures and naming and telling about them.

OPTIONAL: USING DIGITAL COMPONENTS

CD-ROM

Have children take the CD-ROM home and play the games with their families.

ActiveTeach

Demonstrate tracing the letters on the big screen. Invite volunteers to write them.

Math

Objectives: To count items 1–12, to write numbers 9–12

Review: numbers 1–10, animals

TPR: flap arms, hold up fingers, kick, march, point, write

Materials: Class Audio CD A, Workbook

Optional Materials: Sammy the Squirrel puppet, CD-ROM, ActiveTeach, groups of classroom objects

GETTING READY

Introduce the Numbers 11 and 12 (10 minutes)

- Review numbers 1–10 by counting real objects in the class.
- Write the numbers on the board.
- Point to the numbers on the board and count: *1, 2, 3, 4, 5 . . . 10.*
- Then write and say: *11, 12.*
- Walk around the room and identify groups of items. Count them and invite children to repeat after you.
- Then identify groups of items or children and ask: *How many?*

Brainstorm Groups (10 minutes)

- Point to the number 1 on the board.
- Ask children what things come in groups of 1, 2, 3, or 4.
- Brainstorm ideas as a class:
  - 1: nose, head, teacher
  - 2: eyes, legs, ears
  - 3: mom, dad, and baby
  - 4: grandparents, dogs' legs
- Then divide the class into smaller groups. Assign each group a number and have them brainstorm another set for that number only.
- Reconvene and share ideas.

WORKING IN THE BOOK: PAGE 31

A35 7. Listen, say, and trace. Count and write.

- Play the audio of the numbers chant and act it out.
- Play the chant again. Invite children to do the actions and chant with you.

Audio Script

Count to 12 Chant

1, 2, 3, (hold up fingers for counting)
Buzz like a bee. (flap arms and buzz)
4, 5, 6, (hold up fingers for counting)
Do high kicks. (kick)
7, 8, 9, (hold up fingers for counting)
March in a line. (march in place)
10! 10! 10!
Write with a pen. (pretend to write)
11, 12,
Point to yourself. (point to yourself)

- Have children trace the numbers at the top of page 31.
- Explain that the children are counting animals.
- Point to the different animals. Ask: *What animal is this?*
- Do the first one together. Say: *Let's count turtles. 1, 2, 3, 4, . . . 9. Nine turtles.*
- Show children how to write the number 9 in the box by the turtles.
- Have children complete the rest of the page on their own, or as a group.

CONSOLIDATING

Let's Keep Score (10 minutes)

- Have pairs of children take turns tossing a ball back and forth, each time moving farther and farther away from each other.
- While the pairs toss the ball, have the class count how many times they toss the ball without dropping it.

12 Times TPR (5 minutes)

- Have children do actions a different numbers of times.
- For example, have children: jump 12 times, wiggle their ears 11 times, touch their noses 10 times, march 9 times, and so on.

Workbook Page 31

Have children trace the numbers 9–12. Then have children count the groups of helmets and write how many there are in each group. After children color the page, invite partners to share their work by counting the helmets together.

OPTIONAL: USING DIGITAL COMPONENTS

CD-ROM

Have children play the games on the CD-ROM at home to practice numbers.

ActiveTeach

Invite volunteers to use the pen tool to count each group of animals and write the numbers.

MATH

A35 **7** **Listen, say, and trace. Count and write.**

9 10 11 12

Math: counting *1–12* **Writing:** *9–12* **Review:** *1–10*, animals **TPR:** flap arms, hold up fingers, kick, march, point, write

VALUES Stay safe.

A37 **8** **Listen and say. Draw and trace.**

Stay safe.

Values: Stay safe. **Prewriting:** tracing a short sentence

Values

Objective: To learn about the value of staying safe
New Values Language: Stay safe.
Prewriting: tracing a short sentence
Materials: Class Audio CD A, Workbook
Optional Materials: Sammy the Squirrel puppet, CD-ROM, ActiveTeach

GETTING READY

A30 Revisit the Story

- Play the audio and invite children to listen to the story.
- Talk about the kinds of workers the characters want to be. Ask which workers help people or animals.
- Introduce the word *safe*. Tell children that firefighters and police officers help people stay safe.
- Encourage children to act out or talk about ways these workers help people stay safe.

Introduce Staying Safe (10 minutes)

- Prepare a few volunteers to role-play.
- Have them pretend to walk to school. When they get to the crosswalk, have them not stop or look—and just cross the street.
- Have Sammy say: *That's not safe! Please stay safe!*
- Ask the class what the children should have done. (Waited at the crosswalk for a grown-up to help.)
- Have the volunteers role-play the correct way to cross the street.
- Have Sammy say: *Good job! You're staying safe.*
- Brainstorm other ways to stay safe, such as wearing a seatbelt, using sunscreen, not pushing or fighting, wearing a helmet when riding a bike, and not touching the stove.

WORKING IN THE BOOK: PAGE 32

A37 8. Listen and say. Draw and trace.

- Have children look at the pictures on page 32.
- Play the dialogue on the first part of the audio. Ask children to look at the photos as they listen.
- Have volunteers repeat the dialogue with you.

Audio Script

Crossing guard:	You can cross the street. It's safe. There are no cars now.
Kids:	Thank you. You help us stay safe.
Crossing guard:	It's not safe to fight in the street.
Kids:	Stop fighting. It's not safe.

- Then play the chant on the second part of the audio. Have children listen once or twice and chant along with the audio when ready.

Audio Script

Stay Safe Chant

Stay safe at school.
Stay safe in the street.
We stay safe.
We stay safe.

Stay safe at school.
Don't fight in the street.
We stay safe.
We stay safe.

- Talk about each photo with the class and have children discuss whether the children in each photo are staying safe.
- Now point to the faces below each photo. Tell children to draw a smile on the face below the photo where children are staying safe, and a frown under the photo where children are *not* staying safe.
- Finally, have children read and trace the sentence: *Stay safe.*

Talk About It!

- Call attention to "Talk about it!"
- Share something people can do to stay safe. Invite children to talk about ways they can stay safe.

CONSOLIDATING

Act It Out (10 minutes)

- Invite pairs or small groups of children to role-play staying safe and not staying safe.
- If a group role-plays unsafe behavior, cue the class to call out: *Stay safe!*
- If a group acts out staying safe, cue the class to call out: *Good job! You're safe.*

Home Connection

Have children talk with their families about ways to stay safe at home. Back in class, have children draw pictures of one of these ways and share it with the class.

Workbook Page 32

Have children check the box under the picture that shows Sue staying safe. Then have them color the page and say to a partner and then chorally: *Stay safe.*

OPTIONAL: USING DIGITAL COMPONENTS

CD-ROM

Encourage children to play the games and do the activities on the CD-ROM at home to show their families what they're learning about in class.

ActiveTeach

Focus on the two pictures. Use the pointer to highlight who is staying safe and who isn't. Confirm which face should be smiling and which should be frowning.

Review / Assessment

Objectives: To review and assess new unit vocabulary and structures

Materials: Class Audio CD A, Workbook, stickers (in the back of the Student Book and shown on page T108)

Optional Materials: CD-ROM, ActiveTeach, poster board, letter cutouts for *danger*, drawing supplies

GETTING READY

Sing and Move (10 minutes)

- Invite children to sing and move to the various songs and chants from the unit.
- Have children tell which song or chant they liked best.

Play a Review Game (10 minutes)

- Have children sit in a circle.
- Have them ask and answer in turn: *What do you want to be? I want to be a [vet].*
- As each child answers, cue the class to do the gesture for the worker from page T24.

WORKING IN THE BOOK: PAGE 33

9. Stick and say.

- Distribute the stickers (but not the reward sticker).
- Have children open their books to page 33.
- Help children notice the sticker outlines in their books and then stick the correct ones in place. Begin with item 1 and say: *Find the firefighter sticker*. Have children hold up the sticker.
- Say: *Stick the sticker*. Have children stick the sticker and say: *Firefighter.*
- Repeat with the other stickers.

A39 10. Listen and circle.

- Remind children to listen and circle the answer to each question.
- Confirm the answers with the class.

Audio Script

1. I want to be a firefighter.
2. I want to be an artist.
3. I want to be a police officer.
4. I want to be a nurse.

I Can! Use the Reward Sticker

- Help children talk about what they have learned in this unit, using positive language:
  – I can count to twelve. I can write the numbers, too.
  – I know these actions: march, write a [q] in the air, hold up fingers, flap arms, kick, march, pretend to write, point to yourself.
- Distribute the reward stickers.
- Show children where to stick the stickers (on the Unit 3 Good Job! placeholder).

CONSOLIDATING

Congratulations Chant (5 minutes)

- Ask each child to choose something they learned in this unit and then stand together in a circle.
- Have each child chant to tell what he or she learned while the rest of the class claps.

  C1: *I know [the letter v].* (clap, clap)

  C1: *I can [write the numbers 1–12].* (clap, clap)
- End by congratulating the class!

Safety Project: Poster About Preventing Fires

- Have children work in groups of three.
- For each poster, give children poster board, letter cutouts (spelling *danger*), and drawing supplies.
- Have each group brainstorm a dangerous situation or place, such as a fire, electrical outlet, street, or high window ledge.
- Have one child from each group draw a picture of the dangerous situation, one child glue the letters to the poster to spell *danger*, and one glue shapes to the rest of the poster for decoration.

Workbook Page 33

Have children draw themselves as a worker. Have pairs point and say: *What do you want to be? I want to be a/an [astronaut].*

OPTIONAL: USING DIGITAL COMPONENTS

CD-ROM

Have children play the games and do the activities on the CD-ROM at home to show their families what they're learning about in class.

ActiveTeach

Use ActiveTeach to check answers as a class.

REVIEW I can!

9 **Stick and say.** A39 10 **Listen and circle.**

1

2

3

4

Project

Unit 3 GOOD JOB!

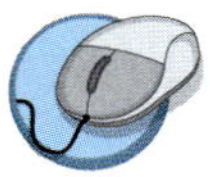

Review/Assessment: *I want to be a [firefighter].* **Project:** health and safety

4 My Town

Unit Overview

Objectives

- ✓ To learn vocabulary about towns
- ✓ To sing songs and chants
- ✓ To do new TPR movements
- ✓ To practice fine and gross motor skills
- ✓ To understand and role-play a story
- ✓ To learn and practice new language structures: *Where does [your dad] work? / [He] works at the [fire station]. / Where does [he] work? / [He] works at a [hospital.]*
- ✓ To recognize and produce the sounds that the letters *w* and *y* stand for at the beginning of words and that *x* stands for in the middle and at the end of words
- ✓ To write the letters *w*, *y*, and *x*
- ✓ To count to 14
- ✓ To learn how to write the numbers 13 and 14
- ✓ To learn the value of asking for help
- ✓ To practice writing a short sentence
- ✓ To practice new language by listening and speaking
- ✓ To learn and review unit vocabulary and language structures

Vocabulary

New: bus, fire station, hospital, police station, post office, school, store, taxi; numbers 13, 14

Review: numbers 1–12; aunt, box, teacher, uncle, windy, yellow

Home-School Connections

Copy the Letter Home for children to bring home to share what they'll be learning in Unit 4 of *My Little Island*. The Letter Home is available online at www.pearsonelt.com/mylittleisland.

Values

Ask for help.

Materials

Student Book pages 34–43; Workbook pages 34–43; Picture Cards 17–24; Class Audio CD A: Tracks 40–52; Program Posters: My Little Island Map, Shapes and Colors All Around, Meet Your New Friends!; stickers (back of Student Book and shown on page T108)

Optional: CD-ROM, ActiveTeach, Big Book, Sammy the Squirrel Puppet

Songs and Chants

- ✓ All Around Town (Class Audio CD A: Tracks 40, 41)
- ✓ *W, X, Y* Cheer (Class Audio CD A: Tracks 45, 46)
- ✓ Count to 14 Chant (Class Audio CD A: Tracks 48, 49)
- ✓ Ask for Help Chant (Class Audio CD A: Tracks 50, 51)

Story

"Where Does He Work?": Sue and Lou play and talk about where Sue's parents work in the community.

Language Structures: *Where does [your dad] work? / [He] works at the [fire station].*

SKILLS

Cross-Curricular Connections

- count to 14, write numbers 11–14, make a building out of shapes
- learn the value of asking for help
- sing, chant, and more to music

Preschool Learning Outcomes

✓ Recognize intonation in questions.

✓ Use short answers to questions.

✓ Understand new language structures.

✓ Recognize and produce the sounds that initial *w* and y and medial and final *x* stands for.

✓ Write the letters *w*, *y*, and *x* in words.

✓ Listen to and follow a story with words.

✓ Make predictions, using pictures.

✓ Sing songs and say chants with TPR.

✓ Join in games and interact.

✓ Talk about self and surroundings.

✓ Develop a positive attitude toward the English language.

Digital Practice

- Have children use the CD-ROM for vocabulary practice in class or at home.
- Use ActiveTeach to go over Student Book pages together as a class.

LEARN BY DOING

TPR

✓ beep horn, drive, flap arms, hold up fingers, kick, march, point, tap knees, turn around, write, write letters in the air

Phonics

✓ Recognize sound-symbol correspondences: initial *w* /w/ and *y* /y/ and medial and final *x* /ks/.

✓ Write the letters *w*, *y*, and *x*.

✓ Complete Phonics page 40.

✓ Listen to the audio.

✓ Sing songs and say chants.

Prereading and Prewriting

✓ Follow a four-page story.

✓ Talk about the characters.

✓ Act out the story to show comprehension.

✓ Practice fine motor skills.

✓ Trace letters and a short sentence.

BULLETIN BOARD DISPLAY

Towns Around the World

✓ Create an interactive bulletin board to celebrate multiculturalism.

Materials

- photos or drawings of places in your town
- photos of towns and cities around the world
- teacher-made place labels
- a cut-out drawing or photo of a taxi
- a cut-out drawing or photo of a bus
- string

Directions

1. Divide the bulletin board into eight equal sections, one for each unit vocabulary word.
2. Label each section with a teacher-made label (*store*, *school*, and so on).
3. Display photos or child-made drawings of the places.
4. Cut out a picture of a bus.
5. Attach it to one end of a long string with the other attached to the top of the bulletin board.
6. Repeat with a picture of a taxi.
7. Have children come to the bulletin board and "drive" the bus or taxi to the different places and tell about them.

4 My Town

A40 ♪ 1 **Listen and sing. Move.**

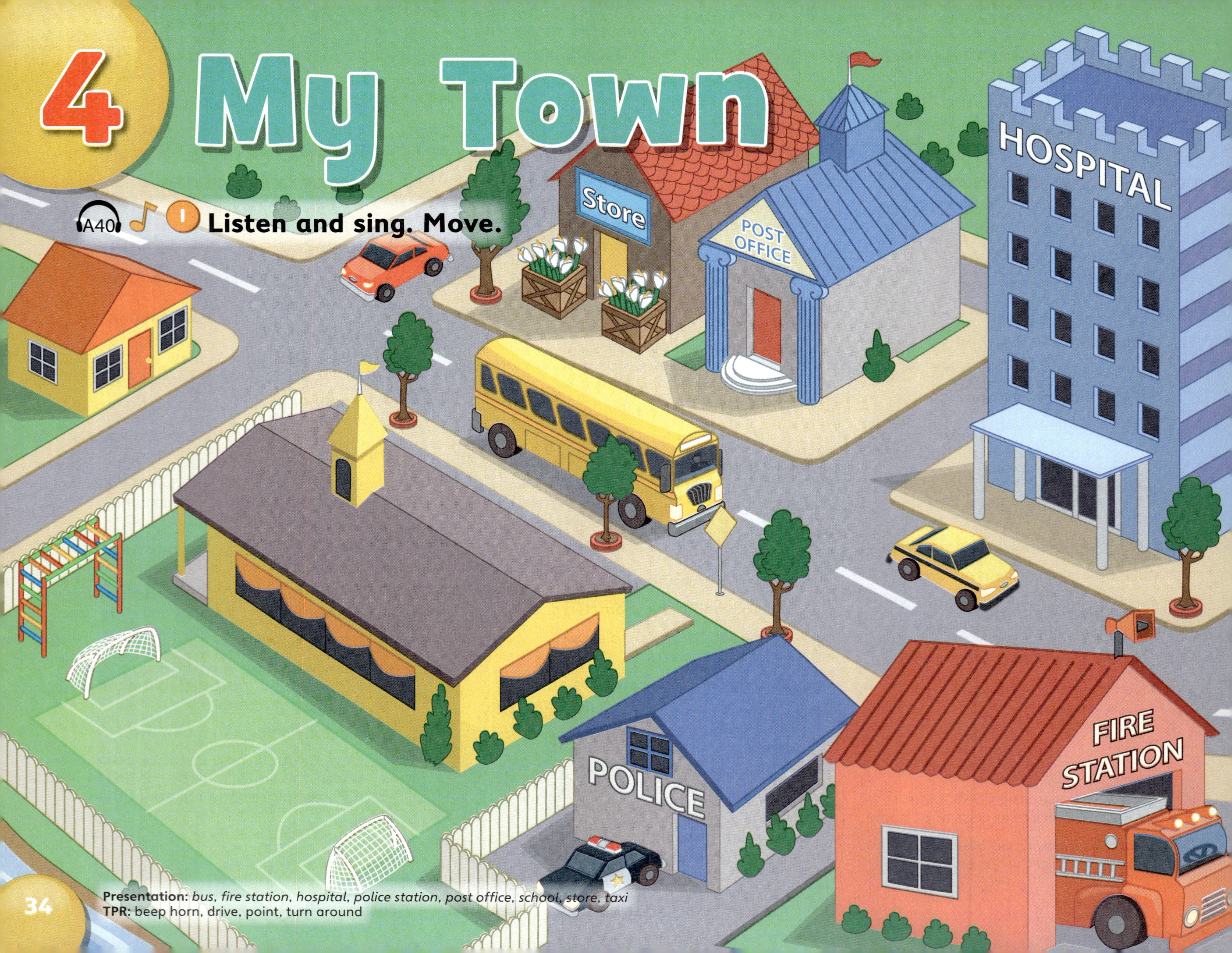

Presentation: *bus, fire station, hospital, police station, post office, school, store, taxi*
TPR: beep horn, drive, point, turn around

Presentation

Objectives: To identify vocabulary in a scene, to learn a song and new TPR actions

New Vocabulary: bus, fire station, hospital, police station, post office, school, store, taxi

TPR: beep horn, drive, point, turn around

Materials: Class Audio CD A, Picture Cards, Workbook

Optional Materials: My Little Island Map poster, CD-ROM, ActiveTeach

GETTING READY

A27 Review Workers (5 minutes)

- Play the song "Time for Work." See page T24.
- Review the different workers children learned about in Unit 3.

Look at the Island Poster (5 minutes)

- Display the poster and review places children have visited.
- Then focus on the places in the town and have children talk about them.
- Ask: *Where do the workers work?*

WORKING IN THE BOOK: PAGE 34

Introduce the Vocabulary

- Have children open their books to page 34.
- Explain that this is Sue and Lou's town. Ask children if they can find the school.
- Use the Picture Cards to reinforce the vocabulary. Hold them up, one at a time.
  - Say: *[Bus].* Have children repeat.
  - Say: *Show me the [bus].* Have children point to the [bus].
- Repeat for the other words.

A40 1. Listen and sing. Move.

- Preteach the actions for the song: turn around, drive, point, and beep the horn.
- Say the line: [*All around town.*] and do the action [turn around].
- Review *Help* by asking children how the workers in the town help people.
- Say: *Let's sing a song.* Play the song.
- Play the song again. Have children sing along and do the actions.

Audio Script

All Around Town

Kids: Town, town,
All around town. (turn around)
In a bus, taxi, or car. (pretend to drive)
Beep, beep! (pretend to beep horn)
All around town.
Doctor, doctor, where are you?
Doctor: In the hospital helping you. (point to other kids)
Kids: Firefighter, firefighter, where are you?
Firefighter: At the fire station helping you. (point to other kids)
Kids: Teacher, teacher, where are you?
Teacher: At the school helping you. (point to other kids)
Kids: Officer, officer, where are you?
Police Officer: At the police station helping you. (point to other kids)
Kids: Postal worker, postal worker, where are you?
Postal Worker: At the post office helping you. (point to other kids)
Kids: Mom, mom, where are you?
Mom: At the store helping you. (point to other kids)
Kids: Dad, dad, where are you?
Dad: In the kitchen waiting for you. (point to other kids)
Welcome home!

CONSOLIDATING

A41 Karaoke (5 minutes)

- Play the karaoke version of the song.
- Use Picture Cards to cue children for the worker.

Place Race (5 minutes)

- Display the unit Picture Cards on the board.
- Have two children play at a time.
- Name a place and have children race to touch the correct card.

Workbook Page 34

Have children trace the police car and color the picture. After children color the page, have them point and say to a partner: *car, police officer,* and *police station.*

OPTIONAL: USING DIGITAL COMPONENTS

CD-ROM

Encourage children to play the games and do the activities on the CD-ROM at home to show their families what they're learning about in class.

ActiveTeach

Use the large format to focus on the different places as they are named in the song. Put the Picture Card images up on the big screen for "Place Race."

Vocabulary

Objectives: To practice new words

New Vocabulary: bus, fire station, hospital, police station, post office, school, store, taxi; numbers 1–8

Materials: Class Audio CD A, Workbook

Optional Materials: Picture Cards, CD-ROM, ActiveTeach, teacher-made name tags for workers

GETTING READY

A40 Review the Song (10 minutes)

- Make name tags of people in the song (doctor, firefighter, teacher, postal worker, police officer, Mom, Dad).
- Place the name tags on seven volunteers.
- Display the Unit 3 Picture Cards (9–16) around the room.
- Play "All Around Town." See page T34.
- Cue the class to sing the chorus and questions and Dad's answer.
- Have volunteers sing their part and walk to the card labeled on their name tag.
- Leave the Picture Cards on display.

Let's Take the Bus (5 minutes)

- Hold the *bus* Picture card over your head and say: *Let's take the bus! Everybody stand up!*
- Chant: Let's take the bus, let's take the bus / Let's take the bus to the [school].
- Hold the *bus* card over your head and lead the group to the [school].
- Invite children to chant with you.

WORKING IN THE BOOK: PAGE 35

A42 2. Listen. Find and number. Say.

- Have children look at the pictures on page 35.
- Play the audio, and have children listen and number the pictures.

Audio Script

1. bus
2. school
3. police station
4. hospital
5. fire station
6. store
7. taxi
8. post office

- Check children's work as a class. Have volunteers point and say: *[1] [bus].*
- For additional practice, say each vocabulary word aloud and have children clap once, pause, clap three times, pause, clap once again, and repeat the word.

CONSOLIDATING

Looking Back (5 minutes)

- Review the Level 2, Unit 5 structure:
  – *The [bed] is in the [bedroom].*
- Gather Picture Cards from Levels 1 and 2 or other pictures of the words (familiar furniture, classroom items, animals, and so on).
- Place these facedown in one pile and the Unit 4 Picture Cards in another.
- Invite a volunteer to pick one picture or card from each pile and help him or her use the two words in a sentence.
- Cue the class to respond: *That's silly!* or *That's okay*. For example:
  – For a pen and a store: The pen is in the store. (That's okay.)
  – For a cow and a store: The cow is in the store. (That's silly!)

Make a Home Connection

Ask children to draw and share pictures of neighborhood places at home.

Workbook Page 35

Have children trace each roadway and tell where each vehicle is going. Have them color the page and then work with a partner to practice target language: *bus, post office, school, store, taxi.*

OPTIONAL: USING DIGITAL COMPONENTS

CD-ROM

Have children play the games on the CD-ROM to demonstrate the new vocabulary they're learning.

ActiveTeach

Use the large digital format to model numbering the boxes on the Student Book page.

VOCABULARY

A42 **2** **Listen. Find and number. Say.**

school

hospital

store

fire station

post office

police station

bus

taxi

Practice: *school, hospital, store, fire station, post office, police station, bus, taxi* **Writing:** *1–8*

Story

Objectives: To read and understand a story, to identify and understand speech bubbles, to learn a new language structure, to listen to and identify the intonation in a sentence, to role-play, to practice new unit vocabulary

New Structures: *Where does [your dad] work? / [He] works at the [fire station].*

Materials: Class Audio CD A, Workbook

Optional Materials: Picture Cards; Sammy the Squirrel puppet; CD-ROM; ActiveTeach; bag, book, table

GETTING READY

Where's Sammy? (10 minutes)

- Review *Where* and the prepositions *in*, *on*, *under*. Introduce the preposition *at*.
- Place Sammy in a bag, on a book, under a table, and at a place (use Picture Cards). Point and ask: *Where's Sammy? He's [in] the [bag].*
- Tell children to close their eyes, and then hide Sammy in different places around the room so he is *in*, *on*, *at*, and *under* something children can name.
- For each place, ask: *Where's Sammy?*
- Invite a volunteer to look for Sammy and then point to him and say: *He's [at] [the hospital].*

Introduce the Story (5 minutes)

- Hold up the Student Book, turned to page 36.
- Ask children to talk about the first page of "Where Does He Work?"
- Explain that Sue and Lou are at the playground on the see-saw and are talking about where their parents work.
- Take children on a picture walk through the rest of the story.

- Have children predict what will happen. Revisit children's predictions later.

WORKING IN THE BOOK: PAGES 36–37

A43 3. Look and listen. Act it out.

- Have children open their books to page 36.
- Play the audio.
- Pause to make sure children are on the correct story page and understand what the children are talking about.
- If needed, help children understand that firefighters (and others like police officers) work in many places to do their jobs and help people.
- Play the story audio again. Point to each speech bubble as the words are spoken.
- Encourage children to speak along with the characters.
- Invite volunteers to act out the story with the audio.

Audio Script

Where Does He Work?

Page 1	Lou:	Where's your mom?
	Sue:	She's at the hospital.
Page 2	Lou:	What does she do?
	Sue:	She's a doctor.
Page 3	Lou:	Where does your dad work?
	Sue:	He's a firefighter. He works at the fire station.
Page 4	Sue:	and a store . . . and a school . . . and . . .
	Lou:	Sue! Let me down, please!

Look at New Language

- Point out the new language the children use to ask and answer about Sue's parents: *Where does your dad work? He works at the fire station.*
- Practice with Sammy. Ask him: *Where does your mom work?*
- Have Sammy answer: *She's a teacher. She works at a [school].*
- Invite partners to practice the dialogue. Help them use words like postal worker (for post office), bus and taxi driver (for bus and taxi), and store clerk (for store).
- Note that you may need to gesture and pantomime to teach postal worker, bus driver, taxi driver, and store clerk.

A43 Listen to the Intonation

- Have children close their eyes and listen while you play the story audio.
- Pause after each speech bubble. Point out how the rise and fall of the speaker's voice differs in questions and answers.
- Have children repeat each question and answer, copying the intonation.

CONSOLIDATING

Role-Play (10 minutes)

- Have pairs of children act out the story.
- First, play the audio and have pairs of children pantomime along with the story.
- Then invite volunteers to act the story out without the audio.

Charades (5 minutes)

- Brainstorm some actions that show what different workers do in the places around town (bus driver steers; store clerk uses cash register).
- Invite volunteers to act one out.
- Ask the class: *Where does [Mary] work?*
- Have the first child to guess, act out what another worker does.

Workbook Page 36

Have children draw lines matching Sue's parents with the places where each works. Have partners point and say: *Where does [she] work? [She] works at a [hospital].*

Workbook Page 37

Have children circle the places where Sue's parents work (the hospital and the fire station). Have children color the page and then practice the target language with a partner: *Where does [he] work? [He] works at the [fire station].*

OPTIONAL: USING DIGITAL COMPONENTS

CD-ROM

Encourage children to use the word-by-word Story Time feature to share the story with their families.

ActiveTeach

Use the big screen to focus on speech bubbles and each word the characters say, using the pointer.

LISTENING

A44 **4** **Listen and circle.**

1

2

3

4

Practice: *Where does [he] work? [He] works at a [hospital].* **Review:** *aunt, teacher, uncle*

Listening

Objectives: To practice listening comprehension, to practice new unit vocabulary and structures

Review: aunt, teacher, uncle

Materials: Class Audio CD A

Optional Materials: Picture Cards, CD-ROM, ActiveTeach, small object to pass around

GETTING READY

A43 Revisit the Story (10 minutes)

- Reread the story "Where Does He Work?" on pages 36–37 together. Challenge a volunteer to retell it.
- Play the audio and have children read along.
- Note on the board where Sue's family members work.

Personalization (5 minutes)

- Invite children to talk about where their family members, including grandparents, aunts, and uncles, work. Review family words as needed.
- Note: you may want to introduce words like *office*.
- Tally on the board how many family members work in each place.

WORKING IN THE BOOK: PAGE 38

A44 4. Listen and circle.

- Have children open their books to page 38.
- Play the dialogues on the audio.
- Have children listen for the number and circle the picture that shows where each person works.

Audio Script

1. Boy: My dad's a nurse.
   Girl: Where does he work?
   Boy: He works at a hospital.
2. Boy: My mom's a teacher.
   Girl: Where does she work?
   Boy: She works at a school.
3. Boy: My uncle's a bus driver.
   Girl: Where does he work?
   Boy: He works in a bus.
4. Boy: My aunt's a police officer.
   Girl: Where does she work?
   Boy: She works at a police station.

CONSOLIDATING

Move It! (5 minutes)

- Display the unit Picture Cards and assign a different child to be: Mom, Dad, Uncle, Aunt, Grandma, Grandpa.
- Teach children this short chant:

  [Mom, Mom] 1, 2, 3. (The Moms stand up.) / [Mom] is a [doctor]. / [Jump] with me. (The Moms jump in place.) / [Mom, Mom] 1, 2, 3. (The Moms keep jumping.) / [Mom] works in a [hospital]. / Now show me. (The Moms point to the hospital card.)
- Continue in this way with other family member, jobs, and places.
- Vary the actions: hop, bend (your knees), arms up, or march.

Pass and Place (5 minutes)

- Have children sit in a circle and display the unit Picture Cards in the center.
- Give children a small object and have them pass it around until you say *stop*.
- Say: *Stop! Where does [Mom] work?*
- Cue the child holding the object to place it on a card and say: *[Mom] works [in] a [taxi].*

Make a Home Connection

Have children talk with their parents about where they work and, if possible, bring in photos of them at work.

OPTIONAL: USING DIGITAL COMPONENTS

CD-ROM

Have children play the games at home to practice their listening skills.

ActiveTeach

Invite volunteers to circle the pictures on the big screen for the whole class to see.

Speaking

Objectives: To practice speaking, to practice new unit vocabulary and structures
Materials: Workbook
Optional Materials: Picture Cards, Sammy the Squirrel puppet, CD-ROM, ActiveTeach

GETTING READY

Guessing Game (5 minutes)

- Model with Sammy.
- Say: *My uncle works at a school. What is he?*
- Have Sammy guess: *He's a teacher.*
- Invite partners to play the game together.

Prepare for the Exercise (5 minutes)

- On the board, display Picture Cards of workers, along with pictures of other workers in one row, and unit Picture Cards and corresponding places for the other workers in another below it.
- Point to the first picture and ask: *Where does [she / the teacher] work?*
- Elicit: *[She] works at a [school].*
- Draw a line from the [teacher] to the [school].
- Invite volunteers to repeat with the other workers and places.

WORKING IN THE BOOK: PAGE 39

5. Match. Ask and answer.

- Have children open to page 39.
- Focus on item 1, which is done as an example. Say: *Where does she work?*
- Call attention to the boy and girl with speech bubbles at the bottom of the page.
- Point to and read the speech bubbles: *Where does she work? / She works at a hospital.*
- Tell children they will work in pairs, using the speech bubble text as a model.
- After asking and answering about where the workers work, tell children to draw a line to match the workers with the other three places.

CONSOLIDATING

Draw and Say (10 minutes)

- Ask children where their parents work. Have them make a drawing of one parent's workplace and, if possible, tape on a photo of the parent at work.
- Have children share their work: *My [mom] works at a [hospital].*

Relay "Crab Walk" Race (10 minutes)

- Display the unit Picture Cards in a row on one side of the room and have children line up in two groups across from it.
- Call out three places in a row: *Bus! Fire Station! School!*
- Have the first child in each group "crab walk" (walk on all fours, stomach in the air) to the bus card, tap it, and then "crab walk" back and tap the next child in line who goes to the second card.
- Continue until the three cards have been tapped and the third child has "crab walked" back to his or her place in line.
- Explain that the first group to finish wins.

Extra Practice Student Book page 96 and T96

For extra practice in speaking, have children turn to page 96 in the back of their books. For teacher support, turn to page T96 in this book.

Workbook Page 38

Have children color the page. Then have them work with a partner to point to each picture and say: *Where does [she] work? [She] works at the [police station].*

Workbook Page 39

Have children circle the differences in Picture B. After children color the page, have partners point to workers and practice saying: *Where does [he] work? [He] works at the [fire station].*

OPTIONAL: USING DIGITAL COMPONENTS

CD-ROM

Have children use the CD-ROM at home to practice speaking skills.

ActiveTeach

Use the large digital format to model matching the workers and places.

SPEAKING

5 **Match. Ask and answer.**

1

2

3

4

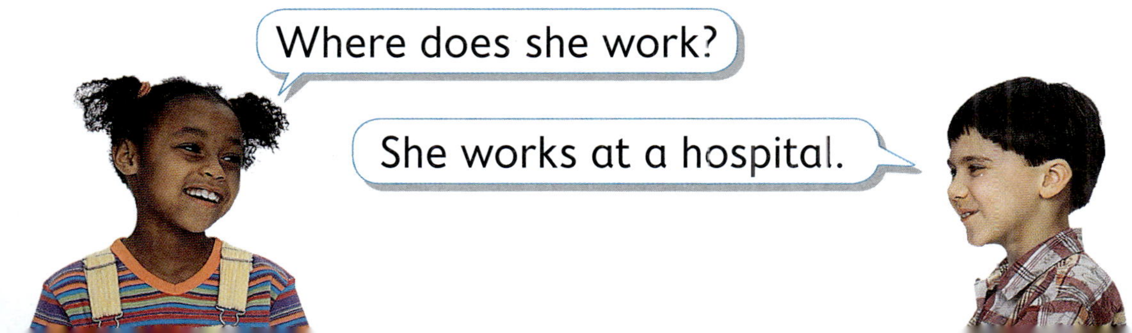

Practice: *Where does [she] work? [She] works at a [hospital].*

PHONICS

A45 A47 6 **Listen. Trace, write, and say.**

w w

windy

x x

box

y y

yellow

Phonics: initial *w*, *y*, medial/final *x* **Prewriting/Writing:** directionality, letter tracing, letters in contexts
Review: *box*, *windy*, *yellow* **TPR:** write letters in the air

Phonics

Objectives: To learn the sounds that *w* and *y* stand for at the beginning of words and that *x* stands for in the middle and at the end of words, to understand sound-symbol correspondences, to recognize left-to-right directionality, to trace and write letters in the context of words

New Sounds and Letters: *w* /w/, *x* /ks/, *y* /y/

Review: box, windy, yellow

TPR: write *w* in the air

Materials: Class Audio CD A, Workbook

Optional Materials: CD-ROM, ActiveTeach, pencils with erasers

GETTING READY

Introduce the Letters (5 minutes)

- Write the letter *w* on the board.
- Say: *This is* w. W *usually stands for* wuh *in words like* windy *and* water.
- Write the letters *w-i-n-d-y*.
- Underline the *w*. Say: *wuh*.
- Run your finger under the word as you slowly say: *Windy*.
- Repeat with the other letters (*x* as in *box*; *y* as in *yellow*).
- Note that the letter *x* rarely appears at the beginning of a word. For now, help children notice that *x* stands for /ks/ at the end of words.

WORKING IN THE BOOK: PAGE 40

A45 A47 6. Listen. Trace, write, and say.

- Have children open to page 40.
- Show children the picture of Sue cheering.
- Jump up and down and pretend to be a cheerleader as you say: *Give me a* w! Cue children to call out: *W!*
- Play the chant and do the actions.
- Play it again and have children respond. Encourage them to repeat the kids' lines.

Audio Script

***W, X, Y* Cheer**

Sue: Give me a *w!*
Fans: *W!*
Sue: What does *w* sound like?
Fans: Wuh!
Sue: Give me a *w* word!
Fans: Wuh . . . *windy!*
Sue: Show me a *w!* (write *w* in the air) Let's hear it for *w!*
Fans: Hooray!

Sue: Give me an *x!*
Fans: *X!*
Sue: What does *x* sound like?
Fans: Ks!
Sue: Give me an *x* word!
Fans: Ks . . . *box!*
Sue: Show me an *x!* (write *x* in the air) Let's hear it for *x!*
Fans: Hooray!

Sue: Give me a *y!*
Fans: *Y!*
Sue: What does *y* sound like?
Fans: Yuh!
Sue: Give me a *y* word!
Fans: Yuh . . . *yellow!*
Sue: Show me a *y!* (write y in the air) Let's hear it for *y!*
Fans: Hooray!

- Focus children on the page again.
- Point to the *w*. Model tracing the letter with your finger. Then have children trace the *w* and write it several times.
- Then point to the word *windy*. Point and say: *Wuh. Windy.*
- Model tracing the *w* at the beginning of the word. Then have children trace it.
- Repeat for the other letters and words.
- Finally, have children take turns pointing to and reading the letters and words on the page.
- For additional practice, have children listen to Class Audio CD A: Track 47.
  - Play the audio, pausing after each word to allow children time to say the initial sound /a/ or /y/ or the medial or final sound that *x* stands for /ks/.

Audio Script

Now listen and say the letters.

windy, window, box, taxi, yellow, yogurt

CONSOLIDATING

"Hand" Writing (10 minutes)

- Use a pencil eraser to write a letter of the alphabet on a volunteer's hand. Model proper pencil grip.
- Have the volunteer guess the letter.
- Continue with other volunteers and familiar letters.
- Reinforce pencil grip with children. Then have them practice "hand" writing with partners.

Workbook Page 40

Have children trace the letters and words and color the pictures. Then have partners share their work by pointing to the letters and pictures and naming and telling about them.

OPTIONAL: USING DIGITAL COMPONENTS

CD-ROM

Have children play the CD-ROM with their families to show them what they know.

ActiveTeach

Demonstrate tracing the letters on the big screen and then have volunteers trace them.

Math

Objectives: To count items 1–14, to write numbers 11–14

Review: numbers 1–12

TPR: flap arms, hold up fingers, kick, march, point, tap your knees, write

Materials: Audio CD A, Workbook

Optional Materials: CD-ROM; ActiveTeach; groups of classroom objects, teacher-made scavenger hunt lists

GETTING READY

Introduce the Numbers 13 and 14 (10 minutes)

- Review numbers 1–12 by counting real objects in the class.
- Write the numbers on the board.
- Point to the numbers on the board and count: *1, 2, 3, 4, 5 . . . 12.*
- Then write and say: *13, 14.*
- Identify groups of items or children and ask: *How many?*

List Game (10 minutes)

- Have children stand in a circle.
- Tell children that they will play a listing game. Explain that you will name a category and a number and that they will take turns saying that number of items in the category: 14 children's names; 13 letters; 12 things in the house (rooms, furniture, and other objects); 11 colors; and so on.
- Count off each item and repeat as children say an item in a category: 1 name, Maria; 2 names, Maria and Sam, and so on.

WORKING IN THE BOOK: PAGE 41

A48 7. Listen, say, and trace. Count and write.

- Play the audio of the numbers chant and act it out.
- Play it again and invite children to chant and do the actions with you.

Audio Script

Count to 14 Chant

1, 2, 3, (hold up fingers for counting)
Buzz like a bee. (flap arms and buzz)
4, 5, 6, (hold up fingers for counting)
Do high kicks. (kick)
7, 8, 9, (hold up fingers for counting)
March in a line. (march in place)
10! 10! 10!
Write with a pen. (pretend to write)
11, 12,
Point to yourself. (point to yourself)
13, 14,
Tap your knees. (tap your knees)

- Have children look at page 41.
- Model tracing the numbers at the top of the page and then have children trace them.
- Point to the different types of toy vehicles and have children identify each by asking: *What is this?*
- Do the first item together. Say: *Let's count fire trucks. 1, 2, 3, 4 . . . 12. Twelve fire trucks.*
- Model writing the number 12 in the box.
- Have children complete the rest of the page on their own, or as a group.

CONSOLIDATING

Scavenger Hunt (10 minutes)

- Tell children they will go on a scavenger hunt.
- Divide the class into groups and give each group a list of things to find. Include review vocabulary in each list, such as 14 red things, 10 crayons, 5 school supplies, and 2 things that start with *p*.
- Tell children beforehand that they will have to put the items back where they found them after the hunt.

Make a Home Connection

Give children a list for a scavenger hunt at home, or have them create their own list.

Workbook Page 41

Have children trace the numbers and count the windows on the bus. Have them write the number in the box and color the page. Finally, have them work in pairs to count the windows aloud together.

OPTIONAL: USING DIGITAL COMPONENTS

CD-ROM

Have children play the games at home to practice numbers.

ActiveTeach

Invite volunteers to use the pen tool to count the number of toy vehicles and to write the numbers.

MATH

A48 7 Listen, say, and trace. Count and write.

11 12 13 14

VALUES Ask for help.

A50 8 **Listen and say. Draw and trace.**

Ask for help.

Values: Ask for help. **Prewriting:** tracing a short sentence

Values

Objective: To learn about the value of asking for help
New Values Language: Ask for help.
Prewriting: Tracing a short sentence
Materials: Class Audio CD A, Workbook
Optional Materials: CD-ROM, ActiveTeach

GETTING READY

A43 Revisit the Story

- Have children listen to the unit story again. See pages T36–T37.
- Discuss ways that firefighters and other workers help their communities.

Introduce Asking for Help (5 minutes)

- Prepare a few volunteers to role-play for the class. Tell them to pretend to play the "List Game" from page T41. Explain that they should act out needing help to name an item from the category and ask each other: *Can you help me?*
- Brainstorm with the class situations when people need to ask for help.

WORKING IN THE BOOK: PAGE 42

A50 8. Listen and say. Draw and trace.

- Have children look at the pictures on page 42.
- Play the dialogue on the first part of the audio and ask children to look at the photos as they listen.
- Have volunteers repeat the dialogue with you.

Audio Script

Girl: I'm learning to skate. Can you help me?
Dad: Yes. I can help. I don't want you to fall.
Girl: Thank you.

- Then play the chant on the second part of the audio. Have children listen and chant along with the audio when they are ready.

Audio Script

Ask for Help Chant
When you're learning something,
Ask for help.
Help! Help! Help!
When you're learning something,
Ask for help.
Help! Help! Help!

- Talk about each photo with the class and have children discuss whether the children in each photo asked for help.
- Now point to the faces below each photo. Tell children to draw a smile on the face below the photo where the child asked for help. Then have them draw a frown under the photo where the child did not.
- Finally, have children read and trace the sentence: *Ask for help.*

Talk about it!

Share a time you asked for help and have children talk about times they asked for help.

CONSOLIDATING

Act It Out (10 minutes)

- Invite pairs or small groups of children to role-play.
- Refer to the situations where people might ask for help from Getting Ready and have groups role-play them.
- If a group does not ask for help, cue the class to say: *Ask for help!* and if the group does, to say: *Good job!*

Which Value Is It? (10 minutes)

- Explain that you will describe a situation about a value or role-play one with volunteers: not wanting to share at school, needing to get across a busy street, having trouble zipping a jacket.
- Tell children to listen carefully and name the value: *Follow rules. Stay safe. Ask for help.*

Workbook Page 42

Have children color the picture and practice the language with a partner: *Ask for help.*

OPTIONAL: USING DIGITAL COMPONENTS

CD-ROM

Have children play the games and do the activities on the CD-ROM at home to show their families what they're learning about in class.

ActiveTeach

Play the live-action videos to reinforce what children are doing in class.

Review / Assessment

Objectives: To review and assess new unit vocabulary and structures

Materials: Class Audio CD A, Workbook, stickers (in the back of the Student Book and shown on page T108)

Optional Materials: Picture Cards; rectangles and triangles cut from colored paper, glue; CD-ROM; ActiveTeach

GETTING READY

Sing and Move (10 minutes)

- Have children sing and move to the various songs and chants from the unit.
- Invite children to tell which song or chant they like best.

Play a Review Game (10 minutes)

- Have children sit in a circle.
- Tell them to pass around the unit Picture Cards until you say: *Stop*.
- Say: *[John], my mom is a [nurse]. Where does she work?*
- Cue [John] to answer: *She works in a [hospital].* Then have [John] look for and point to the *[hospital]* Picture Card.
- Continue with other workers and work places.

WORKING IN THE BOOK: PAGE 35

9. Stick and say.

- Distribute the stickers (but not the reward sticker).
- Have children open to page 43.
- Help children notice the sticker outlines in their books and then stick the correct ones in place. Begin with item 1 and say: *Find the school sticker.*
- Have children hold up the sticker.
- Say: *Stick the sticker.*
- Tell children to stick the sticker and say: *School.*
- Repeat with the other stickers (store, police station, hospital).

A52 10. Listen and circle.

- Remind children to listen and circle the answer to each question.
- Confirm the answers with the class.

Audio Script

1. She's a teacher. Where does she work?
2. He's a bus driver. Where does he work?
3. He's a police officer. Where does he work?
4. She's a nurse. Where does she work?

I Can! Use the Reward Sticker

- Help children talk about what they have learned in this unit. Encourage them to use positive language. (See page T33 for examples.)
- Distribute the reward stickers.
- Show children where to stick the stickers (on the Unit 4 Good Job! placeholder).

CONSOLIDATING

Congratulations Chant (5 minutes)

- Ask children to each choose one thing they learned in the unit (vocabulary, structure, number, letter) or one thing they can do.
- Have children stand in a circle.
- Have the entire class clap and each child take a turn chanting what they learned: *I know* (clap, clap) *[14].* (clap, clap) or what they can do: *I can* (clap, clap) *[write the letters w, x, and y].* (clap, clap)
- End by congratulating the class!

Math Project: Make a Building

- Tell children they are going to make a tall office building and show them the model on page 43.
- Provide rectangles (for the floors) and triangles (for the roof) cut from colored paper and have children work together to glue the shapes down to make their tall building. Have them count the floors in their building.
- Encourage them to talk about the workers in their building.

Workbook Page 43

Have children draw the worker and the place where the person works. After children color the page, have them work with a partner to practice the target language: *Where does [she] work? [She] works at the [school].*

OPTIONAL: USING DIGITAL COMPONENTS

CD-ROM

Have children play the games and do the activities on the CD-ROM at home to show their families what they're learning about in class.

ActiveTeach

Use ActiveTeach to check answers as a class.

REVIEW I can!

9 **Stick and say.** A52 10 **Listen and circle.**

1

2

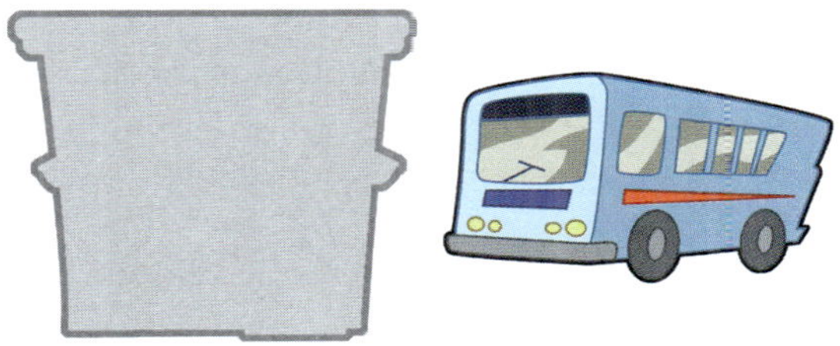

3

4

1+2=3 Project

Unit 4 GOOD JOB!

5 Clothes

Unit Overview

Objectives

- ✓ To learn clothes vocabulary
- ✓ To sing songs and chant
- ✓ To do new TPR movements
- ✓ To practice fine and gross motor skills
- ✓ To understand and role-play a story
- ✓ To learn and practice new language structures: *What [are you] wearing? / [I'm] wearing a [dress].*
- ✓ To recognize and produce the short vowel sound that *e* stands for in the middle of words
- ✓ To learn how to write the letter *e*
- ✓ To count to 16
- ✓ To learn how to write the numbers 15 and 16
- ✓ To learn the value of taking care of one's clothes
- ✓ To practice writing a short sentence
- ✓ To practice new language by listening and speaking
- ✓ To learn and review unit vocabulary and language structures

Vocabulary

New: dress, jacket, pants, shirt, shoes, skirt, socks, sweater; numbers 15, 16

Review: numbers 1–14; colors, shapes; bed, hen, pen

Home-School Connections

Copy the Letter Home for children to bring home to share what they'll be learning in Unit 5 of *My Little Island*. The Letter Home is available online at www.pearsonelt.com/mylittleisland.

Values

Take care of your clothes.

Materials

Student Book pages 44–53; Workbook pages 44–53; Picture Cards 25–32; Class Audio CD A: Tracks 53–65; Program Posters: My Little Island Map, Shapes and Colors All Around, Meet Your New Friends!; stickers (back of Student Book and shown on page T108)

Optional: CD-ROM, ActiveTeach, Big Book, Sammy the Squirrel Puppet

Songs and Chants

- ✓ I Look Great! (Class Audio CD A: Tracks 53, 54)
- ✓ *E* Cheer (Class Audio CD A: Tracks 58, 59)
- ✓ Count to 16 Chant (Class Audio CD A: Tracks 61, 62)
- ✓ Take Care of Your Clothes Chant (Class Audio CD A: Tracks 63, 64)

Story

"The Vacation": Sue talks to her grandma on the phone. Grandma and Grandpa are on vacation. She tells Sue about the weather and what she and Grandpa are wearing.

Language Structures: What [are you] wearing? / [I'm] wearing a [dress]., What [is Grandpa] wearing? / [He's] wearing a [shirt] and [pants].

Review: How's the weather? / It's [sunny].

SKILLS

Cross-Curricular Connections

- count to 16, write numbers 13–16, recognize different shapes
- learn the value of taking care of clothes
- design a T-shirt about things one loves
- sing and chant, move to music

Preschool Learning Outcomes

- ✓ Recognize intonation in questions.
- ✓ Use short answers to questions.
- ✓ Understand new language structures.
- ✓ Recognize and produce the sound that short *e* stands for.
- ✓ Trace and write the letter *e* words.
- ✓ Listen to a story and look at pictures.
- ✓ Make predictions, using pictures.
- ✓ Sing songs and say chants with TPR.
- ✓ Join in games and interact.
- ✓ Talk about self and surroundings.
- ✓ Develop a positive attitude toward the English language.

Digital Practice

- Have children use the CD-ROM for vocabulary practice in class or at home.
- Use ActiveTeach to go over Student Book pages together as a class.

LEARN BY DOING

TPR

- ✓ brush teeth, flap arms, hold up fingers, kick, march, point, punch the air, stretch, tap knees, touch clothes, write, write *e* in the air

Phonics

- ✓ Recognize sound-symbol correspondence: short *e*.
- ✓ Write the letter *e*.
- ✓ Complete Phonics page 50.
- ✓ Listen to the audio.
- ✓ Sing songs and say chants.

Prereading and Prewriting

- ✓ Follow a four-page story.
- ✓ Talk about the characters.
- ✓ Act out the story to show comprehension.
- ✓ Practice fine motor skills.
- ✓ Trace letters and a short sentence.

BULLETIN BOARD DISPLAY

Colorful Clothesline

- ✓ Create a thematic bulletin board to display children's art work.

Materials

- push pins
- string
- clothespins
- teacher-made cut-outs of clothing
- markers
- decorations
- teacher-made or child-made labels

Directions

1. With push pins, hang string across the bulletin board to create a few clotheslines.
2. Prepare several cut-outs of clothing from the unit (dress, jacket, pants, shirt, shoes, skirt, socks, sweater).
3. Invite children to decorate the cut-outs with markers and decorations.
4. Prepare a label for each article of clothing.
5. Sort the cut-outs so all the socks are together, all the shoes are together, and so on.
6. Use the clothespins to "hang" the clothing on the clotheslines and put the labels near the cut-outs (for example, *socks* near the socks).

5 Clothes

A53 ♪ 1 **Listen and sing. Move.**

Presentation: *dress, jacket, pants, shirt, shoes, skirt, socks, sweater* **Review:** *8* **TPR:** hold up 8 fingers, punch the air, stretch, touch clothes

Presentation

Objectives: To identify vocabulary in a scene, to learn a song and new TPR actions

New Vocabulary: dress, jacket, pants, shirt, shoes, skirt, socks, sweater

Review: number 8

TPR: hold up fingers, punch the air, stretch, touch clothes

Materials: Class Audio CD A, Picture Cards, Workbook

Optional Materials: CD-ROM, ActiveTeach, dress-up clothes or clothes from home

GETTING READY

Introduce the Topic: Odd One Out (5 minutes)

- Tell children you are going to draw rows of four pictures and that three of them in each row go together, and one does not: It's the "odd one out."
- Draw a circle, square, triangle, and T-shirt. Elicit that the T-shirt does not belong and is the "odd one out."
- Draw a teddy bear, kite, dress, and ball. Ask which is the "odd one out."
- Continue this way, always making the "odd one out" an article of clothing.
- Ask children what all the rows have in common. Elicit that the "odd one out" is an article of clothing.

Share What You Know (5 minutes)

- Explain that in this unit children will learn language to talk about clothes.
- Invite volunteers to name any clothing words they know in English.
- Walk around the room and talk about what children are wearing.
- Point and say: *Oh, what a nice [dress]. And look, this is a [red shirt].*

WORKING IN THE BOOK: PAGE 44

Introduce Vocabulary

- Have children open to page 44.
- Explain that this is Sue's bedroom and that she and her brother and sister are getting ready for school.
- Use the Picture Cards to reinforce the vocabulary. Say: *[Dress].* Have children repeat. Say: *Show me the [dress].* Have children point to [Sue's sister's dress].
- Repeat with the other words.

A53 1. Listen and sing. Move.

- Preteach the actions for the song: hold up eight fingers, punch the air, stand up and stretch, and touch clothes.
- Say: [*It's the morning*.] and do the action [stand up and stretch].
- Say: *Let's sing a song*. Play the song.
- Play the song again. Invite children to sing along and do the actions when ready.

Audio Script

Sue: It's the morning! (stretch)
I'm up at eight. (hold up 8 fingers)
With my skirt, sweater, and shoes. (touch clothes)
I look grrrrrreat! (punch the air)

Sue's brother: It's the morning! (stretch)
I'm up at eight. (hold up 8 fingers)
With my shirt, pants, and jacket. (touch clothes)
I look grrrrrrreat! (punch the air)

Sue's sister: It's the morning! (stretch)
I'm up at eight. (hold up 8 fingers)
With my dress and socks. (touch clothes)
I look grrrrrrrreat! (punch the air)

CONSOLIDATING

Dress Up Race (10 minutes)

- Have children stand in a circle.
- Put different articles of clothing (two of each) in the middle of the circle.
- Tell children that you will call out two names and an article of clothing and that those two children have to race to find it and put it on.

A54 Karaoke (5 minutes)

- Play the karaoke version of the song.
- Cue each verse with Picture Cards.

Workbook Page 44

Have children draw lines matching Sue and Lou to the different items of clothing. After they color the page, have them work with a partner to practice saying the vocabulary words: *dress, jacket, pants, shirt, shoes.*

OPTIONAL: USING DIGITAL COMPONENTS

CD-ROM

Encourage children to play the games and do the activities on the CD-ROM at home to show their families what they're learning about in class.

ActiveTeach

Use the large digital format to focus on each character and the clothes he or she is wearing.

Vocabulary

Objectives: To practice new vocabulary, to write numbers 1–8

New Vocabulary: dress, jacket, pants, shirt, shoes, skirt, socks, sweater

Materials: Class Audio CD A, Workbook

Optional Materials: Picture Cards, CD-ROM, ActiveTeach

GETTING READY

A53 Review the Song (5 minutes)

- Sing and act out "I Look Great!" with children.
- Display the Picture Cards. Have children point to them as they sing.

Play "I Spy" (5 minutes)

- Review the language structure: *Can you see [the horse]? Yes, I can. / No, I can't.* (Level 2, Unit 8)
- Use the structure to play "I Spy," using children's clothing.
- Say: *Can you see a [dress]? It's [red and yellow]. It has [circles].*
- Cue volunteers to say: *Yes, I can!* or *No, I can't.* Have them gesture to the child who is wearing the item.

WORKING IN THE BOOK: PAGE 45

A55 2. Listen. Find and number. Say.

- Have children look at page 45.
- Remind children to listen and write the numbers.
- Play the audio, pausing after each to allow children time to find and write.

Audio Script

1. socks
2. pants
3. dress
4. jacket
5. skirt
6. shirt
7. shoes
8. sweater

- Check children's work as a class.
- Have volunteers point and say: *[1] [socks].*
- For additional practice, say each vocabulary word aloud and have children clap three times, pause, clap three times again, and repeat the word.

CONSOLIDATING

What's Different? (10 minutes)

- Invite a volunteer to stand up.
- Have children take twenty seconds to study what the volunteer is wearing.
- Then have children close their eyes.
- Change the volunteer's outfit by, for example: rolling a pant leg up, untying a shoe, switching shoes so they're on the wrong feet, un-buttoning a button, having a shirt be inside-out.
- Have children open their eyes and say which article of clothing is different.
- Repeat with other volunteers.

Chain Game (10 minutes)

- Have children stand in a circle to play this memory game.
- Say: *I have [pants].*
- Tell the next child to add an article and say: *I have [pants] and [a sock].*
- Have the next child repeat and add another article: *I have [pants] and [a sock] and [a skirt].*
- See how long children can continue the chain!

Workbook Page 45

Have children find and color Lou's clothes. Have children work in pairs to point and say: *pants, shirt, shoes, socks, sweater.*

OPTIONAL: USING DIGITAL COMPONENTS

CD-ROM

Have children play the games on the CD-ROM to show their families the English words they are learning for clothing.

ActiveTeach

Use the large digital format to model numbering the boxes. To reinforce vocabulary, show and play the audio for the Picture Cards.

VOCABULARY

A55 **2** **Listen. Find and number. Say.**

pants

sweater

skirt

jacket

shoes

socks

shirt

dress

Practice: *pants, sweater, skirt, jacket, shoes, socks, shirt, dress* **Writing:** *I–8*

Story

Objectives: To read and understand a story, to identify and understand speech bubbles, to learn a new language structure, to listen to and identify the intonation in a sentence, to role-play, to practice new vocabulary

New Structures: *What [are you] wearing? / [I'm] wearing a [dress].; What [is Grandpa] wearing? / [He's] wearing a [shirt] and [pants].*

Review: *How's the weather? / It's [sunny].*

Materials: Class Audio CD A, Workbook

Optional Materials: CD-ROM, ActiveTeach

GETTING READY

Talk About Weather (5 minutes)

- Review language used to talk about the weather (Level 2, Unit 9).
- Practice TPR actions for each kind of weather (*sunny:* shade your eyes; *hot:* fan yourself; *cold:* shiver; *snowy:* flutter your fingers downward like snowflakes; *windy:* fly a kite; *rainy:* open an umbrella).
- Model with Sammy. Ask: *How's the weather?* Do an action or gesture to cue his answer: *It's [sunny].*
- Invite volunteers to participate when they are ready.

Introduce the Story (5 minutes)

- Hold up the Student Book, turned to page 46.
- Ask children to talk about the picture on the first page of "The Vacation."
- Explain that Sue is calling her grandma on a cell phone.
- Ask children if they recognize any of the words in the speech bubbles. Invite them to guess what Sue and her grandma are talking about.
- Take a picture walk through the rest of the story and have children predict what will happen. Revisit predictions later.

WORKING IN THE BOOK: PAGES 46–47

A56 3. Look and listen. Act it out.

- Have children open to page 46.
- Play the audio, and pause after each story page to make sure children are on the correct one and understand what Sue and Grandma are talking about.
- If needed, help children understand that the waiter spilled a salad on Grandpa, so he is "wearing" it.
- Ask children: *How's the weather for Sue?* (cold and snowy).
- Play the story again. Point to each speech bubble as the words are spoken.
- Encourage children to speak along with the characters.
- Invite volunteers to act out the story with the audio.

Audio Script

The Vacation

Page 1	Sue:	How's the weather?
	Grandma:	It's sunny.
Page 2	Sue:	What are you wearing?
	Grandma:	I'm wearing a dress.
Page 3	Sue:	What is Grandpa wearing?
	Grandma:	He's wearing a shirt and pants.
Page 4	Grandma:	Oops! Now he's wearing a shirt, pants, and a salad!

Look at New Language

- Point out the new language Sue and Grandma use to ask and answer questions about clothing: *What are you wearing? I'm wearing a dress. What is Grandpa wearing? He's wearing a shirt and pants.*
- Invite partners to take the parts of Sue and Grandma and practice the dialogue.

A56

Listen to the Intonation

- Have children close their eyes and listen while you play the story audio.
- Pause after each question. Point out the different intonation for questions and answers.
- Have children repeat each question and answer, copying the intonation.

CONSOLIDATING

Role-Play (10 minutes)

- Have pairs of children act out the story.
- First, play the audio and have pairs of children pantomime.
- Then invite volunteers to act out the dialogue without the audio.

Continue the Conversation (5 minutes)

- Tell children to imagine that Sue and Grandma keep talking.
- Ask them to imagine what the two characters would say next.
- Have partners work together to create the next few lines of the story.
- Suggest that children talk about Grandpa changing his shirt!

Workbook Page 46

Have children circle the clothing items that Grandpa needs on his vacation. After children color the page, have them work in pairs to practice the structures: *What [is Grandpa] wearing? [He's] wearing a [shirt] and [pants].*

Workbook Page 47

Have children trace Grandma's clothes. Then have them color the page. Finally have them practice the target language with a partner: *What [is Grandma] wearing? [She's] wearing a [dress] and [shoes].*

OPTIONAL: USING DIGITAL COMPONENTS

CD-ROM

Have children review the story at home. Encourage them to use the Story Time feature to focus on individual words.

ActiveTeach

Use the large digital format to focus on the speech bubbles. Point to the speaker, then drag the pointer under each word as it is spoken.

LISTENING

A57 **4** **Listen and find. Then write.**

Practice: *What are you wearing? I'm wearing a [yellow shirt], [blue jacket], and [blue pants].* **Review:** colors **Writing:** *l–4*

Listening

Objectives: To practice listening comprehension, to practice new unit vocabulary and structures

Review: colors, numbers 1–4

Materials: Class Audio CD A

Optional Materials: Sammy the Squirrel puppet, CD-ROM, ActiveTeach, different colored crayons, teacher-made word strips, blindfold, drawing supplies

GETTING READY

Review Colors: Pass and Say (5 minutes)

- Have children sit in a circle.
- Give each child a different colored crayon.
- Tell children you are going to play some music and that they should pass the crayons around until the music stops.
- Play some music, stop it, and say: *Show me [black].*
- Cue children holding a [black] crayon to hold it up and say: *I have [black].* or *This is [black].*
- Continue with other colors.

Build a Sentence (10 minutes)

- Prepare word strips: *I'm, wearing, a, shirt, skirt, jacket, sweater, red, blue, green.*
- Display word strips for the sentence: *I'm wearing a shirt.*
- Help children read the sentence with you by running your finger under each word as you say it.
- Then ask: *What color?* and model the answer: *I'm wearing a red shirt.*
- Take the blue word strip and place before the word *shirt*. Read the new sentence.
- Continue with other sentences. Each time, make sure children see that the color word (adjective) goes before the clothing word (noun).

WORKING IN THE BOOK: PAGE 48

A57 4. Listen and find. Then write.

- Have children open to page 48.
- Explain that Sue is with a friend, Lou, and Lou's dad at the fair.
- Invite children to talk about what the four are wearing. Encourage them to use complete sentences, such as: *[Sue] is wearing [a blue dress]. [Lou] is wearing [a yellow shirt]. [Dad] is wearing [blue pants].*
- Explain that children will listen to the audio in order to identify the characters and write the number for each one in his or her balloon.
- Play the audio. Do the first one together.
- Have children complete the page on their own. (1: Lou; 2: Sue; 3: Dad; 4: Friend)

Audio Script

Narrator:	1. What are you wearing?
Lou:	I'm wearing a yellow shirt, a blue jacket, and blue pants.
Narrator:	Write 1.
Narrator:	2. What are you wearing?
Sue:	I'm wearing a blue dress and red shoes.
Narrator:	Write 2.
Narrator:	3. What are you wearing?
Dad:	I'm wearing a gray shirt, blue pants, and brown shoes.
Narrator:	Write 3.
Narrator:	4. What are you wearing?
Friend:	I'm wearing a purple sweater, a brown skirt, and purple socks.
Narrator:	Write 4.

CONSOLIDATING

Listen and Pick (10 minutes)

- Call for three volunteers to play.
- Blindfold one of them and cue him or her to ask: *What are you wearing?*
- Then disguise your voice and answer for another: *I'm wearing [a green dress] and [black shoes].*
- Remove the blindfold and have the volunteer identify who it is.
- Continue with other volunteers.

Draw and Say (10 minutes)

- Have children draw a person wearing different colored clothing.
- Have them take turns asking and answering: *What's [he / she] wearing? [He / She]'s wearing [blue pants, a red shirt, and green shoes].*

OPTIONAL: USING DIGITAL COMPONENTS

CD-ROM

Have children play the games at home to practice their listening skills.

ActiveTeach

Invite volunteers to write the numbers in the balloons on the big screen for everyone to see.

Speaking

Objectives: To practice speaking, to practice new unit vocabulary and structures

Review: colors

Materials: Workbook

Optional Materials: Sammy the Squirrel puppet, CD-ROM, ActiveTeach, pictures of costumes

GETTING READY

Common Color, Common Clothes (10 minutes)

- Have children sit in a circle.
- Explain that Sammy will tap certain children on the shoulder and that the children he taps should stand up and that the class has to figure out what those children have in common.
- Begin by tapping children who are wearing red. Give a hint, if needed.
- Then tap children who are wearing dresses.
- Repeat with other colors and clothes.

Talk About Costumes (5 minutes)

- Ask children to talk about when they play dress-up and what they wear.
- Introduce some popular costumes and related vocabulary:
  - Princess (crown)
  - Pirate (vest, sword, boots, scarf)
  - Fairy (wings, magic wand)
  - Superhero (cape, mask)
  - Cowboy (hat, boots)
- Refer to Student Book page 49 for princess and pirate pictures, and to books and magazines for others.

WORKING IN THE BOOK: PAGE 49

5. Color. Ask and answer.

- Have children open to page 49.
- Ask children to talk about the picture.
- Explain that Sue and Lou are playing dress-up. Invite children to guess why they are dressing up.
- Invite children to color in Sue and Lou's clothing in different colors.
- Then direct their attention to the boy and girl with the speech bubbles at the bottom of the page.
- Point to and read the speech bubbles: *What's Sue wearing? She's wearing a blue dress.*
- Tell children they will work in pairs to ask and answer questions about the clothing they colored, using the speech bubble text as a model.

CONSOLIDATING

Thumbs-Up or -Down (5 minutes)

- Explain that you and Sammy will talk about someone in the room and that children should agree or disagree by giving a thumbs-up or -down.
- Have Sammy ask: *What's [Amelia] wearing?*
- Say: *[She]'s wearing [green pants and a white sweater].*
- Cue children to give a thumbs-up or a thumbs-down.
- Play a few rounds with Sammy, and then have volunteers take your role.

Let's Move (5 minutes)

- Review some of the actions that children have learned in this and other levels.
- Explain that you and Sammy will describe someone's clothing and children will guess who it is.
- Have Sammy ask: *What's [he] wearing?* Say: *[He's] wearing [black pants] and [a black shirt].*
- Have children guess: *It's [Randy]!*
- Have [Randy] then name an action: *[Jump]!* Cue the class to do the action.

Extra Practice: Student Book page 97 and T97

For extra practice speaking, have children turn to page 97 in the back of their books. For teacher support, turn to page T97 in this book.

Big Book Talk (10 minutes)

- Use the Big Book to get children talking.
- Read "Diddle, Diddle Dumpling" to children a few times and then encourage them to "read" along with you.
- Read the nursery rhyme again, substituting clothing from Unit 5 for the item(s) of clothing in the song. Invite them to create their own rhyme as well.

Workbook Page 48

Have children color the page. Then have them work with a partner to point to each person in the picture and practice the target language: *What's [Sue] wearing? [She's] wearing a [blue dress].*

Workbook Page 49

Have children trace items of clothing in the pictures. Once children have colored the page, have them work with a partner to practice the target language: *What's [Lou] wearing? [He's] wearing a [yellow shirt].*

OPTIONAL: USING DIGITAL COMPONENTS

CD-ROM

Have children use the CD-ROM at home to practice their speaking skills.

ActiveTeach

Use the reproducible activities if children need more practice with unit language.

SPEAKING

5 **Color. Ask and answer.**

EXTRA PRACTICE
Page 97

Practice: *What's [Sue] wearing? [She's] wearing a [blue dress].*
Review: colors

PHONICS

A58 A60 6 **Listen. Trace, write, and say.**

e e

bed

pen

hen

Phonics: short *e* **Prewriting/Writing:** directionality, letter tracing, letters in contexts **Review:** *bed, hen, pen* **TPR:** write *e* in the air

Phonics

Objectives: To learn the short vowel sound that the letter *e* stands for in the middle of words, to understand sound-symbol correspondences, to recognize left-to-right directionality, to trace and write letters in the context of words

New Sounds and Letters: short *e*

Review: bed, hen, pen

TPR: write *e* in the air

Materials: Class Audio CD A, Workbook

Optional Materials: CD-ROM, ActiveTeach, pencils with erasers

GETTING READY

Review Letters (5 minutes)

- Write the alphabet on the board.
- Circle the letters children have already learned: b, c, d, f, g, h, j, k, l, m, n, p, q, r, s, t, v, w, x, y.
- For each letter, have children say the letter, the sound, and a word: *B*, /b/, *bird*.

Introduce the Letter (5 minutes)

- On the board, write *b_d*.
- Say the sound each letter stands for: /b/, /d/.
- Point to the middle space and shrug your shoulders. Run your fingers under each and say: */b/*—(shrug)—*/d/*.
- Write the letter e. Say: *This is* e. E *stands for /e/ in words like* bed.
- Run your finger under the word a few times, and say the sounds slowly: /b/–/e/–/d/.
- Go faster and faster, blending the word, until you are reading: *bed*.
- Erase the *b* and *d*. Write *p* and *n*. Sound out: *pen*.
- Repeat with *hen*.

WORKING IN THE BOOK: PAGE 50

A58 A60 6. Listen. Trace, write, and say.

- Play the "*E* Cheer." Do the actions.
- Invite children to chant and do the actions when they are ready.

Audio Script

***E* Cheer**

Sue: Give me an *e!*
Fans: *E!*
Sue: What does *e* sound like?
Fans: Eh!
Sue: Give me some *e* words!
Fans: Eh . . . *bed!*
Eh . . . *pen!*
Eh . . . *hen!*
Sue: Show me an *e!* (write *e* in the air)
Let's hear it for *e!*
Fans: Hooray!

- Focus children on the page again.
- Point to the e. Model tracing the letter with your finger. Have children trace and then write the letter several times.
- Then point to the word *bed*. Point and say: *eh, bed.*
- Model tracing the e in the middle of the word. Have children trace it.
- Repeat with the other words.
- Have children take turns pointing to and reading the letters and words on the page.
- For additional practice, have children listen to Class Audio CD A: Track 60.
  - Pause after each word to allow children to clap if they hear an *eh* sound.
  - For *pencil*, help children hear the *eh* sound in the first syllable.
- Model once with the words by saying *pen* (clap) and *pan* (don't clap).

Audio Script

Now listen and clap if you hear an *eh* sound.

pet	(clap)
cat	
leg	(clap)
bird	
vet	(clap)
pencil	(clap)

CONSOLIDATING

"Hand" Writing (10 minutes)

- Use a pencil eraser to write a letter of the alphabet on a volunteer's hand. Model proper pencil grip.
- Have the volunteer guess the letter.
- Continue with other volunteers and familiar letters.
- Reinforce pencil grip with children. Then have them practice "hand" writing with partners.
- As a challenge, have children "hand" write words with partners.

Workbook Page 50

Have children color the letter *e* and say the letter and the sound. Then have them trace each letter *e* and take turns saying each word to a partner: *bed*, *pen*, *hen*. Finally, invite children to finish coloring the page.

OPTIONAL: USING DIGITAL COMPONENTS

CD-ROM

Have children play the games at home with their families to show them what they are learning in class.

ActiveTeach

Demonstrate tracing the letters on the big screen. Then invite volunteers to trace and write the letters.

Math

Objectives: To count items 1–16, to write numbers 13–16
Review: numbers 1–14, shapes
TPR: brush teeth, flap arms, hold up fingers, kick, march, point, tap knees, write
Materials: Class Audio CD A, Workbook
Optional Materials: CD-ROM, ActiveTeach, teacher-made number and dot cards (see T21)

GETTING READY

Review and Introduce Numbers (5 minutes)

- Have children count with you to review 1 through 14. Then say: *15, 16* and have children repeat after you.
- Have children count off for more practice.
- Write the numbers 15 and 16 on the board and have the class air-write them.

Review Shapes: Musical Shapes (10 minutes)

- Use tape to make giant shapes on the floor: circle, square, triangle, rectangle, star.
- Point out the shapes. Tell children that you will play music and they should dance around the room until it stops.
- Stop the music and call out a shape: *Circle!*
- Cue everyone to squeeze together to stand in the circle: the goal is for everyone to be in, and nobody out.
- Continue until you call out all shapes.

WORKING IN THE BOOK: PAGE 51

A61 7. Listen, say, and trace. Count and write.

- Play the chant and act it out.
- Play it again and invite children to chant and do the actions with you.

Audio Script
Count to 16 Chant
1, 2, 3, (hold up fingers for counting)
Buzz like a bee. (flap arms and buzz)
4, 5, 6, (hold up fingers for counting)
Do high kicks. (kick)
7, 8, 9, (hold up fingers for counting)
March in a line. (march in place)
10! 10! 10!
Write with a pen. (pretend to write)
11, 12,
Point to yourself. (point to yourself)
13, 14,
Tap your knees. (tap your knees)
15, 16,
Brush your teeth. (pretend to brush teeth)

- Have children look at page 51.
- Model tracing the numbers 15 and 16 at the top of the page and then have children trace them.
- Point to the T-shirts. Have children count and name the shapes: *1, 2, 3, 4 . . . .13, 14. [14] [stars].*
- Show children how to write 14 in the box under the star T-shirt.
- Have children complete the rest of the page on their own, or as a group.

CONSOLIDATING

Group Concentration (10 minutes)

- Use the number and dot cards from page T21. Create new cards for 11–16.
- Divide the class into two groups.
- Shuffle the cards.
- Give the number cards to one group. Give the dot cards to the other group.
- Have the two groups stand facing each other, but not showing their cards.
- Demonstrate how the game is played with a volunteer. Cue him or her to name one child from each group. Explain that if the cards match, the player gets to keep the cards, and if not, the children return to their places.
- Have children from each group take turns and continue the game. Explain that the player with the most pairs of cards at the end wins.

1, Hop, 3, Hop! (5 minutes)

- Have children stand in a circle.
- Have each child count, in turn, to 16.
- Then explain that instead of saying every other number, the child should hop and say: *Hop*. For example: *1, hop, 3, hop, 5, hop . . . .*
- Continue, using different actions.

Workbook Page 51

Have children count the stripes on Sue's skirt. Then have them color the page and practice counting to 16 aloud with a partner.

OPTIONAL: USING DIGITAL COMPONENTS

CD-ROM

Have children play the games at home to practice numbers.

ActiveTeach

Invite volunteers to use the pen tool to count the shapes and write the numbers.

MATH

A61 7 **Listen, say, and trace. Count and write.**

13 14 15 16

VALUES Take care of your clothes.

A63 8 **Listen and say. Draw and trace.**

Take care of your clothes.

Values: Take care of your clothes. **Prewriting:** tracing part of a sentence

Values

Objective: To learn about the value of taking care of your clothes
New Values Language: Take care of your clothes.
Prewriting: Tracing part of a sentence
Materials: Class Audio CD A, Workbook
Optional Materials: Sammy the Squirrel puppet, CD-ROM, ActiveTeach

GETTING READY

A56 Revisit the Story (5 minutes)

- Have children listen to "The Vacation" again.
- Focus on Grandpa's clothes and what happened to them.
- Ask children if they've had accidents with their clothes, such as spilling food on them or tearing them.

Introduce Taking Care of Your Clothes (5 minutes)

- Prepare a few volunteers to role-play for the class.
- Have volunteers act out situations where they do (a child carefully hangs up her coat) and don't take care of their clothes (a child wipes his dirty hands on his shirt).
- Brainstorm with the class other times they do or do not take care of clothes.

WORKING IN THE BOOK: PAGE 52

A63 8. Listen and say. Draw and trace.

- Have children open to page 52.
- Play the dialogue on the first part of the audio and ask children to look at the photos as they listen.
- Have volunteers repeat the dialogue with you.

Audio Script

Mom: Take care of your clothes.
Girl: Yes. Look! I'm putting them away.
Mom: That's great!

- Then play the chant on the second part of the audio. Have children listen and then chant along with the audio when they are ready.

Audio Script

Take Care of Your Clothes Chant
Take care of your clothes
From your head to your toes.
Take care of your clothes.
(Repeat.)

- Talk about each photo with the class and have children discuss whether the child in each photo is taking care of his or her clothes.
- Now point to the faces below each photo. Tell children to draw a smile on the face below the photo where the child is taking care of clothes and a frown where the child is not.
- Finally, have children read the sentence: *Take care of your clothes* and trace the words *your clothes*.

Talk about it!

- Call attention to "Talk about it!"
- Share one way you take care of your clothes and then invite children to talk about ways they take care of their clothes.

CONSOLIDATING

Act It Out (10 minutes)

- Invite pairs or small groups of children to role-play taking or not taking care of their clothes.
- If the group role-plays not taking care of their clothes, cue the class to call out: *Take care of your clothes!* or *Good job!* if they act out taking care.

Make a Home Connection

Create a chart (and provide some stars) that children can take home to reinforce taking care of their clothes (e.g., putting dirty clothes in a hamper). Tell children that every time they take care of their clothes, they should give themselves a star!

Workbook Page 52

Have children trace and name the clothing items that are properly put away *(shirt, jacket,* and *shoes)*. Have children color the picture. Then invite partners to point to and name all the different items of clothing pictured on the page.

OPTIONAL: USING DIGITAL COMPONENTS

CD-ROM

Encourage children to play the games and do the activities on the CD-ROM at home to show their families what they're learning about in class.

ActiveTeach

Focus on the two pictures. Use the pointer to highlight details that show who is taking care of clothes and who is not.

Review / Assessment

Objectives: To review and assess new unit vocabulary and structures

Materials: Class Audio CD A, Workbook, stickers (in the back of the Student Book and shown on page T108)

Optional Materials: CD-ROM, ActiveTeach, pictures of clothes, photocopies of T-shirt outline, drawing supplies

GETTING READY

A Sing and Move (10 minutes)

- Have children sing and move to the various songs and chants from the unit.
- Invite children to tell which song or chant they liked best.

Ask and Answer (5 minutes)

- Gather pictures from magazines and catalogs of people wearing different clothes.
- Hold up each picture and ask: *What's [he / she] wearing?*
- Elicit: *[He's] wearing [green shoes, red pants, and an orange sweater].*
- Then ask individuals: *How about you? What are you wearing?*
- Elicit responses.

WORKING IN THE BOOK: PAGE 53

9. Stick and say.

- Distribute the stickers (but not the reward sticker).
- Have children open to page 53.
- Help children notice the sticker outlines in their books and then stick the correct ones in place. Begin with item 1 and say: *Find the shirt sticker.*
- Have children hold up the sticker.
- Say: *Stick the sticker.*
- Cue children to stick the sticker and say: *Shirt.*
- Repeat with the other stickers (skirt, shoes, jacket).

A65 10. Listen and circle.

- Remind children to listen and circle the answer to each question.
- Confirm the answers with the class.

Audio Script

1. What are you wearing?
   I'm wearing a shirt.
2. What are you wearing?
   I'm wearing a skirt.
3. What are you wearing?
   I'm wearing shoes.
4. What are you wearing?
   I'm wearing a sweater.

I Can! Use the Reward Sticker

- Help children talk about what they have learned in this unit. Encourage them to use positive language. (See page T33 for examples.)
- Distribute the reward stickers.
- Show children where to stick the stickers (on the Unit 5 Good Job! placeholder).

CONSOLIDATING

Congratulations Chant (5 minutes)

- Ask children to each choose one thing they learned in the unit (vocabulary, structure, number, letter) or one thing they can do.
- Have children stand in a circle.
- Have the entire class clap and each child take a turn chanting what they learned: *I know* (clap, clap) *[pants].* (clap, clap) or what they can do: *I can* (clap, clap) *[take care of my clothes].* (clap, clap)
- End by congratulating the class!

Art Project: Design Your Own T-Shirt

- Make a simple outline of a T-shirt.
- Write: *I (heart)* and photocopy enough for each child.
- Cut out enough T-shirts for everyone.
- Brainstorm things children love, such as pets, ice cream, toys, and siblings.
- Have children draw something they love on their T-shirt.

Workbook Page 53

Have children draw themselves wearing their favorite clothes. Invite them to color the page and share their work: *I'm wearing a [sweater] and [pants].*

OPTIONAL: USING DIGITAL COMPONENTS

CD-ROM

Have children play the games and do the activities on the CD-ROM at home to show their families what they're learning about in class.

ActiveTeach

Use ActiveTeach to check answers as a class.

REVIEW I can!

9 **Stick and say.** A65 10 **Listen and circle.**

1

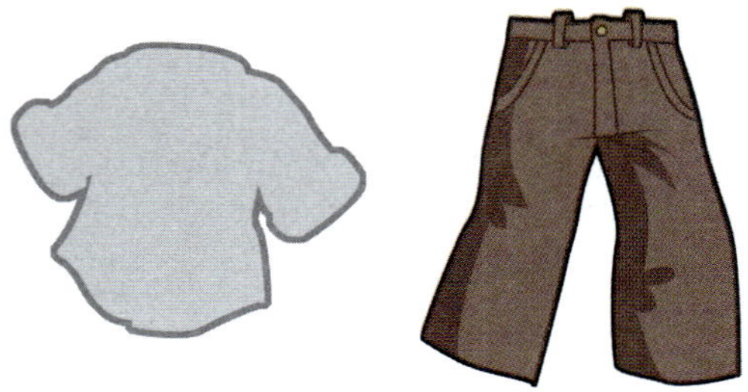

2

3

4

Project

Review/Assessment: *What are you wearing? I'm wearing a [shirt].* **Project:** art

6 Feelings

Unit Overview

Objectives

- ✓ To learn vocabulary used for feelings
- ✓ To sing songs and chant
- ✓ To do new TPR movements
- ✓ To practice fine and gross motor skills
- ✓ To understand and role-play a story
- ✓ To learn and practice new language structures: *How do you feel? / I'm [excited]. How does [Lou] feel? / He's [excited].*
- ✓ To practice sound-symbol correspondence: *a* /a/
- ✓ To recognize and produce the short vowel sound that the letter *a* stands for in the middle of words
- ✓ To write the letter *a*
- ✓ To count to 18
- ✓ To write the numbers 17 and 18
- ✓ To learn the value of not fighting
- ✓ To practice writing a short sentence
- ✓ To practice new language by listening and speaking
- ✓ To learn and review unit vocabulary and language structures

Vocabulary

New: excited, happy, hungry, mad, sad, scared, thirsty, tired; numbers 17, 18

Review: numbers 1–16; food; cat, dad, grandma, grandpa, hand, mom

Home-School Connections

Copy the Letter Home for children to bring home to share what they'll be learning in Unit 6 of *My Little Island*. The Letter Home is available online at www.pearsonelt.com/mylittleisland.

Values

Don't fight.

Materials

Student Book pages 54–63; Workbook pages 54–63; Picture Cards 33–40; Class Audio CD B: Tracks 1–13; Program Posters: My Little Island Map, Shapes and Colors All Around, Meet Your New Friends!; stickers (back of Student Book and shown on page T108)

Optional: CD-ROM, ActiveTeach, Big Book, Sammy the Squirrel Puppet

Songs and Chants

- ✓ Choose a Mask (Class Audio CD B: Tracks 1, 2)
- ✓ *A* Cheer (Class Audio CD B: Tracks 6, 7)
- ✓ Count to 18 Chant (Class Audio CD B: Tracks 9, 10)
- ✓ Don't Fight Chant (Class Audio CD B: Tracks 11, 12)

Story

"The Ride": Sue and Lou go on a rollercoaster at an amusement park, and talk about how they feel before, during, and afterwards.

Language Structures: *How do you feel? / I'm [excited]. How does [Lou] feel? / He's [excited].*

SKILLS

Cross-Curricular Connections

- count to 18, write numbers 15–18
- learn the value of not fighting, make a feelings poster
- sing, chant, and move to music

Preschool Learning Outcomes

- ✓ Recognize intonation in questions.
- ✓ Use short answers to questions.
- ✓ Understand new language structures.
- ✓ Recognize and produce the sound that short *a* stands for.
- ✓ Write the letter *a* in words.
- ✓ Listen to and follow a story with words.
- ✓ Make predictions, using pictures.
- ✓ Sing songs and say chants with TPR.
- ✓ Join in games and interact.
- ✓ Talk about self and surroundings.
- ✓ Develop a positive attitude toward the English language.

Digital Practice

- Have children use the CD-ROM for vocabulary practice in class or at home.
- Use ActiveTeach to go over Student Book pages together as a class.

LEARN BY DOING

TPR

- ✓ brush teeth, cry, cup mouth, drink, eat, flap arms, hold up fingers, jump, kick, march, point, put on mask, question action, shiver, tap knees, write, write *a* in the air, yawn

Phonics

- ✓ Practice sound-symbol correspondences: short *a*.
- ✓ Write the letter *a*.
- ✓ Complete Phonics page 60.
- ✓ Listen to the audio.
- ✓ Sing songs and say chants.

Prereading and Prewriting

- ✓ Follow a four-page story.
- ✓ Talk about the characters.
- ✓ Act out the story to show comprehension.
- ✓ Practice fine motor skills.
- ✓ Trace letters and a short sentence.

Children can use the CD-ROM to teach younger family members English!

BULLETIN BOARD DISPLAY

Make a Face!

✓ Create an interactive bulletin board to practice unit language.

Materials

- teacher-made spinner (paper plate)
- push pin
- teacher-made arrow/pointer
- large paper circle
- shape cut-outs
- tape, Velcro, or sticky tack

Directions

1. Divide the paper plate into eight sections and write a feeling (sad, scared, etc.) in each and attach the paper plate (spinner) to the bulletin board with a push pin in the center.
2. Attach a large circle shape on the bulletin board for a face.
3. Prepare several cut-outs that can be used to add features to the face (to show emotions). For example: a large crescent for a smile (happy); the same crescent upside down (sad); a thought bubble with a drink (thirsty).
4. Keep the cut-outs in envelopes attached to the bulletin board. Put all the mouths in one envelope, all the eyes and eyebrows in another, and so on.
5. Attach the pointer next to the spinner and have children take turns spinning and attaching shapes to "make a face" (mad, sad, etc.). Have them use tape, Velcro, or sticky tack to attach.

6 Feelings

B1 1 **Listen and sing. Move.**

Presentation: *excited, happy, hungry, mad, sad, scared, thirsty, tired*
TPR: cry, cup mouth, drink, eat, jump, put on mask, question action, shiver, yawn

Presentation

Objectives: To identify feelings vocabulary in a scene, to learn a song and new TPR actions

New Vocabulary: excited, happy, hungry, mad, sad, scared, thirsty, tired

TPR: cry, cup mouth, drink, eat, jump, put on mask, question action, shiver, yawn

Materials: Class Audio CD B, Picture Cards, Workbook

Optional Materials: Meet Your New Friends! poster, CD-ROM, ActiveTeach, mask

GETTING READY

Introduce the Topic (5 minutes)

- Make a face (happy, sad, mad, scared, tired) to show different feelings.
- Each time, invite children to guess how you feel. Then ask children to talk about times they feel that way.

Meet Your New Friends! Poster (5 minutes)

- Show the Meet Your New Friends! poster.
- Talk with children about friends and how friends help us when we are sad or scared and how sometimes friends are just happy to be together!

WORKING IN THE BOOK: PAGE 54

Present Vocabulary and TPR

- Have children open to page 54.
- Explain that Sue and Lou are making masks, which show different feelings.
- Show children a real mask, if needed.
- Hold up the Picture Cards, one at a time.
  - Say: *Excited.* Have children repeat.
  - Have children point to the mask for "excited."
  - Teach children the related TPR action from the song: jump up and down.
  - Have children do the action and say: *I'm excited.*
- Repeat with the other vocabulary words.

B1 1. Listen and sing. Move.

- Say: *Let's sing a song.* Play the audio.
- Play the song again. Invite children to sing along and do the actions when they are ready.

Audio Script

Choose a Mask

Sue: Choose, choose, choose a mask.
Put it on and play. (pretend to put on a mask)
Tell us, tell us (cup mouth)
How you feel today. (question action)

Sue & Lou: I'm happy! I'm happy!
Hee, hee, hee, hee, hee!
I'm sad. I'm sad. (pretend to cry)
Boo hoo, boo hoo hoo!
I'm scared. I'm scared. (shiver)
Eeeek! Eeeek! Eeeek!

(Repeat first verse.)

Sue & Lou: I'm mad! I'm mad!
Grrrr! Grrrr! Grrrr!
I'm excited! I'm excited! (jump up and down)
Oh! Oh! Oh! Oh! Oh!
I'm tired. I'm tired. (yawn)
Yaaawn, Yaaawn, Yaaawn.

(Repeat first verse.)

Sue & Lou: I'm thirsty. I'm thirsty. (pretend to drink)
Glug, glug, glug, glug, glug!
I'm hungry! I'm hungry! (pretend to eat)
Yum, Yum, Yum, Yum, Yum!
Join me. Join me.
Please take some!

(Repeat first verse.)

CONSOLIDATING

Practice with TPR (5 minutes)

- Play each line of each verse, one line at a time.
- Challenge children to do the TPR for the feeling, while repeating the line.

Workbook Page 54

Have children draw a smile to show *happy* and a frown to show *sad.* After children color the page, have them work with partners to point to the pictures and say the words.

OPTIONAL: USING DIGITAL COMPONENTS

CD-ROM

Encourage children to play the games and do the activities on the CD-ROM at home to show their families what they're learning about in class.

ActiveTeach

Play the audio for the song and use the big screen to focus on each mask as the feeling is mentioned.

Vocabulary

Objectives: To practice new words, to write numbers 1–8

New Vocabulary: excited, happy, hungry, mad, sad, scared, thirsty, tired

Writing: numbers 1–8

Materials: Class Audio CD B, Workbook

Optional Materials: Picture Cards, CD-ROM, ActiveTeach, paper plates, string, markers, stapler or tape

GETTING READY

B1 Review the Song (5 minutes)

- Sing and act out "Choose a Mask."
- Display the Picture Cards. Have children point to them as they sing.

Make a Mask (10 minutes)

- Gather paper plates, string, and markers.
- Have children choose a feeling and draw a face on a plate for a mask.
- Give children some ideas: mouth up (happy) and down (sad); jagged V-shaped eye brows (mad); wide-open eyes (excited); yawning mouth (tired); little circle mouth and uneven eyebrows (scared).
- Cut out eye holes and nose or mouth holes. Attach two pieces of string to each mask so children can tie it on.

WORKING IN THE BOOK: PAGE 55

B3 2. Listen. Find and number. Say.

- Have children look at the pictures on page 55.
- Remind them that they should listen to the audio and number the pictures.
- Play the audio, pausing for children to find the picture for the feeling and write the number.

Audio Script

1. sad
2. excited
3. happy
4. hungry
5. thirsty
6. tired
7. scared
8. mad

- Check children's work as a class.
- Have volunteers point and say: *[I] [sad].*
- For additional practice, say each vocabulary word aloud and have children clap three times, pause, clap twice, and repeat the word.

CONSOLIDATING

Telephone (5 minutes)

- Have children sit in a line.
- Display the unit Picture Cards at the end of the line.
- Whisper a word to the first child: *Thirsty*.
- Have children whisper the word down the line until it reaches the last child in line who says the word out loud and points to the Picture Card.

Show Me Happy (5 minutes)

- Have children practice making faces and using gestures they learned in the song (on page T54) to show different feelings.
- Say: *Show me happy*.
- Cue the class to make a happy face (and/or gesture).
- Continue this way.

Workbook Page 55

Have children draw lines to match the faces with the people in the picture. Then have children color the page. Have partners point to each face and name the feeling.

OPTIONAL: USING DIGITAL COMPONENTS

CD-ROM

Have children play the games to show their families the words they are learning for feelings.

ActiveTeach

Use the large digital format to model numbering the boxes. For more vocabulary practice, use the Picture Card images and audio.

VOCABULARY

B3 **2** **Listen. Find and number. Say.**

happy

sad

mad

scared

excited

hungry

thirsty

tired

Story

Objectives: To read and understand a story, to identify and understand speech bubbles, to learn new language structures, to listen to and identify the intonation in a sentence, to role-play, to practice new unit vocabulary

New Structures: *How do you feel? / I'm [excited].*

Review: *dad*

Materials: Class Audio CD B, Workbook

Optional Materials: Picture Cards, CD-ROM, ActiveTeach

GETTING READY

Talk About Amusement Parks (5 minutes)

- If possible, show a picture of an amusement park. Ask children if they've ever been to one.
- Ask children to name rides and other activities at amusement parks.
- Finally, invite them to name different feelings they might have there.

Introduce the Story (5 minutes)

- Hold up the Student Book, turned to page 56.
- Focus on the first page of "The Ride." Ask children to talk about the picture.
- Explain that Sue and Lou are at an amusement park. Point to the ride and say: *This is the ride.*
- Ask children if they recognize any of the words in the speech bubbles. Invite them to guess what Sue and Lou are talking about.
- Take a picture walk through the rest of the story.
- Have children predict how Sue and Lou will feel. Revisit predictions later.

WORKING IN THE BOOK: PAGES 56–57

B4 3. Look and listen. Act it out.

- Have children open their books to page 56.
- Play the audio, pausing after each story page to make sure children are on the correct one and understand what Sue and Lou are talking about.
- Play the story again. Point to each speech bubble as the words are spoken.
- Encourage children to speak along with the characters.
- Invite volunteers to act out the story with the audio.

Audio Script

The Ride

Page 1	Lou:	Yay! I'm excited! How do you feel?
	Sue:	I'm excited, too!
Page 2	Sue:	Um . . . I'm scared.
	Lou:	I'm scared, too!
Page 3	Lou:	Now, I'm happy.
	Sue:	I'm happy, too.
Page 4	Dad:	How do you feel?
	Lou:	Good . . . but Dad, I'm hungry!
	Sue:	. . . and I'm thirsty!

Look at New Language

- Point out the new language Sue and Lou use to talk about their feelings: *How do you feel? I'm [scared].*
- Invite partners to practice the dialogue.
- C1 asks: *How do you feel?* C2 answers: *I'm [happy]. How do you feel?* C1 answers.

B4 Listen to the Intonation

- Have children close their eyes and listen while you play the story audio.
- Pause after each sentence. Focus on how the characters use their voices to show emotion or feeling.
- Have children mimic the intonation, using the audio as a model.
- Extend the practice to include the other feeling words. Guide children to use intonation to show other feelings: *I'm [mad / sad / tired].*

CONSOLIDATING

Role-Play (10 minutes)

- Have groups of three children act out the story.
- First, play the audio and have the groups pantomime.
- Then invite volunteers to act it out without the audio.
- Encourage them to pretend to get on the ride, ride it, and get off.

How Do You Feel? (5 minutes)

- Display the unit Picture Cards around the room.
- Invite a volunteer to stand.
- Describe a simple scenario or show a picture of, for example: a mother giving smiling children a yummy dessert. Ask children to imagine they are one of the children.
- Ask the volunteer: *How do you feel?*
- Cue the volunteer to answer: *I'm [happy]* and to race to the *[happy]* card.
- Repeat with other volunteers and scenarios.

Workbook Page 56

Have children write numbers in the boxes to match the scenes at the top of the page with the feelings shown at the bottom of the page. Invite partners to take turns asking and answering: *How do you feel? / I'm [excited].*

Workbook Page 57

Have children check the boxes to show how Sue and Lou feel in the story. Once children have colored the page, have them work with a partner to practice the target language: *How do [Sue and Lou] feel? / [They're] [excited].*

OPTIONAL: USING DIGITAL COMPONENTS

CD-ROM

Have children play the audio for the story at home. Encourage them to use the Story Time feature, playing the story, word by word.

ActiveTeach

Use the large digital format to focus on the speech bubbles. Point to the person speaking, and then drag the pointer under each word as it is spoken.

LISTENING

B5 **4** **Listen and draw.**

Practice: *How do you feel? I'm [scared].* **Review:** *dad, grandma, grandpa, mom*

Listing

Objectives: To practice listening comprehension, to practice new unit vocabulary and structures

Review: dad, grandma, grandpa, mom

Materials: Class Audio CD B

Optional Materials: Picture Cards, CD-ROM, ActiveTeach, masks from T55

GETTING READY

B4 Revisit the Story (10 minutes)

- Challenge children to retell "The Ride" on pages T56–57.
- Then reread the story together.
- Play the audio and have children read along.
- Invite volunteers to act it out.

Prepare for the Exercise (5 minutes)

- Share the masks children made on T55 by having each child show his or hers.
- Invite the class to guess: *How does he / she feel? (Happy / sad / excited, and so on.)*
- Reinforce correct guesses and praise the child who made each mask.

WORKING IN THE BOOK: PAGE 58

B5 4. Listen and draw.

- Have children open their books to page 58.
- Explain that Sue and Lou are at the circus with Sue's family.
- Have children point to and name the different family members.
- Ask children how they think people usually feel at a circus.
- Explain that children will listen and then draw faces on each family member to show how he or she feels.
- Remind children of the ways they showed feelings on their masks. For hungry and thirsty, elicit ideas, such as a thought bubble with food or a drink.
- Praise children's work and check that they can say the feelings they've drawn.

Audio Script

1. How do you feel, Sue?
   Sue: I'm scared!
2. How do you feel, Lou?
   Lou: I'm excited!
3. How do you feel, Dad?
   Dad: I'm hungry!
4. How do you feel, Mom?
   Mom: I'm happy!
5. How do you feel, Grandpa?
   Grandpa: I'm thirsty!
6. How do you feel, Grandma?
   Grandma: I'm tired!

CONSOLIDATING

At the Circus (5 minutes)

- Print out pictures from the Internet showing different events at a circus.
- Ask children to imagine they're at the circus.
- Show each picture and ask children: *How do you feel?*

Pass and Say (10 minutes)

- Have children sit in a circle.
- Hand out the unit Picture Cards.
- Explain that you will play some music and that children should pass the cards around until the music stops.
- Stop the music and ask each child holding a card: *[Cristina], how do you feel?*
- Cue each child to look at the card and answer: *I feel [sad].*
- Model using appropriate facial expressions, intonation, and gestures, and encourage children to do the same when they answer.

OPTIONAL: USING DIGITAL COMPONENTS

CD-ROM

Have children play the games at home to practice their listening skills.

ActiveTeach

Invite volunteers to draw faces on the big screen for the whole class to see how the family members feel at the circus. For more practice, read the audio for the conversations and change the family members' answers.

Speaking

Objectives: To practice speaking, to practice new unit vocabulary and structures

Materials: Workbook

Optional Materials: Picture Cards, Sammy the Squirrel puppet, CD-ROM, ActiveTeach, Audio CD

GETTING READY

Brainstorm (5 minutes)

- Display the unit Picture Cards on the board.
- Point to each and invite children to talk about what makes them feel this way.
- Encourage children to try to use English vocabulary for their answers or to act out what makes them feel a certain way.
- Write their responses, or draw simple pictures of them, near the Picture Cards.

Apply (5 minutes)

- Using the ideas on the board, say: *You see a [monster]. How do you feel?*
- Guide children to answer: *I feel [scared].*

WORKING IN THE BOOK: PAGE 59

5. Match, ask, and answer.

- Have children open to page 59.
- Focus on item 1, which is done as an example. Say: *Lou's excited!*
- Call attention to the boy and girl with speech bubbles at the bottom of the page.
- Point to and read the speech bubbles: *How does Lou feel? He's excited!*
- Tell children they will work in pairs, using the speech bubble text as a model.
- Explain that after asking and answering questions about how the characters on the left feel about the items on the right, children will draw a line from the character to the item.

CONSOLIDATING

Figure It Out (10 minutes)

- Display eight pictures or Picture Cards—one to elicit each feeling.
- Model the activity with Sammy. Explain that you are going to think of a picture and tell Sammy how you feel about it and that Sammy is going to try to guess the picture.
- Have Sammy ask: *How do you feel?*
- Say: *I feel thirsty.*
- Have Sammy point to the pictures, one at a time.
- Have him think out loud: *Hmmm. Thirsty . . . A [bed]? No. A [monster]? No. A [ride]? No. [Juice]? Yes!*
- Invite volunteers to play Sammy's part, your part, or both.

Freeze Dance (10 minutes)

- Review TPR actions from the song "Choose a Mask" (T54) and the facial expressions from the "Show Me Happy" activity (T55).
- Tell children that they will do a freeze dance: that they will dance to some music until it stops. Explain that when the music stops, you will call out a feeling and that children have to freeze and use their bodies and faces to show the feeling. Demonstrate a few for children first.

Extra Practice: Student Book page 98 and T98

For extra practice speaking, have children turn to page 98 in the back of their books. For teacher support, turn to page T98 in this book.

Workbook Page 58

Have children draw faces on the clowns to show feelings, such as happy or sad. Have children color the page and practice the target language with a partner by pointing to the pictures and saying: *How does [he] feel? / [He's] [happy].*

Workbook Page 59

Have children draw lines matching the pictures on the left to the gray images on the right. Then have children color the page and work with a partner to ask and answer: *How does [she] feel? / [She's] [hungry].*

OPTIONAL: USING DIGITAL COMPONENTS

CD-ROM

Have children use the audio feature on the CD-ROM at home. Encourage them to mimic the audio to practice their speaking skills.

ActiveTeach

Use the large digital format to model drawing lines from the characters on the left to the items on the right.

SPEAKING

EXTRA PRACTICE Page 98

5 **Match, ask, and answer.**

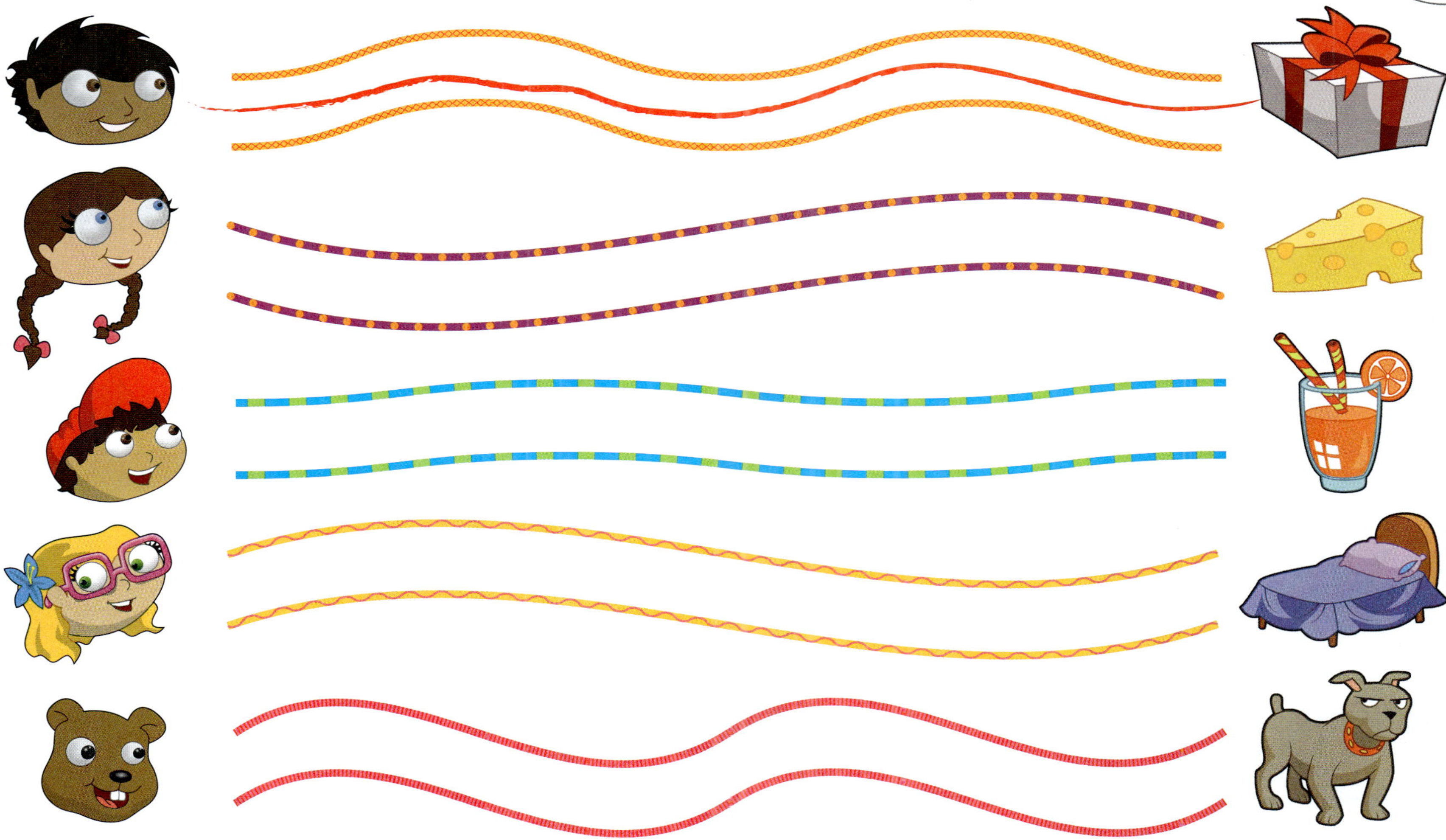

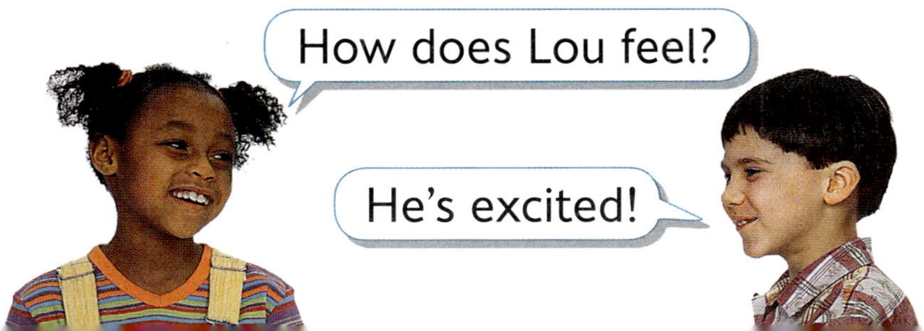

Practice: *How does [Lou] feel? He's [excited].*

PHONICS

B6 B8 6 **Listen. Trace, write, and say.**

a a

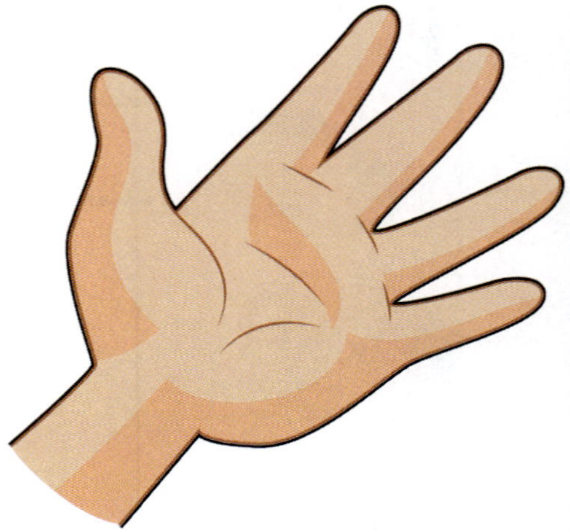

cat dad hand

Phonics: short *a* **Prewriting/Writing:** directionality, letter tracing, letters in contexts **Review:** *cat, dad, hand* **TPR:** write *a* in the air

Phonics

Objectives: To learn the short vowel sound that the letter *a* stands for in the middle of words, to understand sound-symbol correspondences, to recognize left-to-right directionality, to trace and write the letter *a* in a word

New Sounds and Letters: short *a*

Review: cat, dad, hand

TPR: write *a* in the air

Materials: Class Audio CD B, Workbook

Optional Materials: CD-ROM, ActiveTeach, pencils with erasers

GETTING READY

Review Letters (5 minutes)

- Write the alphabet on the board.
- Invite children to point to and say the letters they know.
- For each letter, invite children to say the letter, the sound, and a word: *B*, /b/, *bird*.

Introduce the Letter (5 minutes)

- On the board, write *c__t*.
- Say the sound each letter stands for: /k/, /t/.
- Point to the middle space and shrug your shoulders. Run your fingers under each and say: /k/–(shrug)–/t/.
- Write the letter *a*. Say: *This is* a. A *stands for /a/ in words like* cat.
- Run your finger under the word a few times, and say the sounds slowly: /k/–/a/–/t/.
- Go faster and faster, blending the word, until you are reading: *cat*.
- Erase the *c* and *t*. Write *d* and *d* and follow a similar procedure for *dad*.
- Repeat with *hand*.

WORKING IN THE BOOK: PAGE 60

B6 B8 6. Listen. Trace, write, and say.

- Play the "*A* Cheer". Do the actions.
- Invite children to chant and do the actions when they are ready.

Audio Script

***A* Cheer**

Sue: Give me an *a!*
Fans: *A!*
Sue: What does *a* sound like?
Fans: Ah!
Sue: Give me some *a* words!
Fans: Ah . . . *cat!*
Ah . . . *dad!*
Ah . . . *hand!*
Sue: Show me an *a!* (write *a* in the air)
Let's hear it for *a!*
Fans: Hooray!

- Focus children on the page again.
- Point to the *a* on the top left. Model tracing the letter with your finger. Then have children trace and write the letter several times.
- Then point to the word *cat*. Point and say: *ah, cat*.
- Model tracing the *a* in the middle of the word. Then have children trace it.
- Repeat for the other words.
- Have children take turns pointing to and reading the letters and words.
- For additional practice, have children listen to Class Audio CD B: Track 8. Tell children to listen and clap if a word has *ah*.
  - Model once with the words *pen* (don't clap) and *pan* (clap).

Audio Script

Now listen and clap if you hear an *ah* sound.

apple *(clap)*
grass *(clap)*
clap *(clap)*
fish
backpack *(clap)*
clock

CONSOLIDATING

"Hand" Writing (10 minutes)

- Use a pencil eraser to write a letter of the alphabet on a volunteer's hand. Model proper pencil grip.
- Have the volunteer guess the letter.
- Continue with other volunteers and familiar letters.
- Reinforce pencil grip with children. Then have them practice "hand" writing with partners.
- As a challenge, have children "hand" write words with partners.

Workbook Page 60

Have children color the letter *a* and say the letter and the sound. Then have them trace each letter *a* and take turns saying each word to a partner: *cat, dad, hand*. Finally, invite children to finish coloring the page.

OPTIONAL: USING DIGITAL COMPONENTS

CD-ROM

Have children play the games at home to show their families the sounds and letters they know.

ActiveTeach

Demonstrate tracing the letters on the big screen. Invite volunteers to trace and write the letters.

Math

Objectives: To count items 1–18, to write numbers 15–18

Review: numbers 1–16, food words

TPR: brush teeth, flap arms, hold up fingers, jump, kick, march, point, tap knees, write

Materials: Class Audio CD B, Workbook

Optional Materials: CD-ROM, ActiveTeach, teacher-made number and dot cards (see T21 and T51), 18 crayons, two bags

GETTING READY

Review and Introduce Numbers (5 minutes)

- Have children count with you to review the numbers 1 through 16.
- Then say: *17, 18* and have children repeat.
- Model writing the numbers 17 and 18 on the board and have the class air-write them.

Race to Order (10 minutes)

- Reuse the number cards you made on pages T21 and T51. Create new cards for 17 and 18.
- Divide the number cards into three groups: 1–6, 7–12, 13–18 and display the numbers in each group out of order.
- Invite three volunteers to come to the board: one child per group of cards.
- Cue the three volunteers to put their group of number cards in order. Say: *Go!*
- Announce the winner.

WORKING IN THE BOOK: PAGE 61

B9 7. Listen, say, and trace. Count and write.

- Play the chant and act it out.
- Play it again and invite children to chant and do the actions with you.

Audio Script

Count to 18 Chant

1, 2, 3, (hold up fingers for counting)
Buzz like a bee. (flap arms and buzz)
4, 5, 6, (hold up fingers for counting)
Do high kicks. (kick)
7, 8, 9, (hold up fingers for counting)
March in a line. (march in place)
10! 10! 10!
Write with a pen. (pretend to write)
11, 12,
Point to yourself. (point)
13, 14,
Tap your knees. (tap knees)
15, 16,
Brush your teeth. (pretend to brush teeth)
17, 18.
Jump like a jumping bean. (jump)

- Have children look at page 61.
- Model tracing the numbers 17 and 18 at the top of the page and have children trace them.
- Point to the different foods. Have children count and name the items: *1, 2, 3, 4 . . . 14, 15. [15] [juices].*
- Show children how to write 15 in the box next to the juice box.
- Have children complete the rest of the page on their own, or as a group.

CONSOLIDATING

How Many Bag (Part 1) (5 minutes)

- Put 18 crayons in a bag.
- Invite a volunteer to reach into the bag, feel around briefly, and then guess how many crayons are in it.
- Confirm by removing and counting the crayons for the class.
- Repeat with other volunteers and other items in different quantities.

Compare the Bags (10 minutes)

- Gather two bags and 18 crayons.
- Put [three] crayons in one bag and [four] crayons in another but don't let children see.
- Have children take turns holding each bag and guessing, by feeling how heavy it is, which bag has more crayons.
- Confirm by taking the crayons out one at a time and counting them.
- Repeat with other quantities of crayons.

Workbook Page 61

Have children trace the numbers, count the items, and write numbers to tell how many there are of each. After they color the page, have children work with a partner to point to and name each group: *15 cookies, 16 apples, 17 cars, 18 blocks*.

OPTIONAL: USING DIGITAL COMPONENTS

CD-ROM

Have children play the games and do the activities at home to show their families what they are learning about in class.

ActiveTeach

Invite volunteers to use the pen tool to count each group of food items and write the numbers in the correct boxes.

MATH

B9 7 **Listen, say, and trace. Count and write.**

15 16 17 18

Math: counting 1–18 Writing: 15–18 Review: 1–16, food
TPR: brush teeth, flap arms, hold up fingers, jump, kick, march, point, tap knees, write

VALUES Don't fight.

B11 8 **Listen and say. Draw and trace.**

Don't fight.

Values: Don't fight. **Prewriting:** tracing a short sentence

Values

Objective: To learn about the value of not fighting
New Values Language: Don't fight.
Prewriting: Tracing a short sentence
Materials: Class Audio CD B, Workbook
Optional Materials: CD-ROM, ActiveTeach

GETTING READY

B4 Revisit the Story (5 minutes)

- Read and listen to "The Ride" on pages T56–57 again.
- Review feelings and talk with children about times when they feel a certain way.
- Talk about what people do when they are mad or angry. Explain that sometimes when people get mad or angry, they fight.

Introduce Not Fighting (5 minutes)

- Prepare a few volunteers to role-play for the class. Coach them to use their words when they fight, not actions.
- Have volunteers act out scenarios where they get angry and might fight, such as a brother and sister wanting the same seat in a restaurant; two friends wanting to play with the same toy; two classmates wanting to be first in line.
- Brainstorm with the class other times they might fight.

WORKING IN THE BOOK: PAGE 62

B11 8. Listen and say. Draw and trace.

- Have children open their books to page 62.
- Play the dialogue on the first part of the audio and ask children to look at the photos as they listen.
- Have volunteers repeat the dialogue with you.

Audio Script

Kids: We don't fight.
Dad: That's great! Play nicely. Don't fight!
Kids: Yes, we all play together and we have fun.

- Then play the chant on the second part of the audio. Have children listen and then chant along with the audio when they are ready.

Audio Script

Don't Fight Chant
Please don't fight
When you get mad.
When you fight
It makes me sad.
Please don't fight
A friend or brother.
When you fight
It hurts another.

- Talk about each photo with the class and have children discuss whether the children in each photo are fighting or playing nicely.
- Now point to the faces below each photo. Tell children to draw a smile on the face below the photo where the children are not fighting and a frown under the photo where they are fighting.
- Finally have children read the sentence: *Don't fight* and trace the words.

Talk about it!

- Call attention to "Talk about it!"
- Share something people can do to keep from fighting when they are angry (counting to ten, for example). Invite children to talk about ways they can keep from fighting.

CONSOLIDATING

Act It Out (10 minutes)

- Invite pairs or small groups of children to act out situations in which there is a conflict and people might fight over something.
- Cue the class to call out: *Don't fight!*
- Then have the pairs or groups act out a way to resolve the problem without fighting. Cue the class to call out: *Good job!*

Make a Home Connection

Encourage children to ask people at home what they do to avoid fighting.

Workbook Page 62

Have children color the picture and practice saying: *Don't fight*. Have partners talk about the page.

OPTIONAL: USING DIGITAL COMPONENTS

CD-ROM

Encourage children to play the games and do the activities on the CD-ROM at home to show their families what they're learning about in class.

ActiveTeach

Use the pointer to highlight details that show who is fighting and who is not.

Review / Assessment

Objectives: To review and assess new unit vocabulary and structures

Materials: Class Audio CD B, Workbook, stickers (in the back of the Student Book and shown on page T108)

Optional Materials: Picture Cards, CD-ROM, ActiveTeach, letters of the alphabet cut out from magazines, posterboard

GETTING READY

B Sing and Move (10 minutes)

- Invite children to sing and move to the various songs and chants from the unit.
- Invite children to tell which song or chant they like best.

Quick Review (5 minutes)

- Use unit Picture Cards for a quick review.
- Hold up a card and ask: *How do you feel?*
- Cue the class to answer together: *I feel [tired].*
- Then practice with individuals.
- Show a card and ask: *[Harry], how do you feel?*
- Cue the child to say: *I feel [thirsty].*

WORKING IN THE BOOK: PAGE 63

9. Stick and say.

- Distribute the stickers (but not the reward sticker).
- Have children open their books to page 63.
- Help children notice the sticker outlines in their books and then stick the correct ones in place. Begin with item 1 and say: *Find the happy sticker.*
- Have children hold up the sticker.
- Say: *Stick the sticker.*
- Have children stick the sticker and say: *I'm happy.*
- Repeat with the other stickers (thirsty, excited, mad).

B13 10. Listen and circle.

- Remind children to listen and circle the answer to each question.
- Confirm answers with the class.

Audio Script

1. How do you feel?
   Boy: I'm happy.
2. How do you feel?
   Girl: I'm hungry.
3. How do you feel?
   Boy: I'm excited!
4. How do you feel?
   Girl: I'm scared.

I Can! Use the Reward Sticker

- Help children talk about what they have learned in this unit. Encourage them to use positive language. (See page T33 for examples.)
- Distribute the reward stickers.
- Show children where to stick the sticker (on the Unit 6 Good Job! placeholder).

CONSOLIDATING

Congratulations Chant (5 minutes)

- Ask children to each choose one thing that they learned in the unit (vocabulary, structure, number, letter).
- Have children stand in a circle.
- Have the class clap while each child chants to tell what he or she knows or can do, such as: *I know (clap, clap) [hungry]. (clap, clap) and I can (clap, clap)[count to 18]. (clap, clap)*
- End by congratulating the class!

Social Studies Project: Feelings Poster

- Gather letters of the alphabet cut out from magazines.
- For each poster, have children choose a few feelings to illustrate.
- Show children how to use different letters to make a collage-spelling of each feeling word.
- Then have them draw a picture of something that elicits the feeling (monster-scared) or that is associated with the feeling (drink-thirsty).
- Help children attach the words by the pictures to make a feelings poster.

Workbook Page 63

Have children draw the face to show how they feel. Have them color the page and share their work with a partner: *I feel [tired].*

OPTIONAL: USING DIGITAL COMPONENTS

CD-ROM

Have children play the games and do the activities on the CD-ROM at home to show their families what they're learning about in class.

ActiveTeach

Use ActiveTeach to check answers as a class.

REVIEW I can!

9 Stick and say. B13 10 Listen and circle.

1

2

3

4

Project

Unit 6 GOOD JOB!

Review/Assessment: *How do you feel? I'm [excited].* **Project:** social studies

7 Healthy Food

Unit Overview

Objectives

- ✓ To learn vocabulary for healthy food
- ✓ To sing songs and chant
- ✓ To do new TPR movements
- ✓ To practice fine and gross motor skills
- ✓ To understand and role-play a story
- ✓ To learn and practice new language structures: *What do you want, [Lou]? / I want [an orange] and [a banana], please.*
- ✓ To recognize and produce the short vowel sound that the letter *o* stands for in the middle of words
- ✓ To write the letter *o*
- ✓ To count to 20
- ✓ To write the numbers 19 and 20
- ✓ To learn the value of eating healthy food
- ✓ To practice writing a short sentence
- ✓ To practice new language by listening and speaking
- ✓ To learn and review unit vocabulary and language structures

Vocabulary

New: banana, carrot, fork, lettuce, mango, orange, plate, tomato; numbers 19, 20

Review: numbers 1–18; colors, family members; box, bread, cheese, cookie, doll, hot, salad

Home-School Connections

Copy the Letter Home for children to bring home to share what they'll be learning in Unit 7 of *My Little Island*. The Letter Home is available online at www.pearsonelt.com/mylittleisland.

Values

Eat healthy food.

Materials

Student Book pages 64–73; Workbook pages 64–73; Picture Cards 41–48; Class Audio CD B: Tracks 14–26; Program Posters: My Little Island Map, Shapes and Colors All Around, Meet Your New Friends!; stickers (back of Student Book and shown on page T108)

Optional: CD-ROM, ActiveTeach, Big Book, Sammy the Squirrel Puppet

Songs and Chants

- ✓ Colors on My Plate (Class Audio CD B: Tracks 14, 15)
- ✓ *O* Cheer (Class Audio CD B: Tracks 19, 20)
- ✓ Count to 20 Chant (Class Audio CD B: Tracks 22, 23)
- ✓ Eat Healthy Food Chant (Class Audio CD B: Tracks 24, 25)

Story

"At the Market": Sue and Lou go to the market with Sue's mom. They buy fruits and vegetables.

Language Structures: *What do you want, [Lou]? / I want [an orange] and [a banana], please.*

SKILLS

Cross-Curricular Connections

- count to 20, write numbers 17–20
- learn the value of eating healthy food
- make a food rainbow
- sing, chant, and move to music

Preschool Learning Outcomes

✓ Recognize intonation in questions.

✓ Use short answers to questions.

✓ Understand new language structures.

✓ Recognize and produce the sound that short *o* stands for.

✓ Write the letter *o* in words.

✓ Listen to and follow a story with words.

✓ Make predictions, using pictures.

✓ Sing songs and say chants with TPR.

✓ Join in games and interact.

✓ Talk about self and surroundings.

✓ Develop a positive attitude toward the English language.

Digital Practice

- Have children use the CD-ROM for vocabulary practice in class or at home.
- Use ActiveTeach to go over Student Book pages together as a class.

LEARN BY DOING

TPR

✓ brush teeth, flap arms, hold up fingers jump, kick, look action, march, point, pretend to eat, rub tummy, tap knees, write, write *o* in the air

Phonics

✓ Recognize sound-symbol correspondences: short *o*.

✓ Write the letter *o*.

✓ Complete Phonics page 70.

✓ Listen to the audio.

✓ Sing songs and say chants.

Prereading and Prewriting

✓ Follow a four-page story.

✓ Talk about the characters.

✓ Act out the story to show comprehension.

✓ Practice fine motor skills.

✓ Trace letters and a short sentence.

BULLETIN BOARD DISPLAY

Healthy Food Chart

✓ Create an interactive bulletin board to practice unit language.

Materials

- child-made name tags
- index cards or card-sized paper
- reduced photocopies of Picture Cards
- pictures and photos of food
- thick marker
- scissors
- push pins or tape

Directions

1. Have children write their names on index cards (or card-sized paper).
2. Photocopy the unit Picture Cards, reducing by about half. Make enough copies for everyone in the class.
3. Cut out pictures from magazines or make drawings of foods from Level 1: cake, cheese, juice, milk, water, yogurt and Level 2: apple, bread, chicken, cookies, pasta, salad.
4. Have children attach their name tags to the bulletin board in a column down the left side.
5. Then have them choose pictures of food they like and attach them next to their names.
6. Using a thick marker, have children draw a smiley face by each healthy food.

7 Healthy Food

B14 ♪ 1 **Listen and sing. Move.**

Presentation: *banana, carrot, fork, lettuce, mango, orange, plate, tomato* **Review:** colors, *salad* **TPR:** look action, pretend to eat, rub tummy

Presentation

Objectives: To identify food vocabulary in a scene, to learn a song and new TPR actions
New Vocabulary: banana, carrot, fork, lettuce, mango, orange, plate, tomato
Review: colors, salad
TPR: look action, pretend to eat, rub tummy
Materials: Class Audio CD B, Picture Cards, Workbook
Optional Materials: Sammy the Squirrel puppet, CD-ROM, ActiveTeach, pictures, drawings, or realia of food

GETTING READY

Share What You Know (5 minutes)

- Review food vocabulary children learned in Level I: cake, cheese, juice, milk, water, yogurt and Level 2: apple, bread, chicken, cookies, pasta, salad.
- Show a picture, drawing, or realia for each word. Ask: *What's this?*
- Elicit: *It's [juice / an apple / a cookie].*

Personalize (5 minutes)

- To review structures to talk about food, model this dialogue with Sammy the Squirrel:
  - Sammy: *Do you like [apples]?*
  - Teacher: *Yes, I do. / No, I don't.*
  - Sammy: *How about [cookies]?*
  - Teacher: *I like / don't like [cookies].*
- Have partners practice the dialogue.

WORKING IN THE BOOK: PAGE 64

Introduce Vocabulary

- Have children open to page 64.
- Elicit that Sue and Lou are having lunch or a snack.
- Hold up the Picture Cards, one at a time:
  - Say: *Banana.* Have children repeat and point to the banana on the page.
  - Ask: *What color is it? (Yellow.)*
- Repeat with the other words.

B14 1. Listen and sing. Move.

- Say: *Let's sing a song.* Play the song.
- Play the song again. Invite children to sing along and do the actions.

Audio Script

Colors on My Plate

Lou: Look at the colors.
Look at the colors on my plate! (look action)
I'm very hungry! I can't wait.
There's an orange . . . mango!
Here it comes . . .
From hand to mouth!
(pretend to eat with a fork)
Yum! Yum! Yum! (rub tummy)

Sue: Look at the colors.
Look at the colors on my plate! (look action)
I'm very hungry! I can't wait.
There's a yellow . . . banana.
Here it comes . . .
From hand to mouth!
(pretend to eat with a fork)
Yum! Yum! Yum! (rub tummy)

Sue and Lou: Look at the colors.
Look at the colors in the salad! (look action)
I'm very hungry! I can't wait.
There's a red . . . tomato!
An orange . . . carrot!
Green . . . lettuce.
Here it comes . . .
From hand to mouth!
(pretend to eat with a fork)
Yum! Yum! Yum! (rub tummy)

CONSOLIDATING

B15 Karaoke Review (5 minutes)

- Play the karaoke version of the song to review the food from Levels I and 2.
- Hold up pictures and have children sing about the color: *Look at the colors . . . There's a red . . . apple. . . .*
- For the third verse, help children sing: *Look at the colors of dessert.*

Workbook Page 64

Have children connect the dots to complete the pictures. Then have them draw lines to match the food items. After children color the page, have them practice saying these words with a partner: *banana, carrot, fork, salad, tomato.*

OPTIONAL: USING DIGITAL COMPONENTS

CD-ROM

Encourage children to play the games and do the activities on the CD-ROM at home to show their families what they're learning about in class.

ActiveTeach

Use the large digital format to focus on each food item in the song.

Vocabulary

Objectives: To practice new words, to write numbers 1–8

New Vocabulary: banana, carrot, fork, lettuce, mango, orange, plate, tomato

Materials: Class Audio CD B, Workbook

Optional Materials: Picture Cards, CD-ROM, ActiveTeach

GETTING READY

B14 Review the Song (5 minutes)

- Sing and act out "Colors on My Plate" on page T64.
- Display the unit Picture Cards. Have children point to them as they sing.

Sort By Color (5 minutes)

- Display large sheets of paper in four colors: red, orange, yellow, green.
- Brainstorm food of each color. Write the word and draw simple pictures of each on the appropriate sheet of colored paper.
- For food that belongs in two categories (carrots that are orange with green leaves), put it on both sheets, circling what is (green) and what is (orange).
- Invite children to name other foods that belong in each category and add them to the display.

WORKING IN THE BOOK: PAGE 65

B16 2. Listen. Find and number. Say.

- Have children look at the pictures on page 65.
- Remind them to listen to the audio and number the pictures.
- Play the audio, pausing after each word to allow children time to find the picture of it and write the number.

Audio Script

1. banana
2. mango
3. plate
4. tomato
5. fork
6. orange
7. lettuce
8. carrot

- Check children's work as a class.
- Have volunteers point and say: *[1] [banana].*
- For additional practice, say each vocabulary word aloud and have children clap three times, pause, clap twice, pause, clap once, and repeat the word.

CONSOLIDATING

What's Missing? (10 minutes)

- Display the unit Picture Cards.
- Have children look closely.
- Then say: *Close your eyes!*
- Remove or cover one of the cards.
- Say: *Open your eyes! What's missing?*
- Continue in this way.

Let's Move (5 minutes)

- Display the Picture Cards around the room.
- Review familiar actions and movements, such as walk, march, dance, hop, jump, and stretch.
- Invite a few volunteers to stand. *Say: [Stretch] to the [fork].*
- Then have them use a [stretching] motion to get from their seats to the [*fork*] Picture Card and back.

Workbook Page 65

Have children follow the pattern to draw the item in each empty box. After they color the page, have them work with a partner to practice pointing to the images and saying the vocabulary words.

OPTIONAL: USING DIGITAL COMPONENTS

CD-ROM

Have children play the games to show their families the English words they know for food.

ActiveTeach

Use the large digital format to model numbering the boxes. For more vocabulary practice, use the Picture Card images and audio.

VOCABULARY

B16 **2** **Listen. Find and number. Say.**

tomato

plate

mango

lettuce

banana

carrot

orange

fork

Practice: *tomato, plate, mango, lettuce, banana, carrot, orange, fork* **Writing:** *1–8*

Story

Objectives: To read and understand a story, to identify and understand speech bubbles, to learn new language structures, to listen and identify intonation, to role-play, to practice new unit vocabulary

New Structures: *What do you want, [Lou]? / I want [an orange] and [a banana], please.*

Materials: Class Audio CD B, Workbook

Optional Materials: Picture Cards; CD-ROM; ActiveTeach; pictures of different stores, props for role play

GETTING READY

Activate Prior Knowledge (5 minutes)

- Show pictures of stores and markets.
- Introduce the word *market*. Explain that markets sell fruits and vegetables.
- Ask children if they shop at a market and help choose the food to buy for their families.

Introduce the Story (5 minutes)

- Hold up Student Book page 66.
- Focus on the picture on the first page of "At the Market" and ask children to talk about it.
- Explain that Sue and Lou are at a market with Sue's mom.
- Take a picture walk through the story and have children predict what food the family will buy. Revisit predictions later.

WORKING IN THE BOOK: PAGES 66–67

B17 3. Look and listen. Act it out.

- Have children open to page 66.
- Play the audio, pausing to make sure children understand what's happening.
- Play the story audio again. Point to each speech bubble as the words are spoken.

- Encourage children to speak along with the characters.
- Invite volunteers to act out the story with the audio.

Audio Script

At the Market

Page 1	Mom:	What do you want, Lou?
	Lou:	I want an orange and a banana, please.
Page 2	Mom:	What do you want, Sue?
	Sue:	I want two carrots, please.
Page 3	Sue:	1, 2, 3, 4.
	Mom:	Yes, four, please.
Page 4	Farmer:	What do you want now?
	Lou:	I want a mango, please. I'm hungry!

Look at New Language

- Point out the language structures the characters use to ask and answer questions about food: *What do you want? / I want [a mango].*
- Invite partners to practice the dialogue: *What do you want? / I want [a carrot]. What do you want?*

B17 Listen to the Intonation

- Have children close their eyes and listen while you play the story audio, pausing after each question and answer while noting the intonation.
- Have children repeat each question and answer, copying the intonation.

CONSOLIDATING

Role-Play (10 minutes)

- Have groups of four children act out the story.
- First, play the audio, pausing to let the groups pantomime each role.
- Then invite volunteers to act out the story without the audio. Provide props for them to use as they role-play.

Don't Forget Your Manners! (5 minutes)

- Have three children role-play a different scenario as follows: a farmer who sells the food (from the unit Picture Cards), a shopper who buys it, and a "Good Manners Police Officer" who makes sure the two use good manners and say: *Please* and *Thank you*.
- Guide children through the role play:
  - C1: Hello, what do you want?
  - C2: I want lettuce.
  - C3: Say *please!*
  - C2: I want lettuce, please.
  - C1: Here. (Hands C2 the *lettuce* card.)

    (C2 takes the lettuce, but does not say thank you.)
  - C3: Say *thank you!*
  - C2: Thank you.
- If C2 says *Please* and *Thank you* without being reminded by C3 (the Good Manners Police Officer), then C3 just gives a thumbs-up and smiles.

Make a Home Connection

Encourage children to talk about times they've shopped with their families. Practice target language with children so they can politely ask for something in a store the next time they go: *I want [a mango], please.*

Workbook Page 66

Have children trace the path to the foods that Lou wants. Then have them color the page and tell a partner the names of the foods they found for Lou: *mango, orange, banana.*

Workbook Page 67

Have children circle the items that Sue wants in the story. After they color the page, have partners ask and answer: *What do you want, Sue? / I want [two carrots], please.*

OPTIONAL: USING DIGITAL COMPONENTS

CD-ROM

Have children play the story audio at home. Show them how to use the Story Time feature so they can focus on individual words.

ActiveTeach

Use the large digital format to focus on the speech bubbles. Point to the person speaking, and then drag the pointer under each word as it is spoken.

LISTENING

B18 4 **Listen and match.**

Practice: *What do you want, [Mom]? I want [tomatoes], please.* **Review:** family members

Listening

Objectives: To practice listening comprehension, to practice new unit vocabulary and structures

Review: family members

Materials: Class Audio CD B

Optional Materials: Picture Cards, CD-ROM, ActiveTeach, photocopies of unit story, paper, drawing supplies, teacher-made food labels, play place settings

GETTING READY

B17 Revisit the Story (10 minutes)

- Photocopy and display, out of order, the pages of the story "At the Market" on pages T66–67.
- Invite children to put them back in the correct order.
- Then replay the story audio and have children read along.

Tic-Tac-Toe (10 minutes)

- Divide the class into two teams: X and O. Have each team choose someone to come to the board and write.
- Make a nine-box tic-tac-toe grid on the board. Demonstrate the goal of tic-tac-toe: getting three in a row.
- Show the (*banana*) Picture Card to Team X. Ask: *What do you want?*
- If team X answers correctly and says: *I want a (banana)*, the player from Team X writes an *X* on the grid and nothing if the team gets it wrong.
- Show Team O a different food card.
- Continue this way until a team gets three in a row.

WORKING IN THE BOOK: PAGE 68

B18 4. Listen and match.

- Have children open their books to page 68.
- Point to the foods and elicit the words. Then point to and help children name the people at the bottom of the page: Lou and Lilly and Sue's family members (Mom, Dad, Grandma, Grandpa).
- Explain that children will listen to the audio and draw lines matching the people with the food they want.
- Point out that the first item is done as an example.
- Play the audio and have children finish the page on their own.

Audio Script

Sue:	What do you want, Mom?
Mom:	I want tomatoes, please.
Sue:	What do you want, Lou?
Lou:	I want a banana, please.
Sue:	What do you want, Dad?
Dad:	I want a carrot, please.
Sue:	What do you want, Grandma?
Grandma:	I want a mango, please.
Sue:	What do you want, Grandpa?
Grandpa:	I want lettuce, please.
Sue:	What do you want, Lilly?
Lilly:	I want an orange, please.

CONSOLIDATING

Make Menus (10 minutes)

- Distribute paper and drawing supplies.
- Invite children to create menus, using the foods they know. To help them, display the food Picture Cards.
- Have them draw a picture of each food and copy the word or glue a teacher-made label of it for their menus.

Play Restaurant (10 minutes)

- Tell children they will role-play a restaurant in small groups.
- Set the table with play place settings, if possible, and pretend to be the waiter. Hand out the menus children made.
- Ask each child: *What do you want?*
- Have children answer, in turn: *I want [salad], please.*
- Encourage them to order food while you pretend to take their orders.
- Serve the food and drinks.
- Cue children to say: *Thank you* and then pretend to eat and drink.
- At the end, clear the table and hand them a check. Have children pretend to pay.

OPTIONAL: USING DIGITAL COMPONENTS

CD-ROM

Have children play the games at home with their families to practice listening skills.

ActiveTeach

Invite volunteers to draw lines matching the food to the characters.

Speaking

Objectives: To practice speaking, to practice new unit vocabulary and structures

Review: bread, cheese, cookie

Materials: Workbook

Optional Materials: Picture Cards, Sammy the Squirrel puppet, CD-ROM, ActiveTeach, T-Chart on page T136

GETTING READY

Prepare for the Exercise (5 minutes)

- Display the unit Picture Cards in a row on the board.
- Beneath each card, draw a check box.
- Model with Sammy and ask him: *What do you want?*
- Have Sammy answer: *I want a mango, a fork, a tomato, and lettuce.*
- Draw a check in the box beneath the mango, fork, tomato, and lettuce.
- Erase the check marks and have volunteers take your role and Sammy's. Repeat a few times.

Find Your Partner (10 minutes)

- Prepare a list of foods children know, enough for one food for every two children.
- Whisper the name of a food from your list in each child's ear, being sure to whisper each food twice.
- Tell children to walk around and ask each other: *What do you want?*
- When children find a match, have them stay together as partners for the next activity.

WORKING IN THE BOOK: PAGE 69

5. Ask and answer. Check [✓].

- Have children open to page 69.
- Have children name the foods.
- Next, call attention to the boy and girl with speech bubbles at the bottom of the page.
- Point to and read the speech bubbles: *What do you want? / I want a tomato, please.*
- Point to the check mark for a tomato in the sample answer.
- Then tell children to check what they want (in a different color).
- Next, tell children they will work in pairs, using the speech bubble text as a model, and interview each other to find out what food they each want.

CONSOLIDATING

Make a Chart (5 minutes)

- Make a chart to show how many children checked each food or use the T-Chart on page T136 (for more than two foods, make copies).
- Write each food at the top of a column.
- Ask how many children chose each one and put a check mark for each.
- Help the class count out the results.
- Say: *[12] children want [a carrot / bread].*

Shopping List (10 minutes)

- Tell children they are going to make food shopping lists.
- Help them draw a food, write the word for it, and make a check box.
- Have children use their lists to role-play food shopping. See page T67 for ideas. Or have them take their lists home and use them the next time the family goes food shopping.

Extra Practice: Student Book page 99 and T99

For extra practice speaking, have children turn to page 99 in the back of their books. For teacher support, turn to page T99 in this book.

Workbook Page 68

Have children match the pictures of the people to what they want. After children color the page, have partners role-play to share their work: *What do you want, [Dad]? / I want [chicken], please. What do you want, [Mom]? / I want [salad], please. What do you want, [Grandma]? / I want [juice], please.*

Workbook Page 69

Have children work with a partner to practice the target language: *What do you want? / I want [an orange], please.* Have them check the box for each word they use in a sentence. Then invite children to color the page.

OPTIONAL: USING DIGITAL COMPONENTS

CD-ROM

Have children use the CD-ROM at home. Tell them to mimic the audio to practice their speaking skills.

ActiveTeach

Use the big screen to model checking the food items.

SPEAKING

EXTRA PRACTICE
Page 99

5 Ask and answer. Check ☑.

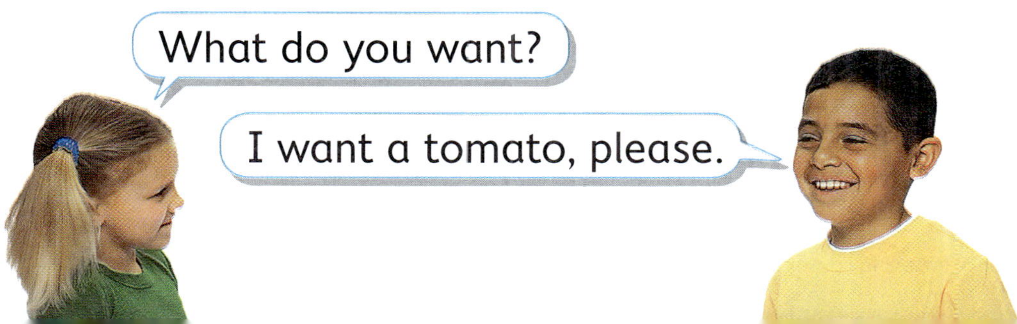

Practice: *What do you want? I want [a tomato], please.*
Review: *bread, cheese, cookie*

PHONICS

B19 B21 6 **Listen. Trace, write, and say.**

o o

hot doll box

Phonics: short *o* **Prewriting/Writing:** directionality, letter tracing, letters in contexts **Review:** *box, doll, hot* **TPR:** write *o* in the air

Phonics

Objectives: To learn the short vowel sound that the letter *o* stands for in the middle of words, to understand sound-symbol correspondence, to recognize left-to-right directionality, to trace and write the letter *o*

New Sounds and Letters: short *o*

Review : box, doll, hot

TPR: write *o* in the air

Materials: Class Audio CD B, Workbook

Optional Materials: CD-ROM, ActiveTeach, pencils with erasers

GETTING READY

Review Letters (5 minutes)

- Write the alphabet on the board.
- Invite children to point to and say the letters they know.
- For each letter, invite children to say the letter, the sound, and a word: *B*, /b/, *bird*.

Introduce the Letter (5 minutes)

- On the board, write *h__t*.
- Say the sound each letter stands for: /h/, /t/.
- Point to the middle space and shrug your shoulders. Run your fingers under each and say: /h/–(shrug)–/t/.
- Write the letter o. Say: *This is* o. O *stands for /o/ in words like* hot.
- Run your finger under the word a few times, saying the sounds: /h/–/o/–/t/.
- Go faster and faster, blending the word, until you are reading: *Hot*.
- Erase the *h* and *t*. Write *d* and *ll* and follow a similar procedure for *doll*.
- Repeat with *box*.

WORKING IN THE BOOK: PAGE 70

B19 B21 **6. Listen. Trace, write, and say.**

- Play the "O Cheer." Do the actions.
- Invite children to chant and do the actions when they are ready.

Audio Script

***O* Cheer**

Sue: Give me an *o!*
Fans: *O!*
Sue: What does o sound like?
Fans: Ah!
Sue: Give me some *o* words!
Fans: Ah . . . *hot!*
Ah . . . *doll!*
Ah . . . *box!*
Sue: Show me an *o!* (write *o* in the air)
Let's hear it for *o!*
Fans: Hooray!

- Focus children on the page again.
- Point to the *o* on the left. Model tracing the letter with your finger. Then have children trace the *o* in the grid and write it several times.
- Then point to the word *hot* on the left. Say: /o/, *hot*.
- Model tracing the *o* in the middle of the word. Then have children trace it.
- Repeat for the other words.
- Have children take turns pointing to and reading the letters and words on the page.
- For additional practice, have children listen to Class Audio CD B: Track 21. Tell children to listen and clap if a word has /o/.
  – Model once with the words *hot* (clap) and *hat* (don't clap).

Audio Script

Now listen and clap if you hear an *ah* sound.

clock *(clap)*
dad
socks *(clap)*
mom *(clap)*
milk
doctor *(clap)*

CONSOLIDATING

"Hand" Writing (10 minutes)

- Use a pencil eraser to write a letter of the alphabet on a volunteer's hand. Model proper pencil grip.
- Have the volunteer guess the letter.
- Continue with other volunteers and familiar letters.
- Reinforce pencil grip with children. Then have them practice "hand" writing with partners.
- As a challenge, have children "hand" write words with partners.

Workbook Page 70

Have children color the letter *o* and say the letter and the sound. Then have them trace each letter *o* and take turns saying each word to a partner: *hot, doll, box*. Finally, invite children to finish coloring the page.

OPTIONAL: USING DIGITAL COMPONENTS

CD-ROM

Have children play the games at home to show their families the sounds and letters they know.

ActiveTeach

Demonstrate tracing the letters on the big screen. Then invite volunteers to trace and write the letters.

Math

Objectives: To count items 1–20, to write numbers 17–20

Review: numbers 1–18

TPR: brush teeth, flap arms, hold up fingers, jump, kick, march, point, tap knees, write

Materials: Class Audio CD B, Workbook

Optional Materials: CD-ROM, ActiveTeach, crayons, a bag, pencils with erasers

GETTING READY

Review and Introduce Numbers (5 minutes)

- Have children count from 1 to 18 with you.
- Then say: 19, 20 and have children repeat.
- Model writing the numbers 19 and 20, and have the class air-write them.

Get in Order (5 minutes)

- Arrange the class in groups of five.
- Whisper a number from 1 to 5 to each child in a group.
- At your signal, have children line up in order (1, 2, 3, 4, 5).
- Have groups race to line up first.
- Play again. This time, have children try to line up without talking.
- Play again, but divide the class into larger groups and use more numbers.

WORKING IN THE BOOK: PAGE 71

B22 7. Listen, say, and trace. Count and write.

- Play the chant and act it out.
- Play it again and invite children to chant and do the actions with you.

Audio Script

Count to 20 Chant

1, 2, 3, (hold up fingers for counting)
Buzz like a bee. (flap arms and buzz)
4, 5, 6, (hold up fingers for counting)
Do high kicks. (kick)
7, 8, 9, (hold up fingers for counting)
March in a line. (march in place)
10! 10! 10!
Write with a pen. (pretend to write)
11, 12,
Point to yourself. (point)
13, 14,
Tap your knees. (tap)
15, 16,
Brush your teeth. (pretend to brush teeth)
17, 18,
Jump like a jumping bean. (jump)
19, 20.
Laugh! Laugh!
Hee, hee, hee! (pretend to laugh)

- Have children look at page 71.
- Model tracing the numbers 19 and 20 at the top of the page and have children trace them.
- Point to the different foods. Have children count and name the items: *1, 2, 3, 4 . . . 20. [20] [carrots].*
- Show children how to write 20 in the box next to the carrot.
- Have children complete the rest of the page on their own, or as a group.

CONSOLIDATING

How Many? Bag (Part 2) (5 minutes)

- Put 20 crayons in a bag.
- Invite a volunteer to reach into the bag, feel around briefly, and then guess how many crayons are in it.
- Confirm by removing and counting the crayons for the class.
- Repeat with other volunteers and other items in different quantities.

"Hand" Writing Numbers (5 minutes)

- Have children practice "writing" on their partner's hand.
- Have children use the eraser side of a pencil to "write" a number their partner's palm.
- Have the partner guess the number.
- Then have them switch.

Workbook Page 71

Have children trace the numbers 17–20. Then have them count the items in each group and write the number in the box. Then have children color the page and tell a partner how many of each item there are: *[19] [mangoes].*

OPTIONAL: USING DIGITAL COMPONENTS

CD-ROM

Have children play the games at home to practice numbers.

ActiveTeach

Invite volunteers to use the pen tool to count the food and write the numbers.

MATH

B22 7 **Listen, say, and trace. Count and write.**

17 18 19 20

VALUES Eat healthy food.

B24 8 **Listen and say. Draw and trace.**

Eat healthy food.

Values: Eat healthy food. **Prewriting:** tracing a short sentence

Values

Objective: To learn about the value of eating healthy food

New Values Language: Eat healthy food.

Prewriting: Tracing a short sentence

Materials: Class Audio CD B, Workbook

Optional Materials: Picture Cards, CD-ROM, ActiveTeach

GETTING READY

B17 Revisit the Story (5 minutes)

- Have children read and listen to "At the Market" again on pages T66–67.
- Have them name the foods the story characters wanted.
- Introduce the words *fruit* and *vegetables*.
- Ask children to name the fruits and the vegetables they see in the story and other fruits and vegetables they know.

Introduce Eating Healthy Food (15 minutes)

- Display all food Picture Cards.
- Help children group the pictures: healthy food and unhealthy food.
- Give partners two copies of the Word Web on page T137 (with *Healthy Food* in the center circle of one and *Unhealthy Food* in the center circle of the other). Have partners draw a picture of four healthy foods and four unhealthy foods on the appropriate webs. Finally, have partners share their webs with the class.
- Talk about eating lots of vegetables and fruit, and not many sweets.

WORKING IN THE BOOK: PAGE 72

B24 8. Listen and say. Draw and trace.

- Have children open to page 72.
- Play the dialogue on the first part of the audio and ask children to look at the photos as they listen.
- Have volunteers repeat the dialogue with you.

Audio Script

Boy: I like chocolate. I don't like fruit.
Girl: Too much chocolate is not good for you. Eat healthy food.

- Then play the chant on the second part of the audio. Have children listen once or twice and chant along with the audio when they are ready.

Audio Script

Eat Healthy Food Chant

Eat fruit: bananas, mangoes.
Eat vegetables: carrots, lettuce.
Eat healthy food.
Feel great!

- Talk about each photo with the class and have children discuss whether the child in each photo is eating healthy food or not.
- Now point to the faces below each photo. Tell children to draw a smile on the face below the photo in which the child is eating healthy food and a frown under the child who is not eating healthy food.
- Finally, have children read and trace the sentence: *Eat healthy food.*

Talk about it!

- Call attention to "Talk about it!"
- Invite children to name some "junk" or unhealthy food.
- Name healthy foods you like and have children name ones they like.

CONSOLIDATING

Act It Out (10 minutes)

- Invite pairs or small groups of children to role-play the unit story "At the Market."
- If children want healthy food, cue the class to say: *Good job!* If not, cue the class to say: *No, no! Eat healthy food!*

Which Value Is It? (10 minutes)

- Explain that you will describe or role-play a situation and that children should listen carefully and name the value: *Follow rules. Stay safe. Ask for help. Don't fight.*

Make a Home Connection

Encourage children to ask their families what healthy food they like and report back.

Workbook Page 72

Have children color the healthy foods on the page and say to a partner: *Eat healthy food.*

OPTIONAL: USING DIGITAL COMPONENTS

CD-ROM

Encourage children to play the games and do the activities on the CD-ROM at home to show their families what they're learning about in class.

ActiveTeach

Focus the pointer on foods that are healthy and not healthy in the photos. Confirm which should be a smiling or a frowning face.

Review / Assessment

Objectives: To review and assess new unit vocabulary and structures

Materials: Class Audio CD B, Workbook, stickers (in the back of the Student Book and shown on page T108)

Optional Materials: Picture Cards, CD-ROM, ActiveTeach, poster board; crayons, markers, paint, or colored paper; pictures of food cut out from magazines; glue

GETTING READY

B Sing and Move (10 minutes)

- Have children sing and move to the various songs and chants from the unit.
- Invite children to tell which song or chant they like best.

Play a Review Game (5 minutes)

- Divide the class into teams.
- Display the unit Picture Cards.
- Have two volunteers from one team ask and answer: *What do you want? / I want [a mango].*
- Have another child on that team point to the picture of the [mango].
- Have teams take turns.
- Give one point for every correct answer.
- The team with the most points wins.

WORKING IN THE BOOK: PAGE 73

9. Stick and say.

- Distribute the stickers (but not the reward sticker).
- Have children open to page 73.
- Help children notice the sticker outlines in their books and then stick the correct ones in place. Begin with item 1 and say: *Find the banana sticker.*
- Have children hold up the sticker.
- Say: *Stick the sticker.*
- Have children stick the sticker and say: *I want a banana.*
- Repeat with the other stickers (plate, fork, orange).

B26 10. Listen and circle.

- Remind children to listen and circle the answer to each question.
- Confirm answers with the class.

Audio Script

1. What do you want?
   I want a mango, please.
2. What do you want?
   I want a plate, please.
3. What do you want?
   I want some lettuce, please.
4. What do you want?
   I want an orange, please.

I Can! Use the Reward Sticker

- Help children talk about what they have learned in this unit. Encourage them to use positive language. (See page T33 for examples.)
- Distribute the reward stickers.
- Show children where to stick the stickers (on the Unit 7 Good Job! placeholder).

CONSOLIDATING

Congratulations Chant (5 minutes)

- Ask children to each choose one thing they learned in the unit (vocabulary, structure, number, letter) or can do.
- Have children stand in a circle.
- Have the class clap while each child chants to tell what he or she knows or can do, such as: *I know (clap, clap) [I want a banana] (clap, clap) and I can (clap, clap) [write an o] (clap, clap)*
- End by congratulating the class!

Health Project: Food Rainbow

- Cut out pictures of food from magazines.
- For each poster, create a rainbow using crayons, markers, paint, or colored paper.
- Help children sort the food pictures by color and glue them to that color band of the rainbow.

Workbook Page 73

Have children draw the fruits and vegetables they want on the plate. Have them color the page and share their work with a partner: *I want [a banana], please.*

OPTIONAL: USING DIGITAL COMPONENTS

CD-ROM

Have children play the games and do the activities on the CD-ROM at home to show their families what they're learning about in class.

ActiveTeach

Use ActiveTeach to check answers as a class or to model circling the correct answers (1. mango; 2. plate; 3. lettuce; 4. orange).

REVIEW I can!

9 **Stick and say.** B26 10 **Listen and circle.**

1

2

3

4

Project

Unit 7 GOOD JOB!

8 The Zoo

Unit Overview

Objectives

- To learn vocabulary about the zoo
- To sing songs and chant
- To do new TPR movements
- To practice fine and gross motor skills
- To understand and role-play a story
- To learn and practice new language structures: *What's that? / It's a [small] [bat].*
- To recognize and produce the short vowel sound that the letter *u* stands for in the middle of words
- To write the letter *u*
- To do simple addition
- To learn the value of including everyone
- To write a short sentence
- To practice new language by listening and speaking
- To learn and review unit vocabulary and language structures

Vocabulary

New: bat, bear, elephant, lion, monkey, penguin, sea lion, zebra

Review: bus, cup, mouse, sun

Home-School Connections

Copy the Letter Home for children to bring home to share what they'll be learning in Unit 8 of *My Little Island*. The Letter Home is available online at www.pearsonelt.com/mylittleisland.

Values

Include everyone.

Materials

Student Book pages 74–83; Workbook pages 74–83; Picture Cards 49–56; Class Audio CD B: Tracks 27–39; Program Posters: My Little Island Map, Shapes and Colors All Around, Meet Your New Friends!; stickers (back of Student Book and shown on page T108)

Optional: CD-ROM, ActiveTeach, Big Book, Sammy the Squirrel Puppet

Songs and Chants

- Animals in the Zoo (Class Audio CD B: Tracks 27, 28)
- *U* Cheer (Class Audio CD B: Tracks 32, 33)
- Adding (Class Audio CD B: Tracks 35, 36)
- Include Everyone Chant (Class Audio CD B: Tracks 37, 38)

Story

"What's That?": Sue and Lou make shadow animal puppets on the wall. Then a real mouse surprises them.

Language Structures: *What's that? / It's a [small] [bat].*

SKILLS

Cross-Curricular Connections

- do simple addition
- learn the value of including everyone
- make an elephant mask
- sing, chant, and move to music

Preschool Learning Outcomes

- ✓ Recognize intonation in questions.
- ✓ Use short answers to questions.
- ✓ Understand new language structures.
- ✓ Recognize and produce the sound that short *u* stands for.
- ✓ Write the letter *u* in words.
- ✓ Listen to and follow a story with words.
- ✓ Make predictions, using pictures.
- ✓ Sing songs and say chants with TPR.
- ✓ Join in games and interact.
- ✓ Talk about self and surroundings.
- ✓ Develop a positive attitude toward the English language.

Digital Practice

- Have children use the CD-ROM for vocabulary practice in class or at home.
- Use ActiveTeach to go over Student Book pages together as a class.

LEARN BY DOING

TPR

- ✓ clap, eat, flap arms, look, make claws, roar, scratch, waddle, write *u* in the air

Phonics

- ✓ Recognize sound-symbol correspondences: short *u*.
- ✓ Write the letter *u*.
- ✓ Complete Phonics page 80.
- ✓ Listen to the audio.
- ✓ Sing songs and say chants.

Prereading and Prewriting

- ✓ Follow a four-page story.
- ✓ Talk about the characters.
- ✓ Act out the story to show comprehension.
- ✓ Practice fine motor skills.
- ✓ Trace letters and a short sentence.

BULLETIN BOARD DISPLAY

Animal Patterns

- ✓ Create a versatile bulletin board display to practice unit language.

Materials

- photocopies of Picture Cards (full-size and reduced)
- children's drawings of animals
- teacher-made or child-made labels
- glue or tape

Directions

1. Photocopy a few copies each of the unit Picture Cards: half full-size and half at a reduced size.
2. Ask children to draw their favorite animals on paper the same size as the Picture Cards.
3. Photocopy each child's drawing once on a reduced setting (so you have the original and a smaller copy).
4. Create, or have children create, a label for each animal.
5. Put labels in a column down the left of a bulletin board and then make a row for each animal.
6. Use the bulletin board throughout the unit to practice patterns. For example, in the bat row, display Picture Card copies and children's drawings: big, big, small, big, big, small. In the bear row, display Picture Card copies and children's drawings: small, big, small, small, big, small, small, big, small.

8 The Zoo

B27 1 **Listen and sing. Move.**

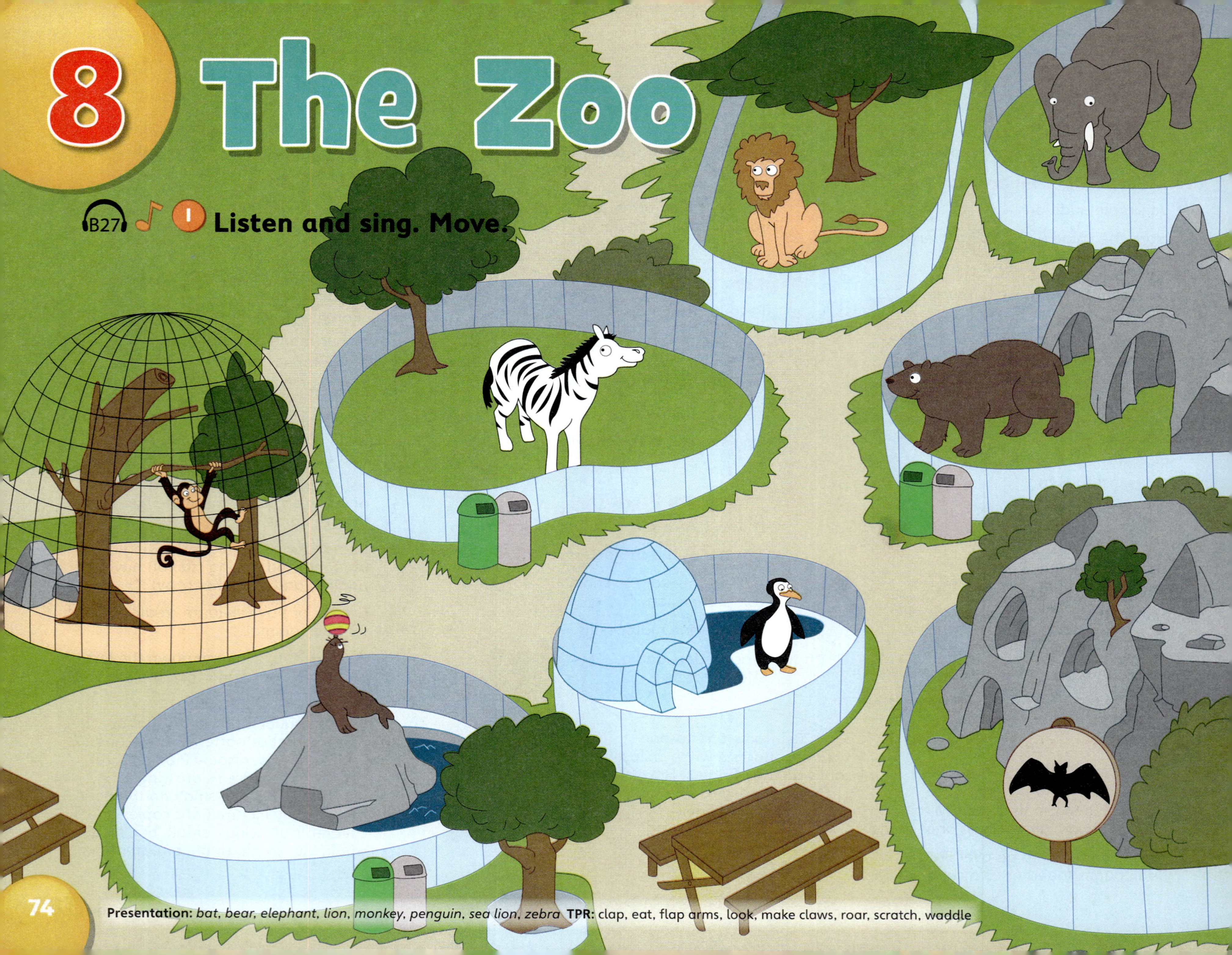

Presentation: *bat, bear, elephant, lion, monkey, penguin, sea lion, zebra* **TPR:** clap, eat, flap arms, look, make claws, roar, scratch, waddle

Presentation

Objectives: To identify vocabulary in a scene, to learn a song and new TPR actions

New Vocabulary: bat, bear, elephant, lion, monkey, penguin, sea lion, zebra

TPR: clap, eat, flap arms, look, make claws, roar, scratch, waddle

Materials: Class Audio CD B, Picture Cards, Workbook

Optional Materials: CD-ROM, ActiveTeach, pictures of animals from Levels 1 and 2, My Little Island Map poster

GETTING READY

Review Animals (5 minutes)

- Review animals from Level 1: bird, cat, dog, fish, mouse, turtle and Level 2: cow, duck, goat, hen, horse, sheep.
- Show or draw a picture for each one.
- Have children move like the animals and say the words.

My Little Island Map (5 minutes)

- Show pictures of zoos and zoo animals and ask children what they think Unit 8 will be about.
- Help children find the zoo on the My Little Island Map poster and ask them if they like going to the zoo.
- Have them name favorite zoo animals.

WORKING IN THE BOOK: PAGE 74

Introduce Vocabulary

- Have children open to page 74.
- Hold up unit Picture Cards, one at a time:
  - Say: *[Bat]*. Have children repeat.
  - Have children point to the [bat] on the page and say: *[Bat]*.

B27 1. Listen and sing. Move.

- Teach children the animal actions in the song.
- Play the audio. Invite children to sing along and do the actions when they are ready.

Audio Script

Animals in the Zoo

Lou: Look, look, what do you see? (look action)
Sue: I see a sea lion—clap, clap, clap! (clap as with flippers)
It's looking at me!
I see a monkey—oooh, oooh, oooh! (scratch like a monkey)
It's looking at me!
Chorus: Animals, animals in the zoo—
Which animal is looking at you?
Sue: Look, look, what do you see? (look action)
Lou: I see a zebra—munch, munch, munch!
It's looking at me!
I see a bear—grrr, grrr, grrr! (make claws with hands)
It's looking at me!
(Repeat chorus.)
Lou: Look, look, what do you see? (look action)
Sue: I see an elephant—pblpbl, pblpbl, pblpbl!
It's looking at me!
I see a lion—roar, roar, roar! (roar like a lion)
It's looking at me!
(Repeat chorus.)
Sue: Look, look, what do you see? (look action)
Lou: I see a bat—squeak, squeak, squeak! (flap arms)
It's looking at me!
I see a penguin—waddle, waddle, waddle! (waddle like a penguin)
It's looking at me!
(Repeat chorus.)

CONSOLIDATING

B28 Karaoke (10 minutes)

- Play the karaoke version of the song.
- Cue children for each verse by holding up a Picture Card of the animal.

Workbook Page 74

Have children draw an animal in each zoo area. Then have them color the page and, with a partner, point to each picture and name the animal.

OPTIONAL: USING DIGITAL COMPONENTS

CD-ROM

Encourage children to play the games and do the activities on the CD-ROM at home to show their families what they're learning about in class.

ActiveTeach

Use the large digital format to focus on each animal as it is named in the song.

Vocabulary

Objectives: To practice new words, to write numbers 1–8

New Vocabulary: bat, bear, elephant, lion, monkey, penguin, sea lion, zebra

Materials: Class Audio CD B, Workbook

Optional Materials: Picture Cards, CD-ROM, ActiveTeach

GETTING READY

B27 Review the Song (5 minutes)

- Have children sing and do the actions for the song "Animals in the Zoo" on page T74.
- Display the Picture Cards. Have children point to them as they sing.

What Color Is It? (5 minutes)

- Review the structures children used in Level 1 to talk about animals: *The [dog] is [brown]. / The [dog] isn't [blue].*
- Have children sit in a circle and pass the unit Picture Cards around until you tell them to stop.
- Say: *Stop.* Ask children to use the structures to say two sentences about the card they are holding.

WORKING IN THE BOOK: PAGE 75

B29 2. Listen. Find and number. Say.

- Have children look at the pictures on page 75.
- Remind them to listen to the audio and number the pictures.
- Play the audio, pausing after each item to allow children time to find the picture and write the number.

Audio Script

1. bear
2. bat
3. zebra
4. elephant
5. monkey
6. penguin
7. lion
8. sea lion

- Check children's work as a class.
- Have volunteers point and say: *[I] [bear].*
- For additional practice, say each vocabulary word aloud and have children clap, pause, clap twice, pause, clap three times, and repeat the word.

CONSOLIDATING

Chain Game (10 minutes)

- Have children stand in a circle to play this memory game.
- Say: *I see a [bat].*
- Have the child to your right say: *I see a [bat] and a [penguin].*
- Have the next child continue the chain: *I see a [bat] and a [penguin] and a [bear].*
- See how long children can keep building the chain!

Animal Charades (10 minutes)

- Play a game of charades.
- Invite one volunteer at a time to do the actions for one of the animals.
- Have the class guess which one it is.

Workbook Page 75

Have children draw the lion's mane, the zebra's stripes, the elephant's trunk, and the bat's wing. Then have children color the page, and then name the animals and the colors with a partner.

OPTIONAL: USING DIGITAL COMPONENTS

CD-ROM

Have children play the games to show their families the animal names they know in English.

ActiveTeach

Use the large digital format to model numbering the boxes on the Student Book page. For more vocabulary practice, use the Picture Card images and audio.

VOCABULARY

B29 **2** **Listen. Find and number. Say.**

bat

penguin

monkey

sea lion

lion

zebra

bear

elephant

Practice: *bat, penguin, monkey, sea lion, lion, zebra, bear, elephant* **Writing:** *1–8*

Story

Objectives: To read and understand a story, to identify and understand speech bubbles, to learn new language structures, to listen to and identify the intonation in a sentence, to role-play, to practice new unit vocabulary

New Structures: *What's that? / It's a [small] [bat].*

Materials: Class Audio CD B, Workbook

Optional Materials: CD-ROM, ActiveTeach, flashlight

GETTING READY

This and That (5 minutes)

- Review: *What's this? / It's a [pencil]. / This is [a pencil].*
- Hold up an item and ask: *What's this?* Cue children to answer: *It's a [book].*
- Then point to something far away. Ask: *What's THAT?*
- Cue the answer: *It's a [window].*
- Reinforce *this* for things that are close, and *that* for things that are far.
- Point and say, and then have children repeat: *This is [my nose]. That is [the window].*

Big and Small (5 minutes)

- Draw big and small shapes on the board.
- Point and say: *Big. Big circle. This is a big circle. Small. Small circle. This is a small circle.*
- Repeat with other shapes.
- Have children stand. Say: *Show me big.*
- Show children how to stretch their bodies and arms as big as they can: *This is big.*
- Repeat with: *Show me small.*

Introduce the Story (5 minutes)

- Hold up the Student Book, turned to page 76.
- Focus on the first page of "What's That?" Ask children to talk about the picture.
- Explain that Sue and Lou are making shadows on the wall.
- Ask children if they recognize any of the words in the speech bubbles. Invite them to guess what the characters are talking about.
- Take a picture walk through the rest of the story.
- Have children predict what happens. Revisit predictions later.

WORKING IN THE BOOK: PAGES 76–77

B30 3. Look and listen. Act it out.

- Have children open to page 76.
- Play the audio and pause at each story page to make sure children are on the correct page and understand what they see.
- Make sure they understand that the real mouse made a big shadow.
- Play the story audio again. Point to each speech bubble as the words are spoken.
- Encourage children to speak along with the characters.
- Invite volunteers to act out the story with the audio.

Audio Script

What's That?

Page 1 Lou: What's that?
Sue: It's a small bat.
Page 2 Sue: What's that?
Lou: It's a big elephant.
Page 3 Sue: What's that?
Lou: It's a big shadow!
Page 4 Lou: It's a small mouse!
Sue: Oh.

Look at New Language

- Point out the new language characters use to ask and answer about what they see: *What's that? It's a [small] [bat]. / It's a [big] [elephant].*
- Invite partners to practice the new language by asking and answering about items around the classroom.

B30 Listen to the Intonation

- Have children close their eyes and listen while you play the story audio.
- Pause after each question and answer, pointing out the different intonation.

CONSOLIDATING

Role-Play (10 minutes)

- Have pairs act out the story.
- First, play the audio and have the pairs pantomime what happens.
- Then invite volunteers to act out the story without the audio.

Make Shadows (10 minutes)

- Use a flashlight in the dark to make shadows against the wall.
- Challenge children to make shadows of the animals in the story.
- Then play a guessing game with shadows. Hold up an item and shine the light on it to make a shadow.
- Ask children to guess what it is.

Workbook Page 76

Have children circle the animals Lou and Sue see in the story. After children color the page, have them work with a partner to practice the target language: *It's a [big] [elephant].*

Workbook Page 77

Have children trace the animals and draw lines to match them with their shadows. Have children color the page and practice the target language with a partner: *What's that? / It's a [small] [bat].*

OPTIONAL: USING DIGITAL COMPONENTS

CD-ROM

Have children play the story audio at home. Encourage them to use the Story Time feature to focus on individual words.

ActiveTeach

Use the large digital format to focus on the speech bubbles. Point to the person speaking, and then drag the pointer under each word as it is spoken.

LISTENING

B31 4 **Listen. Draw a line.**

Practice: *What's that? It's a [big] [elephant].*

Listing

Objectives: To practice listening comprehension, to practice new unit vocabulary and structures

Materials: Class Audio CD B

Optional Materials: Picture Cards, CD-ROM, ActiveTeach, big and small shape cutouts and objects, pictures of different animals (big and small)

GETTING READY

B30 Revisit the Story (10 minutes)

- Replay the story audio from pages T76–77 while children follow along in their books.
- Elicit that Sue is *scared* on the last page. Then ask children if they are scared of any animals.

Sorting Activity (5 minutes)

- Prepare a series of shape cutouts, big and small, and display them on the board in random order.
- Invite volunteers to come to the board and sort the shapes into big and small groups.
- Then give small groups of children big and small objects and have the groups sort them.

WORKING IN THE BOOK: PAGE 78

B31 4. Listen. Draw a line.

- Have children open their books to page 78.
- Point to the different animals and elicit the words for them.
- Explain that children will listen to the audio and draw a line from one animal to the next. Play the audio for item 1 and show children the example line from the word *Start* to the elephant.
- Play the audio and have children follow the example to complete the page. Walk around the room to check that children are drawing lines to the correct animals.

Audio Script

1. What's that?
   It's a big elephant.
2. What's that?
   It's a small penguin.
3. What's that?
   It's a big bear.
4. What's that?
   It's a small bat.
5. What's that?
   It's a big zebra.
6. What's that?
   It's a small monkey.

CONSOLIDATING

Big or Small Animals? (5 minutes)

- Gather pictures and Picture Cards of different animals.
- Invite children to help you arrange them in groups: big animals and small animals.

Let's Move: Big and Small (5 minutes)

- Have children stand in a circle.
- Review actions that children know, such as: *walk, march, hop, jump, dance, stretch, climb, open your eyes, bend your knees, shake your head*.
- Say: *1, 2, 3, Let's move . . . BIG! Walk, walk, walk.*
- Have children walk in a circle, using big actions and gestures.
- Stop and say: *1, 2, 3, Let's move . . . SMALL! Hop, hop, hop.*
- Have children hop in a circle, using small hops.
- Continue this way.

Games

To help children practice their listening skills, have them play selected games on pages T131–135.

Make a Home Connection

Have children go on a scavenger hunt at home to find big and small objects. Make copies of the T-chart on page T136 and write BIG and SMALL for each column head. Give children the charts to draw pictures of the big and small things they find at home.

OPTIONAL: USING DIGITAL COMPONENTS

CD-ROM

Have children play the games at home to practice their listening skills and share what they are learning with their families.

ActiveTeach

Invite volunteers up to the big screen to draw lines connecting the animals.

Speaking

Objectives: To practice speaking, to practice new unit vocabulary and structures

Writing: numbers 1–6

Materials: Workbook

Optional Materials: Picture Cards (including Units 2 and 4), Sammy the Squirrel puppet, CD-ROM, ActiveTeach

GETTING READY

Silly Card Game (10 minutes)

- Place the zoo animal Picture Cards face down in a pile.
- Put the classroom and town Picture Cards (the ones of places from Units 2 and 4) face down in a separate pile.
- Model the activity by choosing a card from each pile and making a sentence. Use the *[elephant]* card and the *[computer room]* card to say: *The [elephant] is in the [computer room].*
- Have volunteers continue this way.

Guessing Game (5 minutes)

- Choose a unit Picture Card but don't show it to the class.
- Describe the animal: *It's [big] and [gray]. What is it?*
- Invite the class to guess: *It's [an elephant]!*
- Allow children to describe an animal when they are ready.
- Continue until everyone has played.

WORKING IN THE BOOK: PAGE 79

5. Ask and answer. Number.

- Have children open to page 79. Use Sammy to help you demonstrate how to do the activity.
- Focus on item 1, which is done as an example. First, call attention to the boy and girl with speech bubbles at the bottom of the page. Tell children that you and Sammy will model how they will work with a partner and use the text in the speech bubbles to do the activity.
- Point to the sea lion and say and ask: *Number 1. What's that?* Have Sammy answer: *It's a big sea lion.*
- Then point to the number *1* in the box by the sea lion. Explain that children will number the rest of the boxes from *2* to *6* in the order of the animals they choose to ask about. Walk around and make sure pairs understand how to do the activity.

CONSOLIDATING

Vocabulary Review (10 minutes)

- Use the same procedure as the one on Student Book page 79 to review vocabulary from other units.
- Display Picture Cards for vocabulary to review on the board.
- Draw a write-in box next to each card.
- Have pairs of children take turns asking and answering about the cards.
- Have children write the numbers in order as they name each card.

Where's the Monkey? (10 minutes)

- On the board, write the word *ZOO*.
- Place the *monkey* Picture Card *in* a bag, *on* a book, *under* a table, and *at* the zoo (near the word *zoo* on the board).
- Each time, point and ask: *Where's the monkey? It's [in] the [bag].*
- Hide a different Picture Card *in*, *on*, or *under* something that children can name, or *at* the zoo.
- Ask: *Where's the [bat]?*
- Invite a volunteer to look for the card. When the volunteer finds it, he or she says: *It's [under] [the table].*

Extra Practice: Student Book page 100 and T100

For extra practice speaking, have children turn to page 100 in the back of their books. For teacher support, turn to page T100 in this book.

Big Book Talk (10 minutes)

- Use the Big Book to get children talking.
- Read the "The Rabbit and the Carrot" to children a few times and then encourage them to "read" along with you.
- Help children talk about things that they share. Invite them to tell the story in their own words.

Workbook Page 78

Have children color the big lion. Have them work with a partner to take turns asking and answering: *What's that? / It's a big lion.*

Workbook Page 79

Have children work with a partner to ask and answer: *What's that? / It's a [big] [zebra].* Then invite them to color the page.

OPTIONAL: USING DIGITAL COMPONENTS

CD-ROM

Have children use the CD-ROM to mimic the audio for practice with their speaking skills at home.

ActiveTeach

Use the big screen to model numbering the boxes.

SPEAKING

5 **Ask and answer. Number.**

EXTRA PRACTICE
Page 100

Practice: *What's that? It's a [big] [sea lion].* Writing: *1–6*

PHONICS

B32 B34 6 **Listen. Trace, write, and say.**

u u

sun cup bus

Phonics: short *u* **Prewriting/Writing:** directionality, letter tracing, letters in contexts **Review:** *bus, cup, sun* **TPR:** write *u* in the air

Phonics

Objectives: To learn the short vowel sound that the letter *u* stands for in the middle of words, to understand sound-symbol correspondences, to recognize left-to-right directionality, to trace and write the letter *u* in the context of words

New Sounds and Letters: short *u*

Review: bus, cup, sun

TPR: write *u* in the air

Materials: Class Audio CD B, Workbook

Optional Materials: CD-ROM, ActiveTeach, pencils with erasers

GETTING READY

Review Letters (5 minutes)

- Write the alphabet on the board.
- Circle the letters children have learned: a, b, c, d, e, f, g, h, j, k, l, m, n, o, p, q, r, s, t, v, w, x, y.
- For each letter, invite children to say the letter, the sound, and a word: *B*, /b/, *bird*.

Introduce the Letter (5 minutes)

- On the board, write *s__n*.
- Say the sound each letter stands for: /s/, /n/.
- Point to the middle space and shrug your shoulders. Run your fingers under each and say: /s/–(shrug)–/n/.
- Write the letter *u*. Say: *This is* u. U *stands for /u/ in words like* sun.
- Run your finger under the word a few times, saying the sounds: /s/–/u/–/n/.
- Go faster and faster, blending the word, until you are reading: *sun*.
- Erase the *s* and *n*. Write *b* and *s* and follow a similar procedure for *bus*.
- Repeat with *cup*.

WORKING IN THE BOOK: PAGE 80

B32 B34 6. Listen. Trace, write, and say.

- Play the "*U* Cheer." Do the actions.
- Invite children to chant and do the actions when they are ready.

Audio Script

***U* Cheer**

Sue: Give me a *u!*
Fans: *U!*
Sue: What does *u* sound like?
Fans: Uh!
Sue: Give me some *u* words!
Fans: Uh . . . *sun!*
Uh . . . *cup!*
Uh . . . *bus!*
Sue: Show me a *u!* (write *u* in the air)
Let's hear it for *u!*
Fans: Hooray!

- Focus children on the page again.
- Point to the *u* on the left. Model tracing the letter with your finger. Next, have children trace the *u* in the grid and then write it several times.
- Then point to the word *sun*. Point and say: *Uh, sun.*
- Model tracing the *u* in the middle of the word. Have children trace it.
- Repeat with the other words.
- Have children take turns pointing to and reading the letters and words on the page.
- For additional practice, have children listen to Class Audio CD B: Track 34. Tell children to listen and clap if they hear a word with /u/.
  - Model once with the words *sun* (clap) and *hat* (don't clap).

Audio Script

Now listen and clap if you hear an *uh* sound.

duck (clap)
jump (clap)
truck (clap)
red
fun (clap)
hot

CONSOLIDATING

"Hand" Writing (10 minutes)

- Use a pencil eraser to write a letter of the alphabet on a volunteer's hand. Model proper pencil grip.
- Have the volunteer guess the letter.
- Continue with other volunteers and familiar letters.
- Reinforce pencil grip with children. Then have them practice "hand" writing with partners.
- As a challenge, have children "hand" write words with partners.

Workbook Page 80

Have children color the letter *u* and say the letter and the sound. Then have them trace each letter *u* and take turns saying each word to a partner: *sun*, *cup*, *bus*. Finally, invite children to finish coloring the page.

OPTIONAL: USING DIGITAL COMPONENTS

CD-ROM

Have children play the games at home with their families to show them the sounds and letters they are learning in class.

ActiveTeach

Demonstrate tracing the letters on the big screen. Then invite volunteers to trace and write the letters.

Math

Objective: To do simple addition
Materials: Class Audio CD B, Workbook
Optional Materials: Sammy the Squirrel puppet, CD-ROM, ActiveTeach, bowl, blocks, big spoon

GETTING READY

How Many Bag (5 minutes)

Warm up by doing the "*How Many?* Bag" activity on page T71.

Introduce Addition (10 minutes)

- For the last turn in "*How Many?* Bag," use three crayons *(1 + 2)*.
- On the board, draw one crayon, a "plus" sign, and two crayons.
- Say: *One plus two equals three.*
- Repeat with other crayon addition sentences.

WORKING IN THE BOOK: PAGE 81

B35 7. Add and draw. Listen and sing.

- Have children open their books to page 81.
- Do the sample item together. Point and say: *One sea lion plus one sea lion equals two sea lions.*
- Follow a similar procedure for the remaining items.
- Point and say: *One plus two equals three.*
- Allow children who are ready to work independently while you work with the others to draw the correct total number of animals.
- Play the song. Invite children to count on their fingers and sing along.

Audio Script

Adding

One plus one equals two.
Two plus one equals three.
Do you see? It's easy to do.
Adding is fun for you and me.
Three plus one equals four.
Three plus three equals six.
Do you see? Let's try more.
Numbers are fun to mix!

CONSOLIDATING

Mix It Up (5 minutes)

- Have available a bowl, a big spoon, and blocks (enough for one to four per child).
- Give each child one to four blocks.
- Invite two volunteers at a time to come to the bowl.
- Have one child drop his or her blocks in the bowl and say: [*Three*]. Cue children to each hold up [three] fingers on one hand.
- Have the other drop his or her blocks in the bowl and say: [*Two*]. Cue children to each hold up [two] fingers on the other hand.
- Stir the blocks with the spoon. Ask: *How many all together?*
- Help children count on their fingers.
- Confirm by taking out all the blocks and counting them.
- Continue this way with other volunteers.

Unscramble (5 minutes)

- Prepare pieces of paper with one to six circles, a plus sign, and an equals sign.
- Display a scrambled equation on the board. For example: [three circles] [five circles] [plus] [equals] [two circles].
- Invite a volunteer to come to the board and unscramble the equation: [three / two circles] [plus] [two / three circles] [equals] [five circles].

Workbook Page 81

Have children add the animals and draw them to show the answer. Have partners point to each answer and tell how many: *[four penguins]*.

OPTIONAL: USING DIGITAL COMPONENTS

CD-ROM

Have children play the games at home to show their families what they are learning in class.

ActiveTeach

Invite volunteers to use the pen tool to count each group of animals and draw the total number.

MATH

B35 7 **Add and draw. Listen and sing.**

VALUES Include everyone.

B37 8 **Listen and say. Draw and trace.**

Include everyone.

Values: Include everyone. **Prewriting:** tracing a short sentence

Values

Objective: To learn about the value of including everyone

New Values Language: Include everyone.

Prewriting: Tracing a short sentence.

Materials: Class Audio CD B, Workbook

Optional Materials: CD-ROM, ActiveTeach, tape

GETTING READY

Review Shapes: Musical Shapes (10 minutes)

- Use tape to make big shapes on the floor.
- Tell children that you will play music and they will dance around the room until the music stops.
- Play and then stop some music, and call out a shape: *[Circle]!*
- Cue everyone to squeeze together to stand in the circle. Tell children the goal is for everyone to be in, nobody out.
- Continue this way.

Introduce Including Everyone (10 minutes)

- Play one more round of Musical Shapes with a few prepared volunteers. This time after the music stops and you call out a shape, don't let one volunteer into it.
- Have the volunteer act sad and hurt. Ask: *How do you feel? (Sad.)*
- Discuss why it's important to include everyone.

WORKING IN THE BOOK: PAGE 82

B37 8. Listen and say. Draw and trace.

- Have children open to page 82.
- Play the dialogue on the first part of the audio and ask children to look at the photos as they listen.
- Have volunteers repeat the dialogue with you.

Audio Script

Kids: Come and play with us.
Adult: That's good. Don't leave anyone out.
Boy: It hurts to be left out.

- Then play the chant on the second part of the audio. Have children listen and then chant along with the audio when they are ready.

Audio Script

Include Everyone Chant

We're all different. We're all the same.
Wherever we are, we're each a star!

- Have children discuss whether the children in each photo are including everyone or not.
- Tell children to draw a smile or frown on the faces below the photos to show whether or not the children in each are including everyone.
- Finally, have children read the sentence: *Include everyone* and trace the words.

Talk about it!

- Call attention to "Talk about it!"
- Invite children to talk about times they can try to include everyone.
- Share some language they can use: *Do you want to play / sit / eat with us?*

CONSOLIDATING

Act It Out (10 minutes)

- Invite small groups of children to role-play ideas from "Talk about it!"
- If children include everyone, cue the class to say: *Good job!* and if not, to say: *No, no! Include everyone!*

Touch the Blue Table (5 minutes)

- Play music and have children walk around until the music stops and you say: *Freeze! Touch the [blue table].*
- Explain that children have to touch the table without moving their feet. Further explain that they can touch it themselves if they are close to it, or by holding hands with other children and making a chain.
- The goal is for everyone to be included.

Workbook Page 82

Have children color the picture and say to a partner: *Include everyone.*

OPTIONAL: USING DIGITAL COMPONENTS

CD-ROM

Have children play the games and do the activities on the CD-ROM at home to show their families what they're learning about in class.

ActiveTeach

Focus on the two photos and use the pointer to highlight details that show who is including everyone and who isn't.

Review / Assessment

Objective: To review and assess new unit vocabulary and structures

Materials: Class Audio CD B, Workbook, stickers (in the back of the Student Book and shown on page T108)

Optional Materials: Picture Cards, Sammy the Squirrel puppet, CD-ROM, ActiveTeach, cutouts (gray circle, pink ovals, white "tusks," long gray strips) string

GETTING READY

B Sing and Move (10 minutes)

- Have children sing and move to the various songs and chants from the unit.
- Invite children to tell which song or chant they like best.

Review Vocabulary and Structures (5 minutes)

- Display the unit Picture Cards around the room.
- Point to one and ask Sammy: *What's that?*
- Have Sammy answer: *It's a [big elephant].*
- Continue, but invite children to ask and answer.

WORKING IN THE BOOK: PAGE 83

9. Stick and say.

- Distribute the stickers (but not the reward sticker).
- Have children open their books to page 83.
- Help children notice the sticker outlines in their books and then stick the correct ones in place. Begin with item 1 and say: *Find the elephant sticker.*
- Have children hold up the sticker.
- Have children stick the sticker and say: *It's a big elephant.*
- Repeat with the other stickers (bat, sea lion, zebra).

B39 10. Listen and circle.

- Remind children to listen and circle the answer to each question.
- Confirm the answers with the class.

Audio Script

1. What's that?
   It's a big elephant.
2. What's that?
   It's a small bat.
3. What's that?
   It's a small monkey.
4. What's that?
   It's a big zebra.

I Can! Use the Reward Sticker

- Help children talk about what they have learned in this unit. Encourage them to use positive language. (See page T33 for examples.)
- Distribute the reward stickers.
- Show children where to stick the stickers (on the Unit 8 Good Job! placeholder).

CONSOLIDATING

Congratulations Chant (5 minutes)

- Ask children to each choose one thing they learned in the unit (vocabulary, structure, number, letter) or one thing they can do.
- Have children stand in a circle.
- Have the class clap while each child chants to tell what he or she knows: *I know* (clap, clap) *[small bat]* (clap, clap) or can do: *I can* (clap, clap) *[add]* (clap, clap).
- End by congratulating the class!

Art Project: Make an Elephant Mask

- Prepare cutouts: gray circle for face with eye holes, pink ovals for ears, white shapes for tusks, and long strips for trunk.
- Help children look at the model, and glue on the other cutouts and draw "eyebrows."
- Show them how to fold the "trunk" like an accordion before gluing it on.
- Attach string to the ears so children can put on their elephant masks.
- Lead children on an elephant march around school.

Workbook Page 83

Have children draw their favorite animal. Then have them color the page and share their work with a partner: *It's a [big] [bear].*

OPTIONAL: USING DIGITAL COMPONENTS

CD-ROM

Have children play the games and do the activities on the CD-ROM at home to show their families what they're learning about in class.

ActiveTeach

Use the big screen to model circling the answers (1. elephant; 2. bat; 3. monkey; 4. zebra) or to check answers as a class.

REVIEW I can!

9 Stick and say. B39 **10** Listen and circle.

1

2

3

4

Project

Unit 8 GOOD JOB!

Review/Assessment: *What's that? It's a [big] [elephant].* Project: art

9 Places

Unit Overview

Objectives

- ✓ To learn vocabulary for places
- ✓ To sing songs and chant
- ✓ To do new TPR movements
- ✓ To practice fine and gross motor skills
- ✓ To understand and role-play a story
- ✓ To learn and practice new language structures: *Where do [bears] live? / [They] live in the [country]. / [Bears] live in the [city], too. / Where does [the mouse] live? / [It] lives in the [field].*
- ✓ To recognize and produce the short vowel sound that the letter *i* stands for in the middle of words
- ✓ To write the letter *i*
- ✓ To do simple subtraction
- ✓ To learn the value of taking care of our world
- ✓ To practice writing a short sentence
- ✓ To practice new language by listening and speaking
- ✓ To learn and review unit vocabulary and language structures

Vocabulary

New: apartment, building, field, forest, mountain, river, street, traffic light

Review: bird(s), cars, ducks, fish, goats, house, milk, mouse, tree(s)

Home-School Connections

Copy the Letter Home for children to bring home to share what they'll be learning in Unit 9 of *My Little Island*. The Letter Home is available online at www.pearsonelt.com/mylittleisland.

Values

Take care of our world.

Materials

Student Book pages 84–93; Workbook Pages 84–93; Picture Cards 57–64; Class Audio CD B: Tracks 40–52; Program Posters: My Little Island Map, Shapes and Colors All Around, Meet Your New Friends!; stickers (back of Student Book and shown on page T108)

Optional: CD-ROM, ActiveTeach, Big Book, Sammy the Squirrel Puppet

Songs and Chants

- ✓ Right Here (Class Audio CD B: Tracks 40, 41)
- ✓ *I* Cheer (Class Audio CD B: Tracks 45, 46)
- ✓ Subtracting (Class Audio CD B: Tracks 48, 49)
- ✓ Take Care of Our World Chant (Class Audio CD B: Tracks 50, 51)

Story

"Where Do Bears Live?": Sue and Lou see a bear on TV. Lou is scared. They look on the computer and learn that bears live in the country. Lou says bears live in the city, too—in the zoo.

Language Structures: *Where do [bears] live? / [They] live in the [country]. / [Bears] live in the [city], too.*

SKILLS

Cross-Curricular Connections

do simple subtraction

learn the value of taking care of our world, make a recycling poster

sing, chant, and move to music

Preschool Learning Outcomes

- ✓ Recognize intonation in questions.
- ✓ Use short answers to questions.
- ✓ Understand new language structures.
- ✓ Recognize and produce the sound that short *i* stands for.
- ✓ Trace and write the letter *i* in words.
- ✓ Listen to and follow a story with words.
- ✓ Make predictions, using pictures.
- ✓ Sing songs and say chants with TPR.
- ✓ Join in games and interact.
- ✓ Talk about self and surroundings.
- ✓ Develop a positive attitude toward the English language.

Digital Practice

Have children use the CD-ROM for vocabulary practice in class or at home.

Use ActiveTeach to go over Student Book pages together as a class.

LEARN BY DOING

TPR

- ✓ point to floor, point to self, trace smile, write *i* in the air

Phonics

- ✓ Recognize sound-correspondences: short *i*.
- ✓ Write the letter *i*.
- ✓ Complete Phonics page 90.
- ✓ Listen to the audio.
- ✓ Sing songs and say chants.

Prereading and Prewriting

- ✓ Follow a four-page story.
- ✓ Talk about the characters.
- ✓ Act out the story to show comprehension.
- ✓ Practice fine motor skills.
- ✓ Trace letters and a short sentence.

Encourage children to have play dates and speak in English over the summer. Children can have fun practicing English together!

BULLETIN BOARD DISPLAY

Peek-A-Boo City and Country

- ✓ Create an interactive bulletin board to practice unit language.

Materials

- children's drawings of animals
- child-made labels
- glue or tape

Directions

1. Brainstorm animals, buildings, places, and other items that are from the city and from the country.
2. Give children four index-card sized pieces of paper and have them draw one thing for the country and one for the city on two of the pieces of paper.
3. On the other two pieces of paper, help each child create a label for *City* and for *Country* and write his or her name on each.
4. Have children put their city and country pictures on the bulletin board, covering them with their labels.
5. Play peek-a-boo. Say: *Peek-a-boo! [Maria] in the [country].*
6. Have [Maria] find her *Country* card, lift the label, and show [her] drawing to the class, and then say: *[The cow] is in the [country].*
7. Continue with other children and their pictures.

9 Places

B40 Listen and sing. Move.

Presentation: *apartment, building, field, forest, mountain, river, street, traffic light* **Review:** *fish, house* **TPR:** point to floor, point to self, trace smile

Presentation

Objectives: To identify vocabulary in a scene, to learn a song and new TPR actions

New Vocabulary: apartment, building, field, forest, mountain, river, street, traffic light

Review: fish, house

TPR: point to floor, point to self, trace smile

Materials: Class Audio CD B, Picture Cards, Workbook

Optional Materials: CD-ROM, ActiveTeach, My Little Island Map poster

GETTING READY

My Little Island Map (5 minutes)

- Display the My Little Island Map poster and help children find the city and the country.
- Introduce: *City* and *Country*, and ask children to point out differences between them as shown on the poster.

Share What You Know (5 minutes)

- Make a two-column chart on board: *City* and *Country* or use the T-Chart on page T136.
- Brainstorm what people can see and do in each place. Attach pictures or make simple drawings.

WORKING IN THE BOOK: PAGE 84

Introduce Vocabulary

- Use the Picture Cards to present unit vocabulary:
  - Say: *[Apartment].* Have children repeat.
  - Have children point to the [apartment] on the page and say: *[Apartment].*

B40 1. Listen and sing. Move.

- Teach the children the actions for the song.
- Play the song audio. Invite children to sing along and do the actions when they are ready.

Audio Script

Right Here

The goat is on the mountain.
The fish is in the river.
The bear is in the forest.
The bird is in the tree.
They are in the country.
(Chorus:)
And I . . . (point to self)
Am happy . . . (trace smile on face)
Right here! (point to floor)

The duck is in the river.
The mouse is in the field.
The bat is in the cave.
The monkey is in the tree.
They are in the country.
(Repeat chorus.)

There are many buildings.
Apartments are inside.
The buildings are so big.
People live up high!
They are in the city.
(Repeat chorus.)

The streets are all around.
Lots of streets are wide.
So many cars and buses—
Traffic lights help guide.
They are in the city.
(Repeat chorus.)

CONSOLIDATING

Picture Cards (5 minutes)

- Display the unit Picture Cards.
- Play the song. Have children point to the cards when the words are sung.

Workbook Page 84

Have children trace the mountains, river, building, and traffic light. Then have them color the page. Finally, have them work with a partner to point to and name the things in the pictures.

OPTIONAL: USING DIGITAL COMPONENTS

CD-ROM

Encourage children to play the games and do the activities on the CD-ROM at home to show their families what they're learning about in class.

ActiveTeach

Use the large digital format to focus on the items from the city and the country.

Vocabulary

Objectives: To practice new words, to write numbers 1–8

New Vocabulary: apartment, building, field, forest, mountain, river, street, traffic light

Materials: Class Audio CD B, Workbook

Optional Materials: Units 8 and 9 Picture Cards; Sammy the Squirrel puppet, CD-ROM, ActiveTeach, drawings and magazine pictures, drawing supplies

GETTING READY

B40 Review the Song (5 minutes)

- Have children sing and do the actions for "Right Here" on page T84.
- Display the Unit 8 Picture Cards. Have children point to the animals as they sing.

Take a Vote (5 minutes)

- Revisit the ideas you listed in Share What You Know on page T84.
- Point to the country column and say: *I like the country.*
- Turn to Sammy: *How about you? Do you like the country or the city?* Have him say: *I like the city.*
- Say: *Let's take a vote.* Write *City* and *Country* on the board.
- Ask children if they like the city or country, and then count the votes and tally them on the board.
- Describe the results: *[Seven] children like the city. [Six] children like the country. More children like the [city].*

WORKING IN THE BOOK: PAGE 85

B42 2. Listen. Find and number. Say.

- Remind children to listen to the audio and number the pictures.
- Play the audio, pausing to allow children to find the pictures and write the numbers.

Audio Script

1. mountain
2. street
3. field
4. apartment
5. forest
6. river
7. traffic light
8. building

- Check children's work as a class.
- Have volunteers point and say: *[I] [mountain].*
- For additional practice, say each vocabulary word aloud and have children clap twice, pause, clap twice again, pause, clap twice again, and repeat the word.

CONSOLIDATING

Sorting Activity (10 minutes)

- Label two sections of the board: *City* and *Country*.
- Use Picture Cards, drawings, and pictures from magazines that show things in the city and country.
- Hold up each picture and cue the class to call out: *City* or *Country*.
- Sort the pictures on the board.

Draw a Place (10 minutes)

- Have children draw a city or a country scene.
- Invite them to share their work: *This is the [city]. This is a [building], a [bus], and a [street].*

Workbook Page 85

Have children match each picture to Lou or Sue. Then have them color the page. Finally, have children work with a partner to point to each picture and name what it shows.

OPTIONAL: USING DIGITAL COMPONENTS

CD-ROM

Have children play the games to show their families words they know for the city and the country.

ActiveTeach

Use the big screen to model numbering the boxes on the Student Book page.

VOCABULARY

B42 **2** **Listen. Find and number. Say.**

apartment

building

street

traffic light

field

forest

mountain

river

Practice: *apartment, building, street, traffic light, field, forest, mountain, river* **Writing:** *1–8*

Story

Objectives: To read and understand a story, to identify and understand speech bubbles, to learn new language structures, to listen to and identify the intonation in a sentence, to role-play

New Structure: *Where do [bears] live? / [They] live in the [country]. [Bears] live in the [city], too.*

Materials: Class Audio CD B, Workbook

Optional Materials: Picture Cards, CD-ROM, ActiveTeach, ball

GETTING READY

Hot Potato (10 minutes)

- Have the class sit in a circle.
- Display the unit Picture Cards so everyone can see them.
- Give one child a ball ("potato") that's easy to pass around.
- Tell children that they will listen to some music and pass the potato around the circle until the music stops.
- Play some music and then stop it.
- Explain that the child holding the potato is out and must leave the circle and call out a vocabulary word: *[Apartment]!*
- Then cue everyone to point to the *[apartment]* Picture Card.
- Play the music and continue until there's one child left: the winner.

Introduce the Story (5 minutes)

- Hold up the Student Book, turned to page 86.
- Focus on the first page of "Where Do Bears Live?". Ask children to talk about the picture.
- Explain that Sue and Lou are watching a television show.
- Ask children if they recognize any of the words in the speech bubbles. Invite them to guess what the characters are talking about.

- Take a picture walk through the rest of the story.
- Have children predict what will happen. Revisit predictions later.

WORKING IN THE BOOK: PAGES 86–87

B43 3. Look and listen. Act it out.

- Have children open their books to page 86.
- Play the audio and pause after each story page to make sure children are on the correct page and understand what's happening.
- Play the story audio again. Point to each speech bubble as the words are spoken.
- Encourage children to speak along with the characters.
- Invite volunteers to act out the story with the audio.

Audio Script

Where Do Bears Live?

Page 1	Lou:	Look at the bear. I'm scared.
	Sue:	It's okay. Bears don't live in the city.
Page 2	Lou:	Where do bears live?
	Sue:	They live in the country.
Page 3	Lou:	Bears live in the city, too.
	Sue:	In the city? Where?
Page 4	Lou:	They live in the zoo.
	Sue:	Oh! Ha! Ha!

Look at New Language

- Point out the structures the characters use to ask and answer about where bears live: *Where do bears live? They live in the [country].*
- Invite partners to practice the exchange by talking about other animals.
- Have children ask about one [bear], as well: *Where does the [bear] live? It lives in the [forest].*
- Encourage children to extend the discussion by including *in the zoo* and *on the farm*.

Listen to the Intonation

B43

- Have children close their eyes and listen while you play the story audio.
- Pause after each question. Point out how the speakers' voices rise and fall in questions and answers.

CONSOLIDATING

Role-Play (10 minutes)

- Have pairs of children act out the story.
- First, play the audio and have pairs of children pantomime.
- Then invite volunteers to act it out without the audio.

What Happens Next? (5 minutes)

- Invite children to guess what might happen next in the story, such as going to the zoo and seeing a bear there.
- After children share their ideas, invite pairs of children to role-play what happens next.

Compare City and Country (5 minutes)

- Give children copies of the Venn diagram on page T138. Help them label one circle *City* and the other *Country*, and the overlapping section *Both*.
- Guide them to draw things from the City and the Country in each circle and things (or animals) under *Both*.

Workbook Page 86

Have children draw a bear and color the page. Then have them practice the target language with a partner: *Where do [bears] live? / [They] live in the [country].*

Workbook Page 87

Have children connect the dots to draw a bear and then color the scene. Have partners name and talk about what they see on the page.

OPTIONAL: USING DIGITAL COMPONENTS

CD-ROM

Have children play and listen to the story at home and invite their families to listen with them.

ActiveTeach

Use the big screen to focus on the speech bubbles. Point to the person speaking, and then drag the pointer under each word as it is spoken.

LISTENING

B44 **4** **Listen and write a number.**

Practice: *Where does [the mouse] live? [It] lives in the [field]. Where do [goats] live? [They] live in the [mountains].* **Review:** *bird, fish, goats, mouse, tree*

Listening

Objectives: To practice listening comprehension, to practice new unit vocabulary and structures

Review: bird, fish, goats, mouse, tree

Materials: Class Audio CD B

Optional Materials: Picture Cards; Sammy the Squirrel puppet, CD-ROM, ActiveTeach, Picture Cards or pictures of Sue, mouse, goat, bear, bird, fish

GETTING READY

B43 Phonics Review (10 minutes)

- Open the Student Book to the story on pages 86–87. (Use ActiveTeach for this activity, if possible.)
- Name a letter: *[L]*. Have children say the sound: /l/ and play the audio for a page from the story.
- Ask children to listen for a word with /l/ at the beginning. Then have them look at their books and find the word (*look, live*).
- Follow a similar procedure for other sounds: /b/, *bear*; /s/, *city, scared*; /k/, *country*.

Prepare for the Exercise (5 minutes)

- Display Picture Cards for field, mountain, forest, apartment, and river in a 3 X 2 grid on the board. Draw a tree in the sixth place.
- Gather Picture Cards or pictures for Sue and for a mouse, goat, bear, bird, and fish.
- Ask and answer the questions from Class Audio CD B: Track 44 with Sammy: *Where do [goats] live? / They live in [the mountains].*
- Note that in Level 2, children learned that goats live on a farm. Explain that wild "mountain goats" live on mountains.
- Place an animal card or picture of Sue next to each place card.

WORKING IN THE BOOK: PAGE 88

B44 4. Listen and write a number.

- Have children open their books to page 88.
- Point to the different scenes and elicit the place words.
- Explain that children will listen to the audio and write numbers to show the order that they heard each place mentioned.

Audio Script

1. Where does the mouse live?
   It lives in the field.
2. Where do goats live?
   They live in the mountains.
3. Where do bears live?
   They live in the forest.
4. Where does Sue live?
   She lives in an apartment.
5. Where does the bird live?
   It lives in a tree.
6. Where do fish live?
   They live in the river.

CONSOLIDATING

Draw the Animal (5 minutes)

- When children finish the activity, have them draw the animals in the scenes on the page.
- Invite volunteers to point, ask, and answer: *Where [does] [the mouse] live? / [It lives] in the [field].*

Clap, Clap, Hop (10 minutes)

- Review TPR and other actions children know.
- Have children sit in a circle. Walk around the circle clapping and saying: *Clap, clap, clap. . . .*
- After a few claps, tap someone on the shoulder and say: *Hop*. Have that child stand and hop around the circle saying: *Hop, hop, hop. . . .*
- Then cue that child to walk around clapping and then tap another child on the shoulder and continue the game.

OPTIONAL: USING DIGITAL COMPONENTS

CD-ROM

Have children play the games at home to practice their listening skills.

ActiveTeach

Use the big screen to help children do the numbering activity.

Speaking

Objectives: To practice speaking, to practice new unit vocabulary and structures
Review: ducks, fish, goats, mouse
Materials: Workbook
Optional Materials: Picture Cards, CD-ROM, ActiveTeach, Class Audio CD B, teacher-made word cards

GETTING READY

Listening Review (10 minutes)

- Revisit the listening lesson from each unit in the Student Book and play the audio. (If possible, use ActiveTeach.)
- Have partners choose one activity to "perform" for the class.

Prepare for the Exercise (10 minutes)

- On the board, draw a two-column chart. In one column, draw: 1 duck, 2 goats, and 3 bears.
- In the other column, display the Picture Cards for *forest*, *river*, and *mountain*.
- Invite partners to ask and answer about the animals: *Where does [the duck] live? Where do [goats] live?*
- Then have volunteers draw a line from the animal(s) to the place.

WORKING IN THE BOOK: PAGE 89

5. Match animals to homes. Ask and answer.

- Have children open their books to page 89.
- Focus on item 1 which is done as an example. Say: *They live in the river.*
- Call attention to the boy and girl with speech bubbles.
- Point to and read the speech bubbles: *Where do ducks live? They live in the river.*
- Tell children they will work in pairs, using the speech bubble text as a model.
- Explain that after asking and answering about the animal(s) on the left and their home(s) on the right, they will draw a line from the animal(s) to its/their home(s). (Note that both ducks and fish live in the river.)
- Check to be sure that children matched the mouse to the field, the fish to the river, the goats to the mountain, and the bears to the forest.

CONSOLIDATING

Count the Animals (5 minutes)

- Have children count each group of animals in Exercise 5: *1, 2. Two ducks. 1. One mouse. 1, 2, 3. Three goats. 1, 2, 3, 4, 5. Five fish. 1, 2. Two bears.*
- Point to the river. Ask: *How many of these animals live in the river?*
- Encourage children to count on their fingers to figure it out.
- Reinforce the equation on the board. Draw pictures with a plus sign and equals sign.
- Point and say: *Two* (point to each duck) *plus* (point to the plus sign) *four* (point to each fish) *equals* (point to the equals sign) *six* (point to each duck and fish in the sum).

Make a Connection (5 minutes)

- Create word cards for the words in the following sentences. Make the cards the same size.
  – Where do bears live?
  – Where do teachers work?
  – Where do students read?
- Display the sentences on the board so the words line up (*Where* under *Where*, and so on) and ask children if they notice any similarities.
- Then switch the subjects around to make different (silly) questions, for example: *Where do ducks read?*

Extra Practice: Student Book page 101 and T101

For extra practice speaking, have children turn to page 101 in the back of their books. For teacher support, turn to page T101 in this book.

Workbook Page 88

Have children draw lines to match the animals to the places where they live. Then have children color the page and practice the target language with a partner: *Where do [fish] live? / [They] live in the [river].*

Workbook Page 89

Have children trace the paths to match Sue and the animals to the places where they live. Have partners ask and answer: *Where does the [duck] live? / [It] lives in the [river].*

OPTIONAL: USING DIGITAL COMPONENTS

CD-ROM

Have children use the CD-ROM at home and mimic the audio to practice speaking skills.

ActiveTeach

Use the big screen to model matching the animal(s) to its/their home(s).

SPEAKING

5 **Match animals to homes. Ask and answer.**

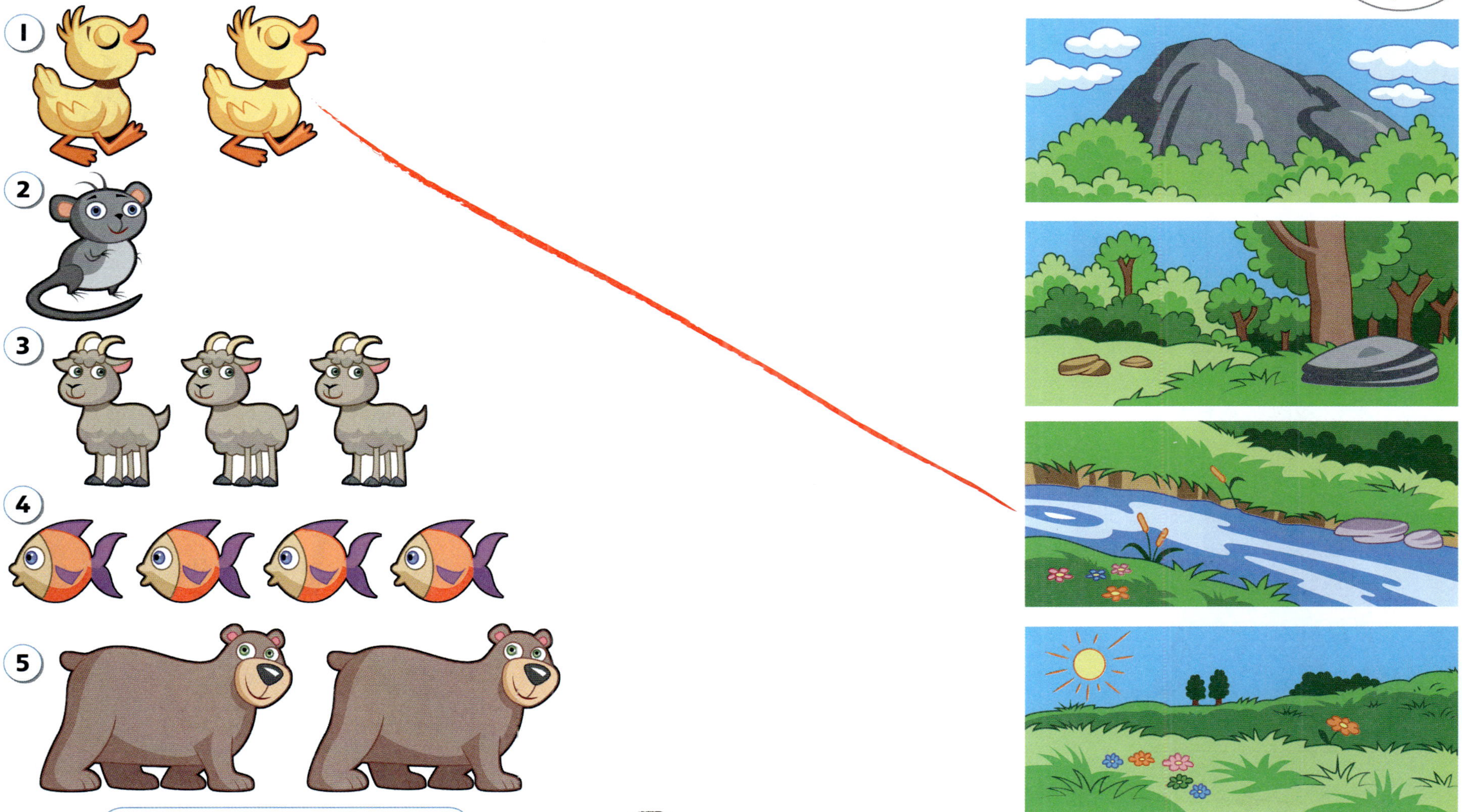

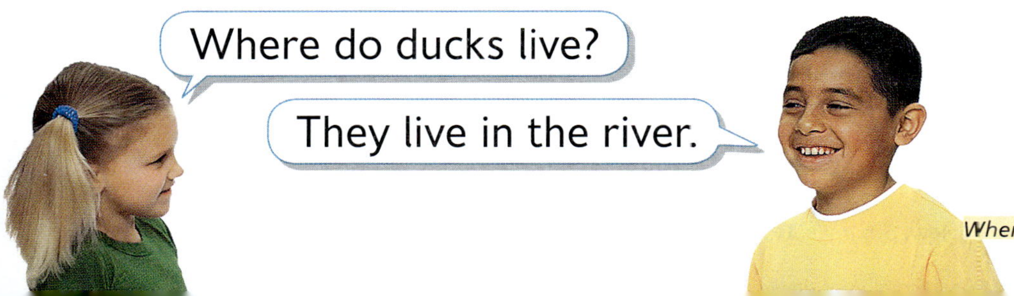

Practice: *Where do [ducks] live? [They] live in the [river]. Where does [the mouse] live? [It] lives in the [field].* **Review:** ducks, fish, goats, mouse

PHONICS

B45 B47 **6 Listen. Trace, write, and say.**

i i

s i t

f i s h

m i l k

Phonics: short *i* **Prewriting/Writing:** directionality, letter tracing, letters in contexts **Review:** *fish*, *milk* **TPR:** write *i* in the air

Phonics

Objectives: To learn the short vowel sound that the letter *i* stands for in the middle of words, to understand sound-symbol correspondences, to recognize left-to-right directionality, to trace and write the letter *i*

New Sounds and Letters: short *i*

Review: fish, milk

TPR: write *i* in the air

Materials: Class Audio CD B, Workbook

Optional Materials: CD-ROM, ActiveTeach, pencils with erasers

GETTING READY

Review Letters (5 minutes)

- Write the alphabet on the board.
- Circle the letters children have learned: a, b, c, d, e, f, g, h, j, k, l, m, n, o, p, q, r, s, t, u, v, w, x, y.
- For each letter, invite children to say the letter, the sound, and a word: *B*, /b/, *bird*.

Introduce the Letter (5 minutes)

- On the board, write *s__t*.
- Say the sound each letter stands for: /s/, /t/.
- Point to the middle space and shrug your shoulders. Run your fingers under each and say: /s/–(shrug)–/t/.
- Write the letter *i*. Say: *This is* i. I *stands for /i/ in words like* sit.
- Run your finger under the word a few times, saying the sounds: /s/–/i/–/t/.
- Go faster and faster, blending the word, until you are reading: *sit*.
- Erase the *s* and *t*. Write *f* and *sh* and follow a similar procedure for *fish*.
- Repeat with *milk*.

WORKING IN THE BOOK: PAGE 90

B45 B47 6. Listen. Trace, write, and say.

- Play the "*I* Cheer." Do the actions.
- Invite children to chant and do the actions when they are ready.

Audio Script

***I* Cheer**

Sue: Give me an *i!*
Fans: *I!*
Sue: What does *i* sound like?
Fans: Ih!
Sue: Give me some *i* words!
Fans: Ih . . . *sit!*
Ih . . . *fish!*
Ih . . . *milk!*
Sue: Show me an *i!* (write *i* in the air)
Let's hear it for *i!*
Fans: Hooray!

- Focus on the page again.
- Point to the *i* on the left. Model tracing the letter with your finger. Next, have children trace the *i* in the grid and then write it several times.
- Then point to the word *sit*. Point and say: *ih, sit*.
- Model tracing the *i* in the middle of the word. Have children trace it.
- Repeat with the other words.
- Have children take turns pointing to and reading the letters and words on the page.
- For additional practice, have children listen to Class Audio CD B: Track 47. Tell children to listen and clap if they hear a word with /i/.
  - Model once with the words *sit* (clap) and *pen* (don't clap).

Audio Script

Now listen and clap if you hear an *ih* sound.

windy *(clap)*
blocks
sun
scissors *(clap)*
sister *(clap)*
window *(clap)*

CONSOLIDATING

"Hand" Writing (10 minutes)

- Use a pencil eraser to write a letter of the alphabet on a volunteer's hand. Model proper pencil grip.
- Have the volunteer guess the letter.
- Continue with other volunteers and familiar letters.
- Reinforce pencil grip with children. Then have them practice "hand" writing with partners.
- As a challenge, have children "hand" write words with partners.

Workbook Page 90

Have children color the letter *i* and say the letter and the sound. Then have them trace each letter *i* and take turns saying each word to a partner: *sit*, *fish*, *milk*. Finally, invite children to finish coloring the page.

OPTIONAL: USING DIGITAL COMPONENTS

CD-ROM

Have children play the games to show their families the sounds and letters they are learning in class.

ActiveTeach

Demonstrate tracing the letters on the big screen. Then invite volunteers to write the letters.

Math

Objective: To do simple subtraction
Review: birds, cars, trees
Materials: Class Audio CD B, Workbook
Optional Materials: CD-ROM, ActiveTeach, bag, blocks

GETTING READY

Review Addition (5 minutes)

- Write a simple picture addition problem on the board: (one block) + (two blocks) = (three blocks).
- Point and read: *One plus two equals three.*
- Repeat with a few other problems.
- At the end, circle the equals sign. Remind children that the two sides of the equation are equal.

Introduce Simple Subtraction (10 minutes)

- Place four blocks in a bag as you count: *1, 2, 3, 4.*
- Then take one out. Ask children how many are left. Take them out and count to confirm.
- Repeat with 3 – 2 = 1.
- Tell children you are going to write a math sentence to show what happened.
- Draw three blocks followed by a minus sign, two blocks, an equals sign, and one block.
- Point and read: *Three minus two equals one.*
- Repeat with a few other examples.

WORKING IN THE BOOK: PAGE 91

B48 7. Subtract and draw. Listen and sing.

- Have children open their books to page 91.
- Do the sample item together. Point and say: *Two traffic lights minus one light equals one light.*
- Reinforce by drawing two lights on the board: *Two.* Erase one and say: *Minus one.* Point and count: *Equals one.*
- Have children who are ready continue on their own while you work with the others.
- Play the song. Show children how to hold up their fingers and curl them down to show subtraction.
- Play it again and invite children to count on their fingers and sing along.

Audio Script

Subtracting
Minus, minus.
Two minus one equals one.
We take away numbers.
Isn't this fun?
Minus, minus.
Five minus four equals one.
We take away numbers.
Isn't this fun?

CONSOLIDATING

Sit and Stand (10 minutes)

- Have three children stand. Say: *Three.*
- Have two more stand: *Plus two.*
- Count them all: *Equals five.*
- Repeat with a few more addition problems, but cue the class to tell you the equation each time.
- Then try some subtraction problems.
- Have five children stand: *Five.*
- Cue two to sit: *Minus two.*
- Count: *Equals three.*
- Repeat and have children tell you the equation each time.

Show Me (10 minutes)

- Divide the class into small groups.
- Give each group an addition or subtraction sentence.
- Tell groups to show the equation using fingers, blocks, or drawings.

Workbook Page 91

Have children draw the items to show the answers. Have partners point to each answer and name it: *[three apples].*

OPTIONAL: USING DIGITAL COMPONENTS

CD-ROM

Have children play the games and do the activities on the CD-ROM at home to show their families what they are learning in class.

ActiveTeach

Invite volunteers to use the pen tool to count and subtract from each group of items and then draw the answer.

MATH

B48 7 **Subtract and draw. Listen and sing.**

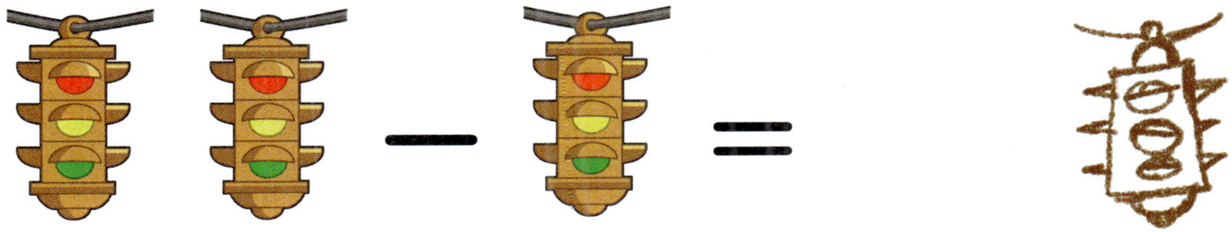

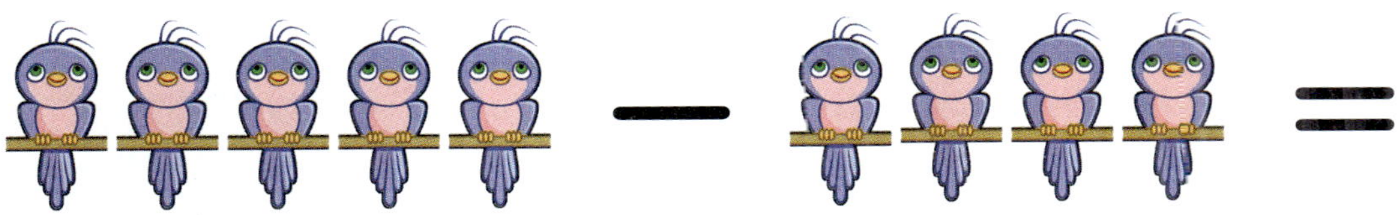

VALUES Take care of our world.

B50 8 **Listen and say. Draw and trace.**

Take care of our world.

Values: Take care of our world. **Prewriting:** tracing a short sentence

Values

Objective: To learn about the value of taking care of our world

New Values Language: Take care of our world.

Prewriting: Tracing a short sentence

Materials: Class Audio CD B, Workbook

Optional Materials: Sammy the Squirrel puppet, CD-ROM, ActiveTeach

GETTING READY

B43 Revisit the Story (5 minutes)

- Revisit "Where Do Bears Live?" on pages T86–87.
- Ask children to name other zoo animals that also live in the wild.
- Talk with children about why it's important to take care of the environment for the animals.

Introduce Taking Care of Our World (10 minutes)

- Pretend you are going on a trip to the forest.
- As you walk through the forest, throw your trash in the river. Make a fire, but leave it burning when you leave. Break tree branches and stomp on berries as you walk away.
- Then pretend to be a bear walking through the same forest.
- Take a drink from the river (make a face and spit it out). Approach the fire and run away (look scared). Pass the broken tree branches and squashed berries (look hungry and sad because there's no food).
- Introduce the language: *Take care of our world.* Explain that we share the world with bears and other animals, so we need to do our part to take care of it.

WORKING IN THE BOOK: PAGE 92

B50 8. Listen and say. Draw and trace.

- Have children look at the pictures on page 92.
- Play the dialogue on the first part of the audio and ask children to look at the photos as they listen.
- Have volunteers repeat the dialogue with you.

Audio Script

Girls: We're picking up our trash.
Adult: Thank you. You're keeping the river clean.
Girls: We want to take care of our world.

- Then play the chant on the second part of the audio. Have children listen and then chant along with the audio when they are ready.

Audio Script

Take Care of Our World Chant

Take care of our forests.
They're nice and green.
Take care of our rivers.
Let's keep them clean.

- Tell children to draw a smile or frown on the faces below the photos to show whether or not the children are taking care of their world.
- Finally, have children read the sentence: *Take care of our world* and trace the words.

Talk about it!

- Invite children to talk about ways they can help take care of our world, such as pick up litter and trash and water trees and plants.
- Extend the discussion to talk about how children can take care of the school environment (such as the classroom and school yard).

CONSOLIDATING

Act It Out (10 minutes)

- Invite small groups of children to do a role play using ideas from "Talk about it!"
- If children practice the value, cue the class to say: *Good job!* and if not, to say: *No, no! Take care of our world.*

Make a Home Connection

Have children ask their families about ways they can help take care of our world and report back to class.

Workbook Page 92

Have children color the litter and practice saying with a partner: *Take care of our world.*

OPTIONAL: USING DIGITAL COMPONENTS

CD-ROM

Have children play the games and do the activities on the CD-ROM at home to show their families what they're learning about in class.

ActiveTeach

Use the big screen to check answers as a class.

Review / Assessment

Objectives: To review and assess new unit vocabulary and structures
Materials: Class Audio CD B, Workbook, stickers (in the back of the Student Book and shown on page T108)
Optional Materials: CD-ROM, ActiveTeach, poster board, art supplies

GETTING READY

B Sing and Move (10 minutes)

- Have children sing and move to the unit songs and chants.
- Invite children to tell which song or chant they like best.

WORKING IN THE BOOK: PAGE 93

9. Stick and say.

- Distribute the stickers (but not the reward sticker).
- Have children open their books to page 93.
- Help children notice the sticker outlines and clues in their books and then stick the correct ones in place. Begin with item 1 and say: *Find the forest sticker.*
- Have children hold up the sticker.
- Have children stick the sticker and say: *It's a forest.*
- Repeat with the other stickers (city, river, mountains).

B52 10. Listen and circle.

- Remind children to listen and circle the answer to each question.
- Confirm answers with the class.

Audio Script

1. Where do bears live?
   They live in the forest.
2. Where do goats live?
   They live in the mountains.
3. Where do fish live?
   They live in the river.
4. Where does the mouse live?
   It lives in the field.

I Can! Use the Reward Sticker

- Help children talk about what they have learned in this unit. Encourage them to use positive language. (See page T33 for examples.)
- Distribute the reward stickers.
- Show children where to stick the stickers (on the Unit 9 Good Job! placeholder).

CONSOLIDATING

Congratulations Chant (10 minutes)

Do the Congratulation Chant (see page T83) to celebrate the English children have learned in Unit 9 and during the entire year.

Social Studies Project: Make a Recycling Poster

- Discuss which items can be recycled in your community and why it's important to recycle.
- Provide children with art supplies.
- Have children create posters to remind families and friends to recycle.

Workbook Page 93

Have children draw a picture to show where they live. Have children color the page. Then invite partners to share their work by saying: *I live in the [city].*

OPTIONAL: USING DIGITAL COMPONENTS

CD-ROM

Have children play the games and do the activities on the CD-ROM at home to show their families what they're learning about in class.

ActiveTeach

Use ActiveTeach to check answers as a class. Then play the live-action video for Unit 9 for the class.

REVIEW I can!

9 Stick and say. B52 **10 Listen and circle.**

1

2

3

4

Project

Review/Assessment: *Where do [bears] live? [They] live in the [forest]. Where does [the mouse] live? [It] lives in the [field].* **Project:** social studies

EXTRA PRACTICE

Match. Ask and answer.

Practice: *Where do you [sing]? In the [music room].*

Unit 2: Extra Practice

Objective: To reinforce the speaking practice on page 19

Vocabulary/Structures: *Where do you [sing]? / In the [music room].*

Optional Materials: Class Audio CD A, CD-ROM, ActiveTeach, Picture Cards, ball

GETTING READY

Ball Toss (5 minutes)

- Display the Unit 2 Picture Cards on the board.
- Have children line up.
- Toss a ball to the first child in line (C1).
- C1 walks to the board and points to an action card: *Where do you [read]?*
- C1 tosses the ball to C2.
- C2 walks to the board and points to the answer card: *In the [classroom].*
- C2 tosses the ball to C3.
- C3 walks to the board and points to another action card: *Where do you [sing]?*
- Continue this way with all children.

A18 Practice Intonation (5 minutes)

- Play the audio for Exercise 4 on page 18.
- Focus on the different intonation for questions and answers.
- Have children repeat each question and answer after listening to the audio.
- Alternate between having children repeat chorally and having pairs speak individually.

WORKING IN THE BOOK: PAGE 94

Match. Ask and answer.

- Have children open to page 94.
- Focus on the boy and girl with speech bubbles at the bottom of the page.
- With a prepared volunteer, read the speech bubble text aloud.
- Explain that partners will follow this question and answer model to complete the page, substituting other vocabulary.
- Read the speech bubble text again and have children repeat.
- Then point out the line matching the singing boy with the picture of the music room.
- Have partners complete the page together and then come together as a class to check answers.

CONSOLIDATING

Extension (5 minutes)

- Extend the speaking practice to focus on familiar vocabulary from Level 2, Unit 5 (bathroom, bedroom, dining room, kitchen, living room).
- Pretend to eat some food. Ask: *Where do you eat?*
- Cue the response: *In the dining room / kitchen.*
- Repeat with other actions for rooms, such as *cook*, *watch TV*, *sleep*, *brush your teeth*, *wash your hands*, and *read*. Use gestures and act out each one to clarify the meaning.

Make a Home Connection

Have children practice at home by asking and answering questions about what family members do in rooms at home.

OPTIONAL: USING DIGITAL COMPONENTS

CD-ROM

Have children listen to and repeat audio activities on the CD-ROM at home to reinforce their speaking skills.

ActiveTeach

Use the pointer to focus on the speech bubbles. Cover the words *sing* and *music room*. Write in *read* and *classroom*. Read the new question and answer aloud to model substituting other vocabulary.

Unit 3: Extra Practice

Objective: To reinforce the speaking practice on page 29

Vocabulary/Structures: *I want to be an [artist].*

Optional Materials: Class Audio CD A, CD-ROM, ActiveTeach

GETTING READY

Make Eye Contact (5 minutes)

- Explain that usually, when people talk to each other, they make eye contact, or look directly at each other, and demonstrate with a volunteer. [Note that you might want to adjust this if children are from a culture where eye contact is not acceptable.]
- Have children practice asking and answering: *What do you want to be? I want to be [an artist].*
- Each time, encourage children to make eye contact with each other while speaking.

A30 Practice Intonation (5 minutes)

- Play the audio for Exercise 5 on page 29.
- Focus on the different intonation for the questions and answers.
- Have children repeat the questions and answers after listening to the audio.
- Play the audio a few times.

WORKING IN THE BOOK: PAGE 95

Look and draw. Say.

- Have children open to page 95.
- Focus on Lou and his speech and thought bubbles at the bottom of the page.
- Explain that partners will follow this model to complete the page, substituting other vocabulary in their answers.
- Read the speech bubble aloud and have children repeat.
- Then point to Lou's thought bubble. Explain that it shows a drawing of an artist because he wants to be an artist.
- Focus on the two pictures at the top of the page, where Sue is holding a stethoscope and Lou is holding a firefighter's hat. Explain that people often have different ideas of what they want to be and that Lou has two ideas on this page.
- Help children use those clues to figure out what Sue and Lou want to be.
- Have them draw a doctor in Sue's thought bubble and a firefighter in Lou's.
- Then have partners practice the line in Lou's speech bubble, substituting *doctor* and *firefighter*.
- Display the unit Picture Cards and have children work with partners and take turns pointing and saying what they want to be.

CONSOLIDATING

Silly Animal Extension (5 minutes)

- Extend the speaking practice to focus on animal vocabulary that children learned in Levels 1 and 2: bird, cat, cow, dog, duck, fish, goat, hen, horse, mouse, sheep, turtle.
- Pretend to fly like a bird. Say: *I want to be a bird. What do you want to be?*
- Cue a prepared volunteer to pretend to gallop like a horse and answer: *I want to be a horse.*
- Have partners ask and answer.

Make a Home Connection

Have children practice asking and answering questions with family members.

OPTIONAL: USING DIGITAL COMPONENTS

CD-ROM

Have children listen to and repeat the audio activities on the CD-ROM at home to reinforce their speaking skills.

ActiveTeach

Use the pointer to focus on the speech / thought bubbles. Cover the words *an artist*. Write in *a doctor*. Read the new line aloud to model substituting other vocabulary.

UNIT 3

EXTRA PRACTICE

Look and draw. Say.

Practice: *I want to be an [artist].*

UNIT 4

EXTRA PRACTICE

Trace and say. Ask and answer.

1

fire station

2

school

3

post office

4

police station

One. Where does he work?

He works at a fire station.

Practice: *Where does [he] work? [He] works at a [fire station].*

Unit 4: Extra Practice

Objective: To reinforce the speaking practice on page 39

Vocabulary/Structures: *Where does [he] work? / [He] works at a [fire station].*

Optional Materials: Class Audio CD A, CD-ROM, ActiveTeach, Sammy the Squirrel puppet

GETTING READY

Speak a Little Louder (5 minutes)

- Help children develop confidence in speaking by improving their ability to project their voices.
- Have partners stand facing each other.
- C1 says: *My [mom] is a [firefighter]. Where does [she] work?*
- C2 answers: *[She] works at a [fire station].*
- Have them switch roles.
- Then have them stand as far away from each other in the classroom as they can.
- Have them ask and answer again. Cue them to speak louder because they are farther away.

A44 Practice Intonation (5 minutes)

- Play the audio for Exercise 4 on page 38.
- Focus on the different intonation for the questions and answers.
- Have children repeat each question and answer after listening to the audio.
- Alternate between having children repeat chorally and having pairs speak individually.

WORKING IN THE BOOK: PAGE 96

Trace and say. Ask and answer.

- Have children open to page 96.
- Point to each place. Say the name and run your finger under the word.
- Explain that children will trace the words.
- Then have children say the words and trace them.
- Focus on the girl and boy with speech bubbles at the bottom of the page.
- Read the speech bubbles aloud. Explain that partners will follow this model to complete the page, substituting other vocabulary to complete the different items.
- Read the speech bubbles again and have children repeat.
- Have partners practice together independently.

CONSOLIDATING

Extension (5 minutes)

- Use Sammy the Squirrel to extend the practice by focusing on the vocabulary for places at school that children learned in Unit 2.
- Say: *My brother is a student. Where does he [play]?*
- Have Sammy answer: *In the playground.*
- Have partners practice asking and answering about their brothers or sisters, as well as cousins and friends.

Make a Home Connection

Have children practice asking and answering questions about workers and the places they work in the community with family members.

OPTIONAL: USING DIGITAL COMPONENTS

CD-ROM

Have children listen to and repeat the audio activities on the CD-ROM at home to reinforce their speaking skills.

ActiveTeach

Use the pointer to focus on the speech bubbles. Cover the words *One*, *he*, and *fire station*. Write in Two, *he*, and *school*. Read the new question and then the answer aloud to model substituting other vocabulary. Be sure to cover *He* and *fire station* in the answer.

Unit 5: Extra Practice

Objective: To reinforce the speaking practice on page 49

Vocabulary/Structures: *What's [he] wearing? / [He's] wearing a [blue] [shirt].*

Optional Materials: Class Audio CD A, CD-ROM, ActiveTeach, ball, index cards or small pieces of paper

GETTING READY

Ball Toss (5 minutes)

- Have children stand in a circle.
- Toss a ball to one child (C1).
- Gesture to another child in the circle. Ask: *What's [Paula] wearing?*
- C1 answers: *[She's] wearing [a blue dress].*
- C1 tosses the ball to C2 and asks about a different child: *What's [Rocco] wearing?*
- Continue this way with all children.

A57 Practice Intonation (5 minutes)

- Play the audio for Exercise 4 on page 48.
- Focus on the different intonation for questions and answers.
- Have children repeat each question and answer after the audio.
- Alternate between having children repeat chorally and having pairs speak individually.

WORKING IN THE BOOK: PAGE 97

Color. Ask and answer.

- Have children open to page 97.
- Have children use the color key to color in Lou's outfit.
- For example, Lou's shirt has the number *1*. The number 1 in the color key is blue, so children color Lou's shirt blue.
- Focus on the boy and girl with speech bubbles at the bottom of the page.
- Read the speech bubbles aloud. Explain that partners will follow this model to complete the page, substituting other colors and clothes.
- Read the speech bubbles again and have children repeat.
- Have partners complete the page together.
- Reconvene to check the page with the class to be sure that children colored Lou's pants red, his socks orange, and his shoes green.

CONSOLIDATING

Extension (5 minutes)

- Extend the speaking practice to review language from previous units.
- Write question cards and answer cards with questions and answers from Units 2-5:

  Where do you play?
  In the playground.

  What do you want to be?
  I want to be an artist.

  Where does a nurse work?
  In a hospital.

  What's she wearing?
  She's wearing green.
- Give the question cards to four children and the answer cards to four others. (If children cannot read their cards, tell them what to say.)
- The children with question cards read their questions aloud and show them to the group.
- The children with answer cards do the same.
- Cue the class to match the questions and answers.

Make a Home Connection

Have children practice asking and answering questions with family members.

OPTIONAL: USING DIGITAL COMPONENTS

CD-ROM

Have children listen to and repeat the audio activities on the CD-ROM at home to reinforce their speaking skills.

ActiveTeach

Use the pointer to focus on the speech bubbles. Cover the words *One*, and *a blue shirt*. Write in *Two* and *red pants*. Read the new question and answer aloud to model substituting other vocabulary.

UNIT 5

EXTRA PRACTICE

Color. Ask and answer.

Practice: *What's [he] wearing? [He's] wearing a [blue] [shirt].*

UNIT 6

EXTRA PRACTICE

Ask and answer.

Practice: *How does [he] feel? He's [mad].*

Unit 6: Extra Practice

Objective: To reinforce the speaking practice on page 59

Vocabulary/Structures: *How does [he] feel? / [He's] [mad].*

Optional Materials: Class Audio CD B, CD-ROM, ActiveTeach, Sammy the Squirrel puppet

GETTING READY

Focus on Posture (5 minutes)

- Model with Sammy the Squirrel.
- Slouch and look down while you say: *Hi, Sammy.*
- Have Sammy say: *Teacher, please stand up straight.*
- Stand up straight, hold your head up, and say: *Hi Sammy*. This time, make your voice a little clearer and louder.
- Explain that it's important to stand up straight when you are speaking.
- Have children practice using proper posture when speaking during this lesson.

B5 Practice Intonation (5 minutes)

- Play the audio for Exercise 4 on page 58.
- Focus on the different speakers' intonation and pronunciation for the questions and the answers.
- Have children repeat each line, imitating the pronunciation and intonation for the questions and answers.
- Alternate between having children repeat chorally and having pairs speak individually.
- Encourage children to be expressive when they speak to show how they feel.

WORKING IN THE BOOK: PAGE 98

Ask and answer.

- Have children open to page 98.
- Explain that the scene shows Lou and his family at a wedding.
- Focus on the girl and boy with speech bubbles at the bottom of the page.
- Read the speech bubbles aloud. Explain that partners will follow this model to complete the page, substituting other vocabulary to complete the different items.
- For each one, ask children to name how the person feels. (*1: he's mad; 2: she's tired; 3: he's happy; 4: she's excited; 5: he's hungry; 6: she's thirsty*).
- Read the speech bubbles again and have children repeat.
- Then have partners complete the page together.

CONSOLIDATING

Extension (5 minutes)

- Extend the speaking practice to focus on other vocabulary and structures.
- Point to different references on the page and ask questions like the following:

  Is this [a cake]?
  Is it [green]?
  Where's [the cake]?
  How many [noses]?
  Can you see [a white dress]?
  What's this?
  What color is it?
  Is the [dress] [blue]?

Make a Home Connection

Have children practice asking and answering questions about how their family members are feeling.

OPTIONAL: USING DIGITAL COMPONENTS

CD-ROM

Have children listen to and repeat the audio activities on the CD-ROM at home to reinforce their speaking skills.

ActiveTeach

Use the pointer to focus on the speech bubbles. Cover the words *One*, *he*, *He's*, and *mad*. Write in *Two*, *she*, *She's*, and *tired*. Read the new question and answer aloud to model substituting other vocabulary.

Unit 7: Extra Practice

Objective: To reinforce the speaking practice on page 69

Vocabulary/Structures: *What do you want? / I want [a carrot], please.*

Optional Materials: Class Audio CD B, CD-ROM, ActiveTeach, Sammy the Squirrel puppet, Picture Cards

GETTING READY

B18 Practice Intonation (5 minutes)

- Play the audio for Exercise 4 on page 68.
- Focus on the different intonation for the questions and answers.
- Have children repeat each question and answer after listening to the audio.
- Alternate between having children repeat chorally and having pairs speak individually.

Listen Carefully (5 minutes)

- Have partners practice asking and answering: *What do you want? / I want [an orange], please.*
- Model the activity with Sammy and a few volunteers.
- Have Sammy and C1 practice the conversation.
- Then have Sammy cover his eyes so he can't see.
- Sammy asks: *What do you want?*
- C1, C2, and C3 each take turns answering.
- Sammy has to identify C1 by the sound of his or her voice.
- Then invite children to play the same game.

WORKING IN THE BOOK: PAGE 99

Trace and say. Ask and answer.

- Have children open to page 99.
- Have children point to the different foods and say the words.
- Show them how to trace the words.
- Have children trace the words.
- Focus on the girl and boy with speech bubbles at the bottom of the page.
- Read the speech bubbles aloud. Explain that partners will follow this model to complete the page, substituting other vocabulary.
- Read the speech bubbles again and have children repeat.
- Then have partners practice the dialogue, substituting the different foods shown on the page.

CONSOLIDATING

Extension (5 minutes)

- Extend the practice to focus on other vocabulary. Display a variety of Picture Cards and realia that children can name.
- Model with Sammy. Ask: *What do you want?*
- Sammy answers: *I want [the book].* Hand him [the book].
- Then have children practice with Sammy or with partners.

Make a Home Connection

Have children practice asking and answering with family members about items at home.

OPTIONAL: USING DIGITAL COMPONENTS

CD-ROM

Have children listen to and repeat the audio activities on the CD-ROM at home to reinforce their speaking skills.

ActiveTeach

Use the pointer to focus on the speech bubbles. Cover the words *One* and *a carrot*. Write in *Two* and *a mango*. Read the new question and answer aloud to model substituting other vocabulary. Continue with the other words.

UNIT 7

EXTRA PRACTICE

Trace and say. Ask and answer.

1  carrot

2 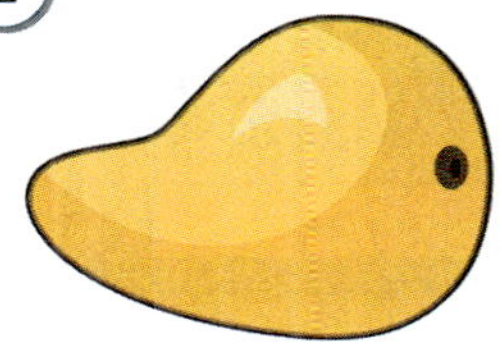 mango

3  orange

4  salad

5  banana

6  juice

One. What do you want?

I want a carrot, please.

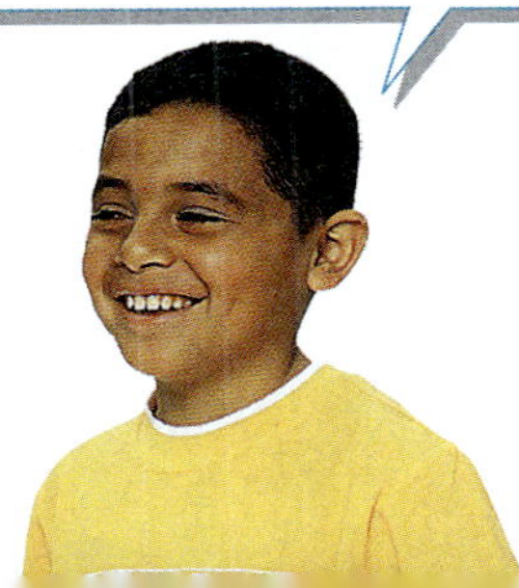

Practice: *What do you want? I want [a carrot], please.*

UNIT 8 EXTRA PRACTICE

Ask and answer.

Practice: *What's that? It's a [big] [lion].*

Unit 8: Extra Practice

Objective: To reinforce the speaking practice on page 79

Vocabulary/Structures: *What's that? / It's a [big] [lion].*

Optional Materials: Class Audio CD B, CD-ROM, ActiveTeach, Picture Cards, ball

GETTING READY

Ball Toss (5 minutes)

- Display the Unit 8 Picture Cards on the board.
- Have children line up.
- Toss a ball to the first child in line (C1).
- C1 walks to the board, points to an animal card, and asks: *What's that?*
- C1 tosses the ball to C2.
- C2 answers: *It's a [lion].*
- C2 walks to the board, points to a different card, and asks: *What's that?*
- C2 tosses the ball to C3. C3 answers.
- Continue this way with other children.

B31 Practice Intonation (5 minutes)

- Play the audio for Exercise 4 on page 78.
- Focus on the different intonation for questions and answers.
- Have children repeat each question and answer after listening to the audio.
- Alternate between having children repeat chorally and having pairs speak individually.

WORKING IN THE BOOK: PAGE 100

Ask and answer.

- Have children open to page 100.
- Focus on the girl and boy with speech bubbles at the bottom of the page.
- Read the speech bubbles aloud. Explain that partners will follow this model to complete the page, substituting other vocabulary.
- Read the speech bubbles again and have children repeat.
- Have partners complete the page together.
- Reconvene to check partners' responses as a class.

CONSOLIDATING

Extension (5 minutes)

- Extend the speaking practice to focus on other vocabulary. Display Picture Cards for vocabulary from other units that you want children to practice.
- Invite volunteers to come to the board, point to a Picture Card, and ask: *What's that?*
- Cue the class to respond together, or invite individuals to respond one at a time.

Make a Home Connection

Have children practice asking and answering questions with family members.

OPTIONAL: USING DIGITAL COMPONENTS

CD-ROM

Have children listen to and repeat the audio activities on the CD-ROM at home to reinforce their speaking skills.

ActiveTeach

Use the pointer to focus on the speech bubbles. Cover the words *One* and *big lion*. Write in *Two* and *small bat*. Read the new question and answer aloud to model substituting other vocabulary.

Unit 9: Extra Practice

Objective: To reinforce the speaking practice on page 89

Vocabulary/Structures: *Where do [goats] live? / They live in the [mountains].*

Optional Materials: Class Audio CD B, CD-ROM, ActiveTeach, Sammy the Squirrel puppet, Picture Cards, blindfold

GETTING READY

Spin and Point (5 minutes)

- Display the Unit 9 Picture Cards on the board.
- Have children stand in a circle and invite a volunteer to the center.
- The volunteer chooses a Picture Card.
- Place a blindfold over the volunteer's eyes and have the volunteer make a pointing gesture.
- Spin the volunteer in a circle and then stop.
- Have the volunteer ask whomever he or she is pointing to, to say a sentence about the Picture Card.
- That child then comes to center to get the blindfold and the game continues.

B44 Practice Intonation (5 minutes)

- Play the audio for Exercise 4 on page 88.
- Focus on the different intonation for questions and answers.
- Have children repeat each question and answer after listening to the audio.
- Alternate between having children repeat chorally and having pairs speak individually.

WORKING IN THE BOOK: PAGE 101

Match. Ask and answer.

- Have children open to page 101.
- Focus on the girl and boy with speech bubbles at the bottom of the page.
- Read the speech bubbles aloud. Explain that partners will follow this model to complete the page, substituting other vocabulary.
- Read the speech bubbles again and have children repeat.
- Have partners complete the page together by asking and answering questions and by matching the animals to the scenes.
- Reconvene to check answers as a class.

CONSOLIDATING

Extension (5 minutes)

- Extend the speaking practice by playing a guessing game.
- Whisper an animal name in each child's ear.
- Sammy asks a child: *Where do you live?*
- The child answers based on the animal you named.
- The class has to guess the animal.

Make a Home Connection

Have children practice asking and answering questions with family members about animals and their homes.

OPTIONAL: USING DIGITAL COMPONENTS

CD-ROM

Have children listen to and repeat the audio activities on the CD-ROM at home to reinforce their speaking skills.

ActiveTeach

Use the pointer to focus on the speech bubbles. Cover the words *goats* and *the mountains*. Write in *ducks*, and *rivers*. Read the new question and answer aloud to model substituting other vocabulary.

UNIT 9

EXTRA PRACTICE

Match. Ask and answer.

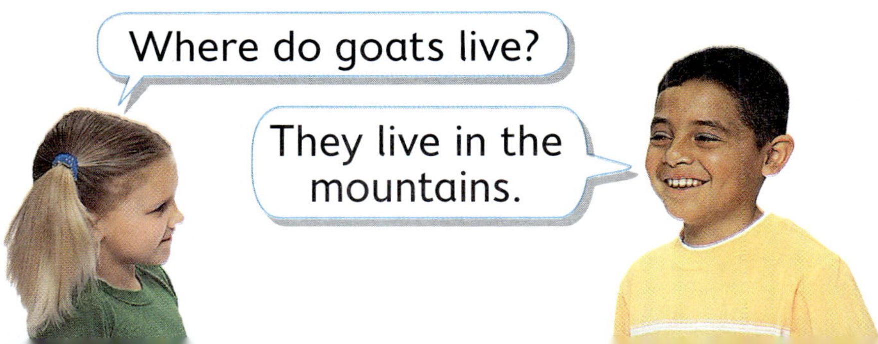

Practice: *Where do [goats] live? They live in the [mountains].*

HOLIDAYS New Year's

B53 Cut and paste. Sing.

Cutouts on page 107

Presentation: *Happy New Year* **Review:** *clock*

Holidays: New Year's

Objectives: To talk about New Year's, to learn New Year's words and phrases, to sing a song

New Holidays Structure: Happy New Year!

Review: clock

Materials: Class Audio CD B, scissors, paste or glue

Optional Materials: large pieces of stiff paper cut into triangles, art supplies, decorations for party hats, tape, ActiveTeach

GETTING READY

Share What You Know (10 minutes)

- Talk about holidays.
- Ask children to name holidays they know and celebrate.
- Ask if anyone celebrates New Year's. How do they celebrate?
- Tell children that in some places around the world, people stay up late (until midnight) the night before (New Year's Eve) and have parties to celebrate the holiday. Explain that at midnight, everyone says, "Happy New Year!" and uses noisemakers to celebrate.

WORKING IN THE BOOK: PAGE 102

B53 Cut and paste. Sing.

- Have children open to page 102.
- Point to the scene and ask children what they think is happening.
- Explain that Sue and Lou are at a New Year's party.
- Point to the clock. Help children understand that it's midnight . . . time to celebrate.
- Point out the balloons, Sue's party hat, and Sue's noisemaker.
- Ask: *Where's Lou's hat? Where's Lou's noisemaker?*
- Have children turn to page 107.
- Help children cut out the hat and noisemaker and glue them to page 102.
- Say: *Let's learn a song.*
- Play the song a few times.
- Encourage children to join in when they're ready.

Audio Script

New Year's

Fireworks sparkle, sparkle bright
Every year on New Year's night.
Once a year we stay up late. Oh, we love to celebrate.
Fireworks sparkle, sparkle bright
Every year on New Year's night.

CONSOLIDATING

Make a Party Hat (15 minutes)

- Prepare large pieces of stiff paper, cut into triangles for hats.
- Distribute art supplies and other decorations.
- Have children decorate the triangles on one side.
- As each child finishes, wrap the triangle around his or her head for fit, and then tape it closed.
- Have children wear their hats to sing "New Year's" one more time.

OPTIONAL: USING DIGITAL COMPONENTS

ActiveTeach

Use ActiveTeach to show children where to paste or glue Lou's hat and noisemaker.

Holidays: Valentine's Day

Objectives: To talk about Valentine's Day, to learn Valentine's Day words and phrases, to sing a song

New Holidays Structures: Happy Valentine's Day

Review: mom

Materials: Class Audio CD B, scissors, paste or glue

Optional Materials: red or pink paper cut into a heart shape, markers, decorations, ActiveTeach

GETTING READY

Share What You Know (10 minutes)

- Talk about holidays.
- Ask children to name holidays they know and celebrate.
- Ask if anyone celebrates Valentine's Day. How do they celebrate?
- Tell children that people sometimes send Valentine's cards to people they love and that sometimes people give presents, too, like chocolate, balloons, flowers, or toys.

WORKING IN THE BOOK: PAGE 103

B55 Cut and paste. Sing.

- Have children open to page 103.
- Point to the scene and ask children what they think is happening.
- Read the speech bubble aloud and have children repeat.
- Explain that it's Valentine's Day.
- Have children turn to page 107.
- Tell children to choose one of the gifts: the teddy bear or the pair of balloons. Have them cut one of them out and paste or glue it onto Sue's mom's hands on page 103.
- Say: *Let's learn a song.*
- Play the song a few times.
- Encourage children to join in when they're ready.

Audio Script

Valentine's Day

Today we give out cards and treats,
Cards and treats, cards and treats.
Today we give out cards and treats
And say "I love you!"

CONSOLIDATING

Make a Valentine (15 minutes)

- For each child, you will need one piece of red or pink paper cut into a heart. To do this, fold the paper in half and then cut out a half heart shape and then open it out.
- Distribute markers and decorations.
- Have children choose someone they love and make a Valentine for him or her.
- Write sentences on the board for children to copy. Talk about what each one means and have children practice saying it:

  Dear [Mommy],
  Happy Valentine's Day.
  I love you.
  Love,
  [Gillian]

OPTIONAL: USING DIGITAL COMPONENTS

ActiveTeach

Focus on the speech bubble and then show children where to glue the cutout of the present they chose.

HOLIDAYS Valentine's Day

B55 **Cut and paste. Sing.**

Cutouts on page 107

Holidays: Easter

Objectives: To talk about Easter, to learn Easter words and phrases, to sing a song

New Holidays Vocabulary: Easter, egg

Review: flower, grass, pink; blue, green, red, yellow

Materials: Class Audio CD B

Optional Materials: ActiveTeach, scissors, paste or glue, colored paper, markers, decorations

GETTING READY

Share What You Know (10 minutes)

- Talk about holidays.
- Ask children to name holidays they know and celebrate.
- Ask if anyone celebrates Easter. How do they celebrate?
- Explain that children often go on Easter egg hunts at Easter. Explain that they look for eggs hidden by an Easter bunny and collect the eggs in Easter baskets.

WORKING IN THE BOOK: PAGE 104

B57 Find and color the eggs. Cut and paste. Sing.

- Have children open to page 104.
- Say: *Today is Easter. Lou and Sue are on an Easter egg hunt. Sue is dressed as an Easter bunny. Help them find the eggs.*
- Have children find the eggs in the picture and color them.
- Then have children turn to page 109.
- Have them cut out the flowers, eggs, chocolate bunny, and girl.
- Show them how to glue the eggs in Lou's basket. Tell them to glue the flowers, bunny, and girl anywhere they want.

- Say: *Let's sing a song about Easter.*
- Play the song a few times. Encourage children to join in when they are ready.

Audio Script

Easter

The Easter Bunny came.
He hid the eggs away.
Here come the children.
They will have fun today.
Put the eggs in baskets.
Count them one by one.
Laugh and play and sing
under the shining sun.

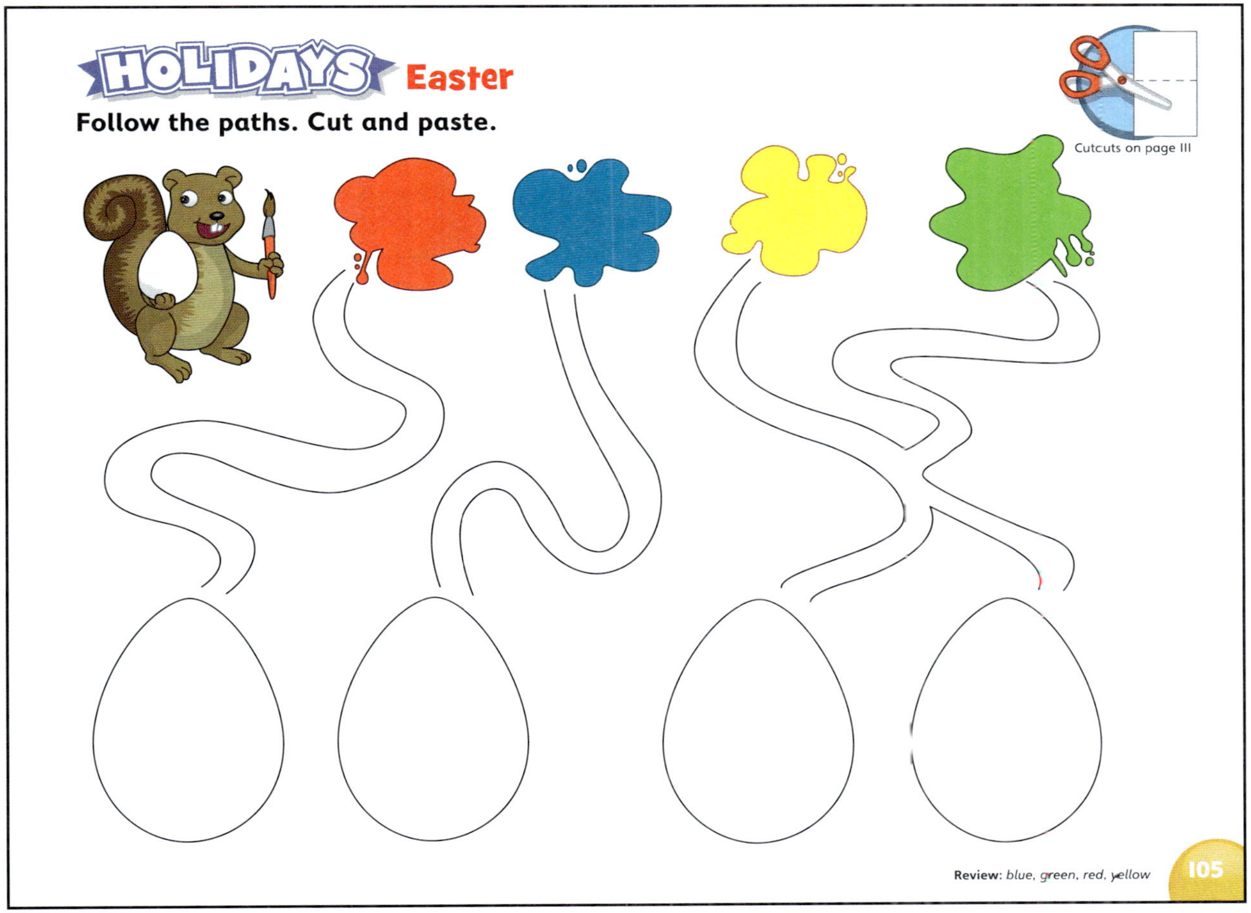

WORKING IN THE BOOK: PAGE 105

Follow the paths. Cut and paste.

- Have children turn to page 105.
- Point to each different color. Ask children: *What color is this?*
- Point to the empty egg shapes at the bottom of the page.
- Have children turn to page 111.
- Help them cut out the eggs.
- Show them how to match the egg cutouts with the colors and say: *Touch [red]. Follow the path.* (Use a red crayon to trace the red path to the egg.) *Glue the red egg here.*

CONSOLIDATING

Easter Egg Hunt (15 minutes)

- Cut out oval egg shapes from different colored paper.
- Have children decorate the oval shapes to look like pretty Easter eggs.
- Gather the eggs.
- Have children put their heads down so they can't see.
- Hide the eggs around the room.
- Invite children to go on an Easter egg hunt around the room. Tell them to look only for their own egg.
- As each child finds his or her egg, have them describe the location: *It's [under] the [red table].*

OPTIONAL: USING DIGITAL COMPONENTS

ActiveTeach

Use ActiveTeach to show children where to glue the cutouts and how to follow the paths.

Cutouts and Stickers

The cutouts for the Holiday lessons that begin on Student Book page 107 and are shown on page T107 of this book are available for use on Student Book pages 102–105. The stickers—at the back of the Student Book and shown on page T108—are available for use with the review lessons in units 2–9.

Cutouts

Cutout	Find on page:	Holiday	Use on lesson page:
party hat	107	New Year's	102
noisemaker	107	New Year's	102
teddy bear	107	Valentine's Day	103
balloons	107	Valentine's Day	103
flowers	109	Easter	104
Easter eggs	109	Easter	104
chocolate bunny	109	Easter	104
girl in Easter clothes	109	Easter	104
red Easter egg	111	Easter	105
yellow Easter egg	111	Easter	105
blue Easter egg	111	Easter	105
green Easter egg	111	Easter	105

Stickers

Sticker	Unit	Use on page:
music room	2	23
classroom	2	23
computer room	2	23
playground	2	23
firefighter	3	33
astronaut	3	33
police officer	3	33
vet	3	33
school	4	43
store	4	43
police station	4	43
hospital	4	43
shirt	5	53
skirt	5	53
shoes	5	53
jacket	5	53
happy	6	63
thirsty	6	63
excited	6	63
mad	6	63
banana	7	73
plate	7	73
fork	7	73
orange (n)	7	73
elephant	8	83
bat	8	83
sea lion	8	83
zebra	8	83
forest	9	93
city	9	93
river	9	93
mountains	9	93
Good job!	2–9	23, 33, 43, 53, 63, 73, 83, 93

Cutouts

Cut out one or more for page 102.

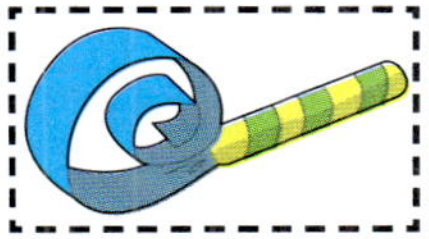

Cut out one or more for page 103.

Cut out one or more for page 104.

Cut out for page 105.

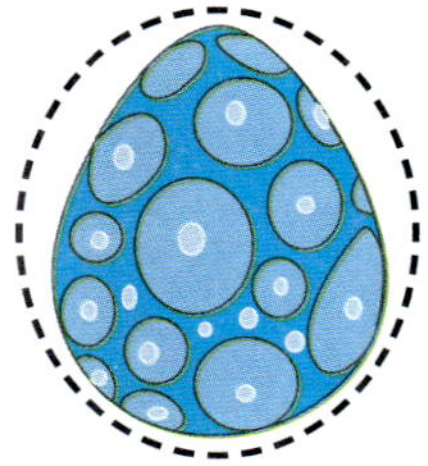

Stickers

Unit 2, page 23

Unit 3, page 33

Unit 4, page 43

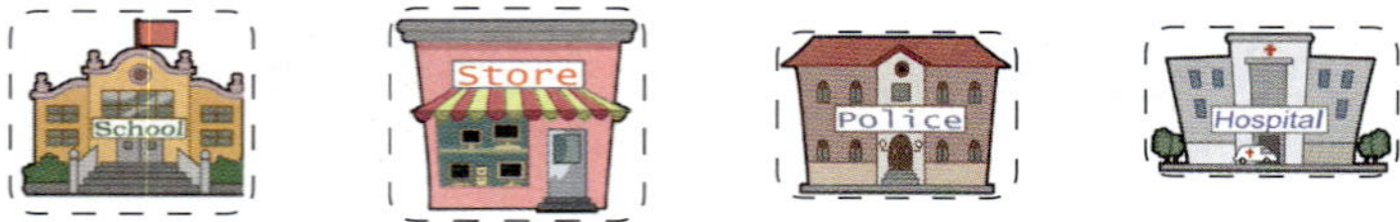

Unit 5, page 53

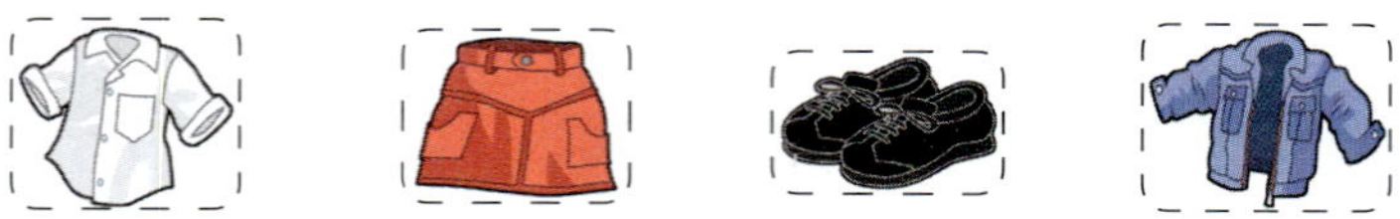

Unit 6, page 63

Unit 7, page 73

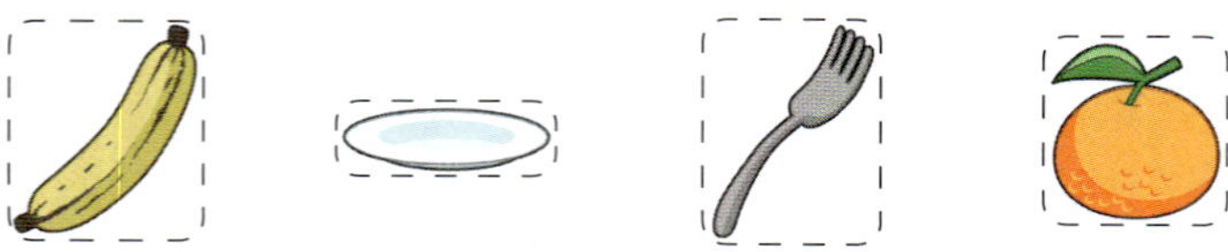

Unit 8, page 83

Unit 9, page 93

Good job!

Resources

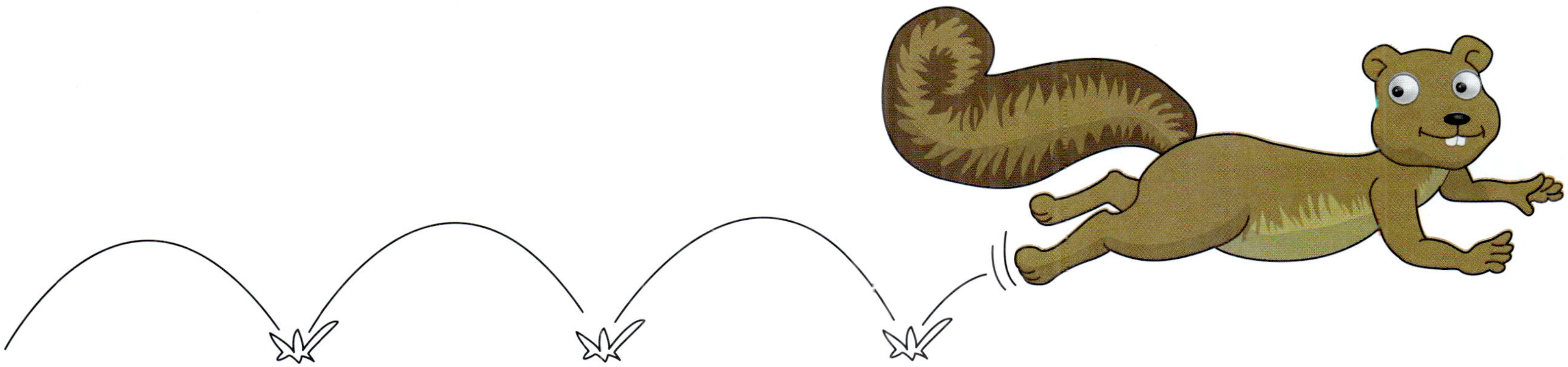

Workbook Pages

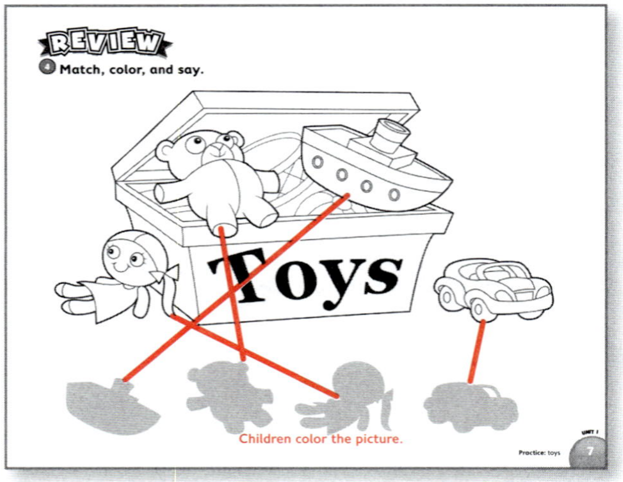

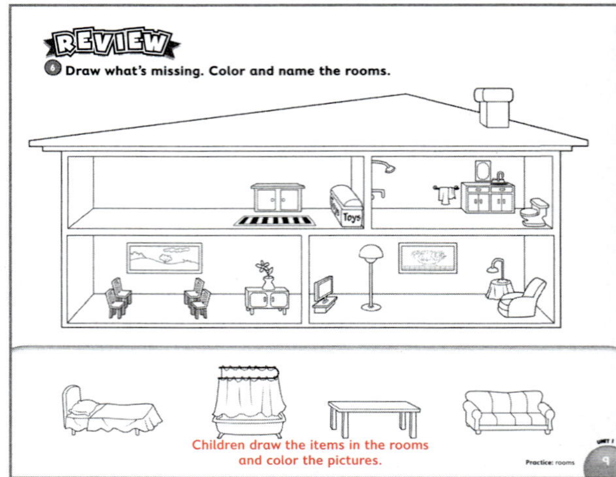

REVIEW

7 Match, color, and say.

Children color the picture.

10 Practice: food items

REVIEW

8 Trace, color, and say.

Children color the pictures.

UNIT 1 Practice: animals, body parts 11

REVIEW

9 Connect the dots. Color and say.

Children color the picture.

12 Practice: weather

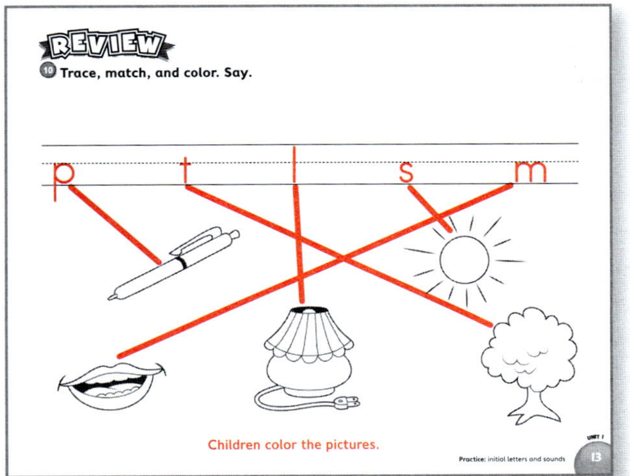
REVIEW

10 Trace, match, and color. Say.

p t l s m

Children color the pictures.

UNIT 1 Practice: initial letters and sounds 13

2 At School

1 Look and number. Color and say.

1 2 3 4

3 4 2 1

Children color the pictures.

14 Practice: classroom, computer room, music room, play, playground, read, sing, use the computer

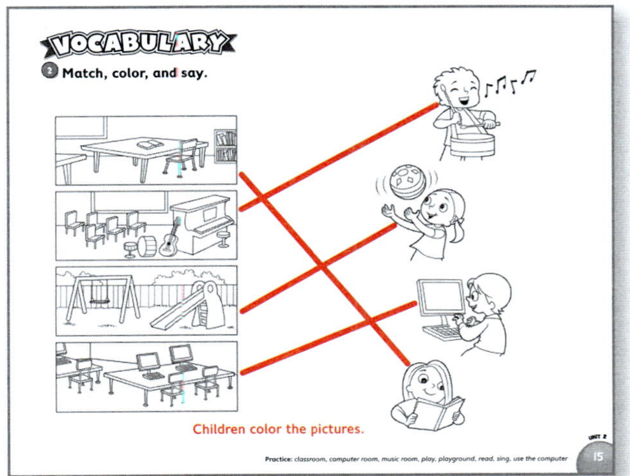
VOCABULARY

2 Match, color, and say.

Children color the pictures.

UNIT 2 Practice: classroom, computer room, music room, play, playground, read, sing, use the computer 15

Workbook Pages

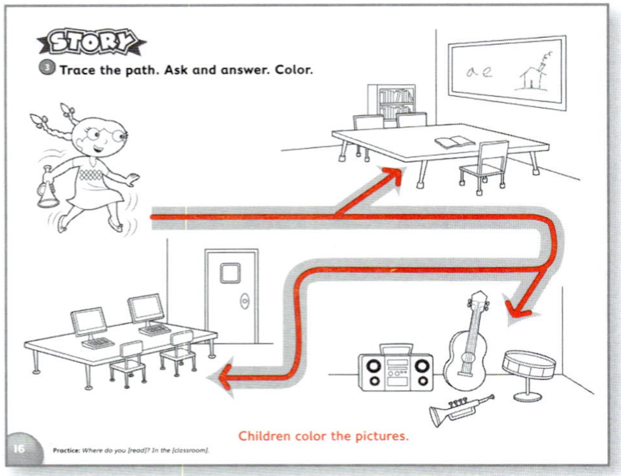

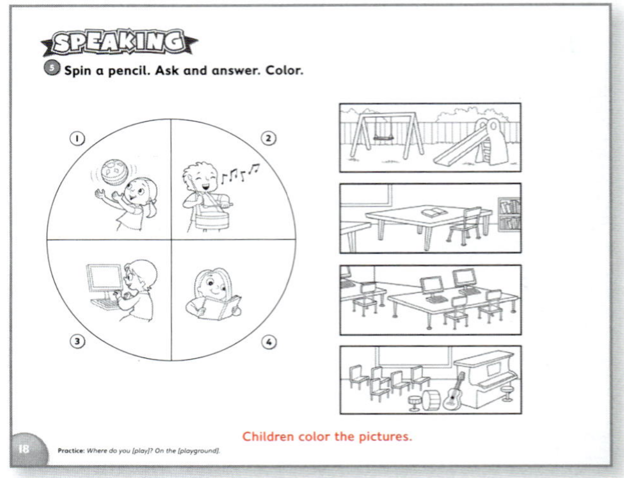

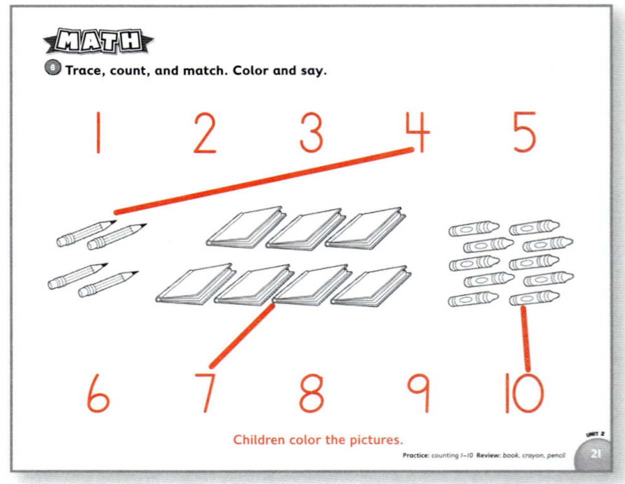

VALUES
9 Color and say.

Children color the picture.
22 **Values:** Follow rules.

REVIEW I can!
10 Draw your favorite place at school.
Color and say.

Children draw here and color the pictures.
UNIT 2
Review: *Where do you [play]? On the [playground].* 23

3 Workers
1 Connect the dots. Color and say.
Children color the picture.
24 **Practice:** firefighter

VOCABULARY
2 Match, color, and say.
Children color the pictures.
UNIT 3
Practice: artist, dentist, doctor, police officer **Review:** teacher 25

STORY
3 Circle what Sue wants to be in the story. Color and say.
Children color the pictures.
26 **Practice:** *I want to be a [police officer].*

STORY
4 Trace, color, and say.
Children color the picture.
UNIT 3
Practice: *I want to be a [firefighter].* 27

Workbook Pages

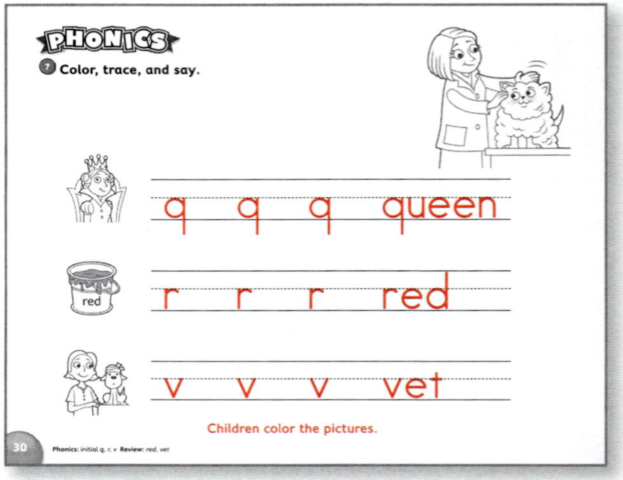

4 My Town
1 Trace, color, and say.
POLICE
Children color the picture.
34
Practice: police station Review: car

VOCABULARY
2 Follow the roads. Color and say.
STORE
BUS
POST OFFICE
SCHOOL
TAXI
Where are they going?
Children color the pictures.
35

STORY
3 Match and color. Ask and answer.
Where does she work?
FIRE STATION
HOSPITAL
Children color the pictures.
36

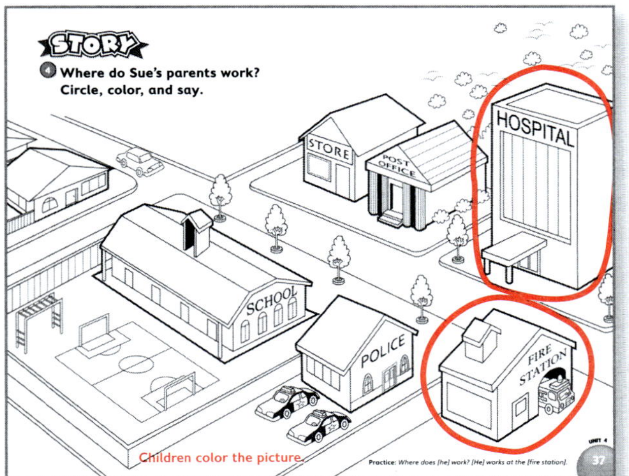
STORY
4 Where do Sue's parents work?
Circle, color, and say.
STORE
POST OFFICE
HOSPITAL
SCHOOL
POLICE
FIRE STATION
Children color the picture.
37

SPEAKING
5 Where does he/she work? Color and say.
1
2
3
4
Children color the picture.
38

SPEAKING
6 Circle the differences in Picture B. Color and say.
A
B
FIRE STATION
HOSPITAL
SCHOOL
STORE
FIRE STATION
HOSPITAL
POLICE
STORE
Children color the pictures.
39

Workbook Pages

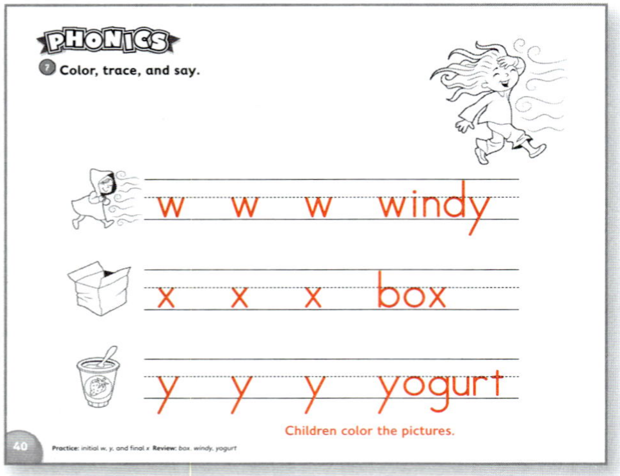

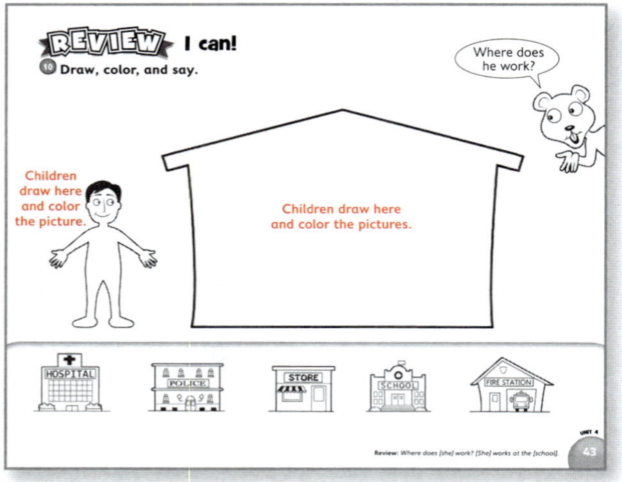

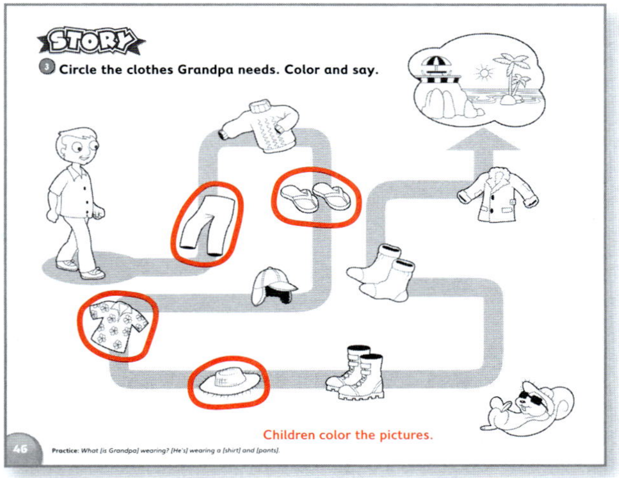
STORY
3 Circle the clothes Grandpa needs. Color and say.
Children color the pictures.
46
Practice: What [is Grandpa] wearing? [He's] wearing a [shirt] and [pants].

STORY
4 Trace Grandma's clothes. Color and say.
Children color the picture.
UNIT 5
Practice: What [is Grandma] wearing? [She's] wearing a [dress] and [shoes].
47

SPEAKING
5 Color. Ask and answer.
Children color the pictures.
48
Practice: What is [Sue] wearing? [She's] wearing a [blue dress].

SPEAKING
6 Trace, color, and say.
Children color the picture.
UNIT 5
Practice: What's [Lou] wearing? [He's] wearing a [yellow shirt].
49

PHONICS
7 Color, trace, and say.
e
bed
pen
hen
Children color the pictures.
50
Phonics: medial e Review: bed, hen, pen

MATH
8 Trace. Count the stripes. Write and color.
15 16
16
Children color the picture.
UNIT 5
Practice: counting 1–16
51

Workbook Pages

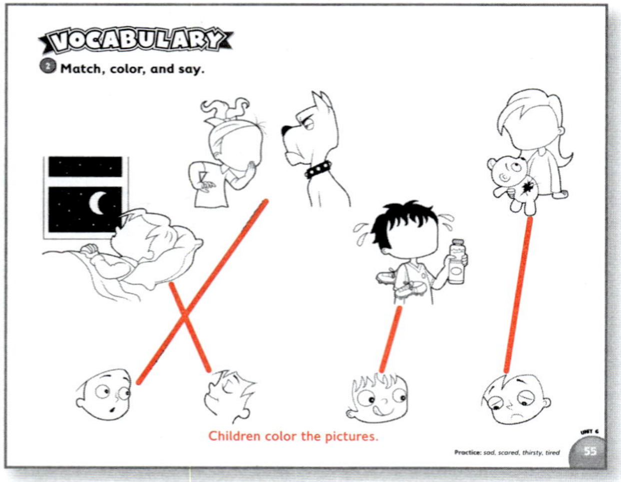

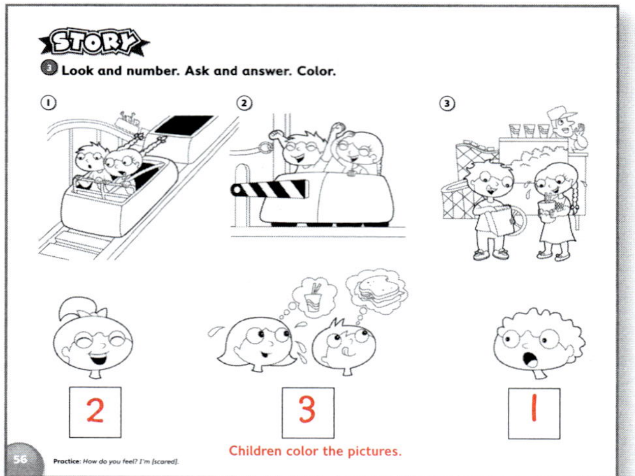

SPEAKING
5 Draw how they feel. Ask and answer. Color.
Children draw faces and color the pictures.
58
Practice: How does [he] feel? [He's] [happy].

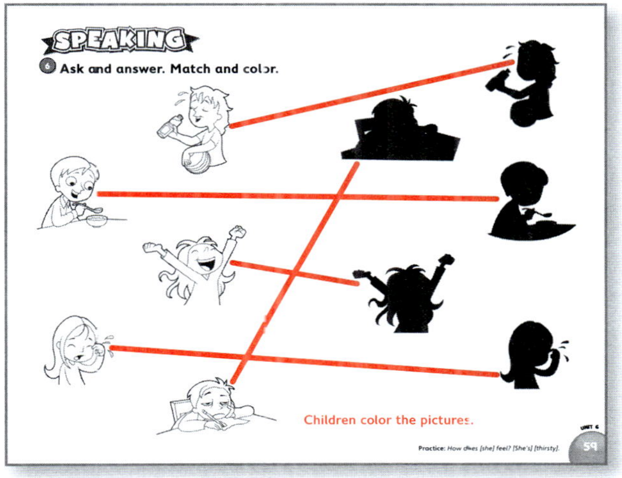
SPEAKING
6 Ask and answer. Match and color.
Children color the pictures.
UNIT 6
Practice: How does [she] feel? [She's] [thirsty].
59

PHONICS
7 Color, trace, and say.
a
cat
dad
hand
Children color the pictures.
60
Phonics: medial a Review: cat, dad, hand

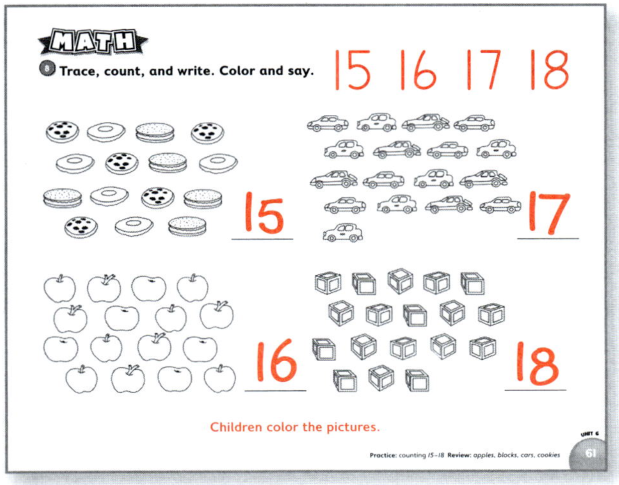
MATH
8 Trace, count, and write. Color and say.
15 16 17 18
15
17
16
18
Children color the pictures.
UNIT 6
Practice: counting 15–18 Review: apples, blocks, cars, cookies
61

VALUES
9 Color and say.
Don't fight!
Children color the picture.
62
Values: Don't fight.

REVIEW I can!
10 Draw how you feel. Color and say.
Children draw here and color the pictures.
UNIT 6
Review: How do you feel? I'm [tired].
63

Workbook Pages

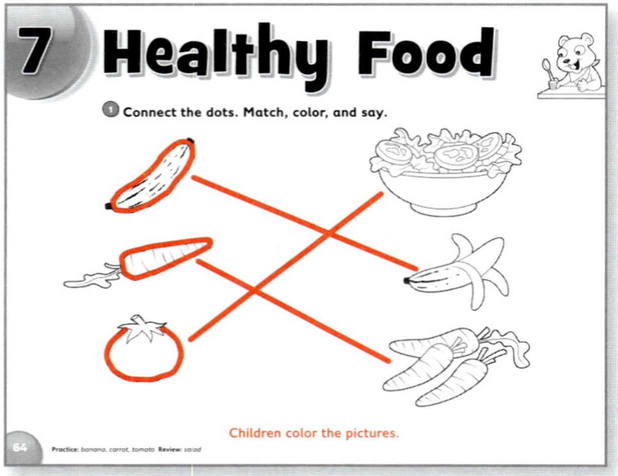

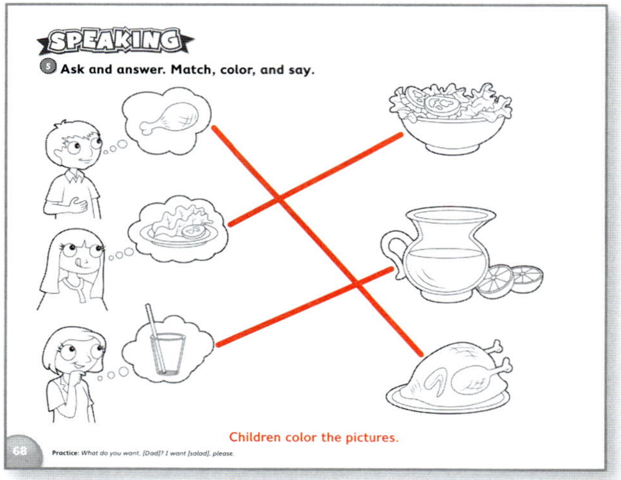

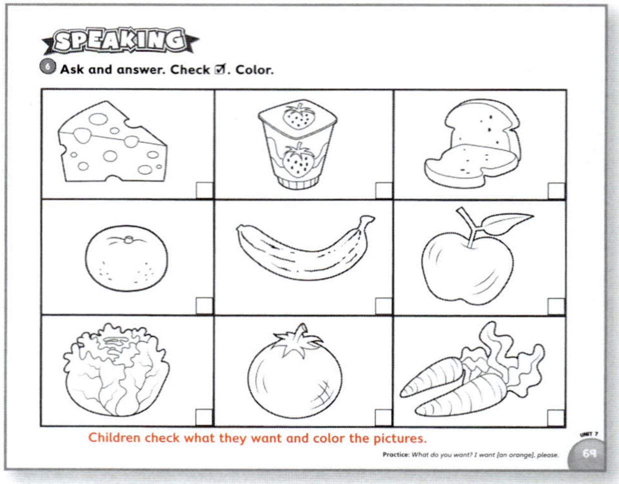

PHONICS

7 Color, trace, and say.

o

hot doll box

Children color the pictures.

70 Phonics: medial o Review: *box, doll, hot*

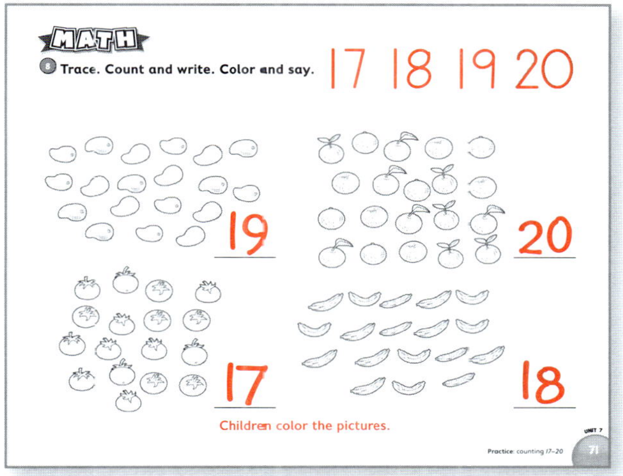

MATH

8 Trace. Count and write. Color and say. 17 18 19 20

19 20

17 18

Children color the pictures.

Practice: counting *17–20* UNIT 7 71

VALUES

9 Color the healthy food and say.

Eat healthy food.

Children color the banana, the carrot, the orange, the mango, and the salad.

72 Values: Eat healthy food.

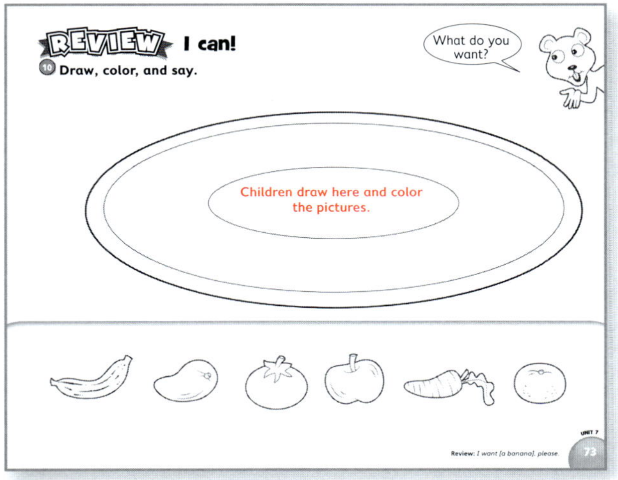

REVIEW I can!

10 Draw, color, and say.

What do you want?

Children draw here and color the pictures.

Review: *I want [a banana], please.* UNIT 7 73

8 The Zoo

1 Match, color, and say.

Children color the pictures.

74 Practice: *bear, monkey, penguin*

VOCABULARY

2 What's missing? Draw, color, and say.

Children draw and color the pictures.

Practice: *bat, elephant, lion, zebra* UNIT 8 75

Workbook Pages

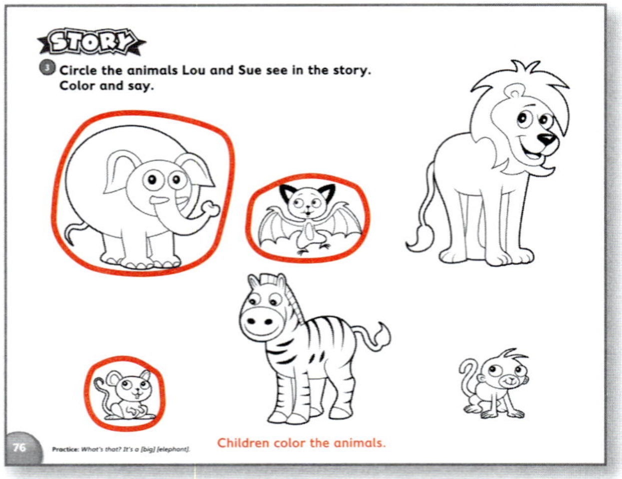

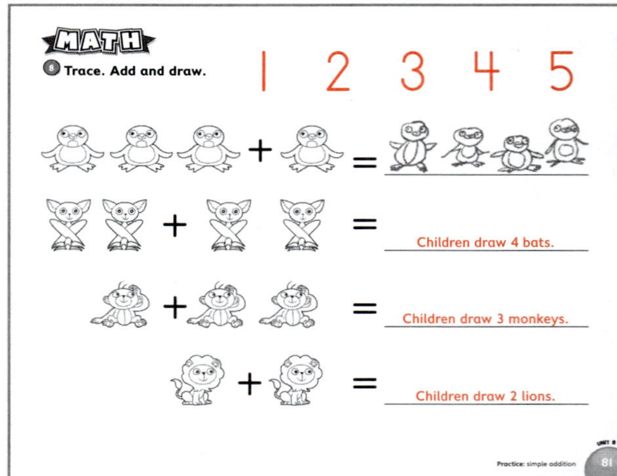

VALUES
9 Color and say.
Include everyone.
Children color the picture.
82
Values: Include everyone.

REVIEW I can!
10 Draw your favorite animal. Color and say.
Children draw here and color the pictures.
UNIT 8
Review: It's a [big] [bear].
83

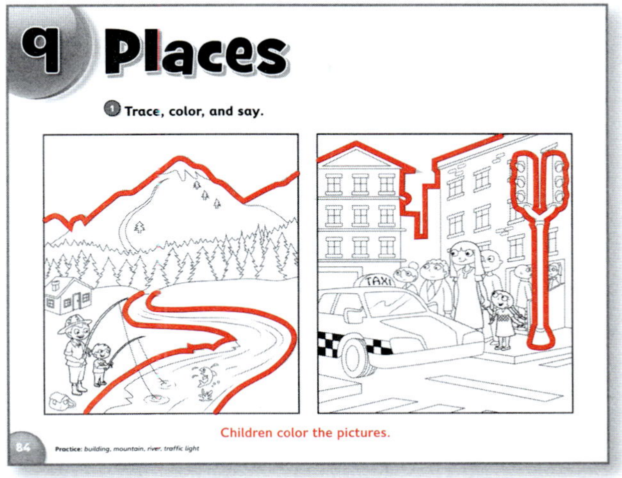
9 Places
1 Trace, color, and say.
TAXI
Children color the pictures.
84
Practice: building, mountain, river, traffic light

VOCABULARY
2 Match, color, and say.
Children color the pictures.
UNIT 9
Practice: apartment, building, field, forest, mountain, river, street, traffic light
85

STORY
3 Draw a bear. Color and say.
Children draw here.
ZOO
Where do bears live?
They live in the country.
Children color the picture.
86
Practice: Where do [bears] live? [They] live in the [country].

STORY
4 Connect the dots. Color and say.
Children color the picture
UNIT 9
Practice: [Bears] live in the [city], too.
87

Workbook Pages

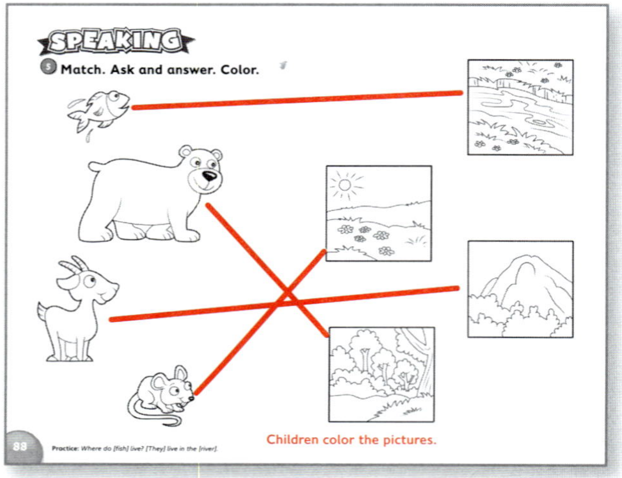

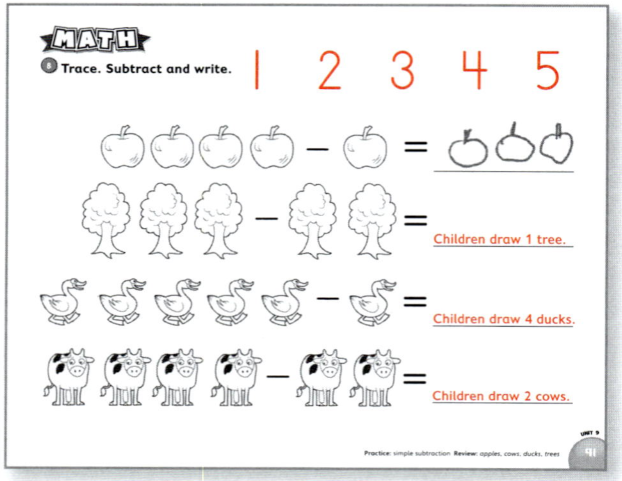

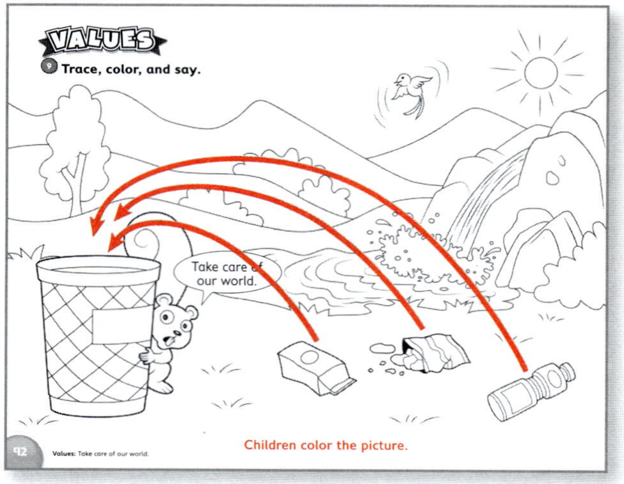

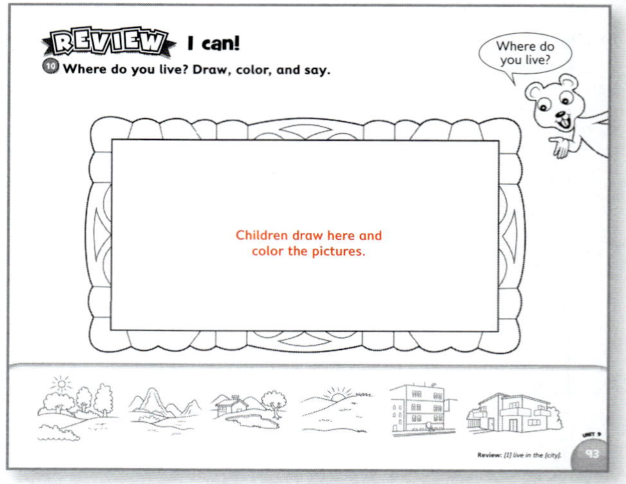

Letters Home: General Letter Home

Dear parents/guardians,

Welcome to the third level of *My Little Island*. We hope that your child will continue to enjoy learning English with this engaging and exciting program.

The program's carefully developed lessons offer a wide range of activities that will give your child a solid foundation for learning English. The focus on using and associating natural gestures and actions with vocabulary helps children bring meaning to the words they are learning.

In the third book of the program, your child will explore the island with two new characters—Lou and Sue—and will learn vocabulary and language structures related to these unit themes:

- ✓ At School
- ✓ Workers
- ✓ My Town
- ✓ Clothes
- ✓ Feelings
- ✓ Healthy Food
- ✓ The Zoo
- ✓ Places

At this level, children will be reviewing sound-symbol correspondences for consonant letters and sounds, will learn new ones, and will go on to learn vowel letters and short vowel sounds.

Three lessons for each thematic unit will help your child develop listening and speaking skills. You'll probably notice that your child enjoys engaging in conversation! You can help your child by talking about each unit's vocabulary and content. You can also listen to the program's CD-ROM and Songs and Chants CD with your child.

Your child learns a lot in the classroom, but support at home is essential to success. Here are few things you can do:

- ✓ talk with your child about what he/she is learning about in English class
- ✓ encourage your child to "teach" you new words, as well as songs and chants
- ✓ be enthusiastic about your child's achievements and progress
- ✓ be supportive of small steps as these will lead to bigger ones

We wish your child great success and a wonderful time learning English with *My Little Island*.

Sincerely,

____

*Note to teachers: Letters for units 1–9 can be found on the website: www.pearsonelt.com/mylittleisland.

Picture Card Index

1. classroom
2. computer room
3. music room
4. play
5. playground
6. read
7. sing
8. use the computer
9. artist
10. astronaut
11. dentist
12. doctor
13. firefighter
14. nurse
15. police officer
16. vet
17. bus
18. fire station
19. hospital
20. police station
21. post office
22. school
23. store
24. taxi
25. dress
26. jacket
27. pants
28. shirt
29. shoes
30. skirt
31. socks
32. sweater
33. excited
34. happy
35. hungry
36. mad
37. sad
38. scared
39. thirsty
40. tired
41. banana
42. carrot
43. fork
44. lettuce
45. mango
46. orange
47. plate
48. tomato
49. bat
50. bear
51. elephant
52. lion
53. monkey
54. penguin
55. sea lion
56. zebra
57. apartment
58. building
59. field
60. forest
61. mountain
62. river
63. street
64. traffic light

Video Scripts

Live-action videos appear on the program's CD-ROM and ActiveTeach. The narrated scripts for them follow.

Unit 2: At School

Narrator: Ann is in the school playground.
She's playing with a yellow ball.
She wants to play with a friend.
Who's this?
It's Ashley.
They say, "Hello.
How old are you?"
"I'm six," says Ann.
"I'm six, too," says Ashley.
They play with the ball.
They have fun.
Who's this?
It's Tom!
He wants to play, too.
Tom is hiding.
Oh no! The ball goes over the wall.
But here it is again.
Ann and Ashley look over the wall.
Who's there?
They look and look, but no one is there.
Ann throws the ball over the wall again.
Ann and Ashley look again.
Tom jumps up.
Hello, Tom!
They run around the playground.
They play with the ball.
Here is the teacher.
Tom has to go now.
Here is the teacher again.
"Hold my hands," she says.
Ann and Ashley have to go, too.
The ball is in the playground.
Play time is over.

Unit 3: Workers

Narrator: Here is the town.
It's very, VERY busy.
Maya is going to the dentist.
We're almost there, Maya.
They look at a very tall building.
Be careful! There are lots of cars.
What is the gardener doing?
There is a cat in the tree.
It's white.
It won't come down.
Here is the garbage man.
Come down, little cat.
The tree is too tall.
Here is a police officer.
The cat is sitting in the tree.
Here is a firefighter.
The cat is still sitting in the tree.
The firefighter climbs up the tree.
Oh no!
Here are a doctor and a nurse.
The cat is STILL sitting in the tree.
Here's a loud truck!
The cat jumps out of the tree.
The workers all go away.
Here comes the dentist.
How's your tooth, Maya?

Video Scripts

Unit 4: My Town

Narrator: Emma and Abby are at the amusement park with grandpa.
They go on the Ferris wheel.
Are you coming with us, Grandpa?
No! Grandpa wants to watch Emma and Abby.
They go up high in the sky.
Look! It's an airport!
There's a big plane.
There's a train station.
And a bus station.
There are some taxis.
One, two, three.
Emma and Abby can see lots of things.
Look! Mountains.
Can you see the beach?
Hey, my dad works at that store!
Look! There's grandpa!
He looks so small!
He has something in his hands.
What is it?
It's two little lollipops.
Now the lollipops look very big!
Yummy!
Thank you, Grandpa!

Unit 5: Clothes

Narrator: Charlie is reading his book.
Molly and Sean come in.
They want to play outside.
Get dressed, Charlie!
Charlie looks at his clothes.
He wants his T-shirt and his shorts.
Oh no! What are you wearing, Charlie?
You wear a T-shirt and shorts in the summer.
What are you going to wear now, Charlie?
Molly and Sean are still waiting.
Oh no! Charlie has a jacket, pants, boots, socks, gloves, a scarf, and a hat.
You wear them in winter, Charlie!
It's fall now.
Charlie puts his jacket, pants, boots, socks, gloves, scarf, and hat away again.
What can he wear?
Ah, Charlie knows what to wear.
Look at Charlie.
He's wearing Dad's jacket and hat.
They are too big.
That's silly, Charlie!
Charlie is ready now. Hooray!
They look outside.
Oh no! It's raining!
They take their jackets off.
Here is the toy box.
Let's play with some toys.

Unit 6: Feelings

Narrator: It's fall.
The children want to make acorn dolls.
They are excited.
The children are in the woods.
They're looking for acorns.
Look at the leaves.
What colors can you see?
Red, brown, yellow.
Look over there. Green!
Dan is looking for acorns.
Look! Kate has an acorn.
Sean is looking for acorns.
Look! He has an acorn, too.
The children take the acorns to the teacher.
Now, they have three acorns.
One, two, three.
Sean looks for another acorn.
Oh look! A chestnut.
Teacher is happy!
Two chestnuts.
But we need acorns.
Oh no! Sean falls into a hole.
Teacher is looking for acorns, too.
"But where's Sean?" she thinks.
Teacher and the children are scared.
Is Sean OK?
They look for Sean.
Look! Two more acorns.
And here's Sean!
Let's count all of the acorns.
One, two, three, four, five acorns.
Great!

Unit 7: Healthy Food

Narrator: It's rainy outside.
What can Lucy and Mike play?
Here's the toy box.
Mike has an idea.
Let's play "Restaurant."
Mike has a white shirt.
Lucy has a red and white apron.
There is a table and chairs.
Lucy puts a cup on the table.
Mike puts a plate, knife, fork, and spoon on the table.
The restaurant is ready.
Mom is going to the restaurant.
She wants to look nice.
Hurry up, Mom!
Lucy and Mike want to play.
Welcome to our restaurant!
"Thank you!" says Mom.
Sit here, please.
Lucy brings Mom the menu.
What do you want, Mom?
Lucy writes it down.
Here's some juice.
Here's a carrot.
Mike brings lots of yummy things to eat.
Eat your fruits and vegetables, Mom!
Mom likes the restaurant.
Lucy brings Mom the check.
Mom has a good idea.
Let's have desert! Yummy!

Video Scripts

Unit 8: The Zoo

Narrator: Adam, Emma, and Dad are at the zoo.
They are excited.
What's that?
It's a big elephant.
It's gray.
What sound do elephants make?
They trumpet like an elephant.
Here's a lion.
What sound do lions make?
Adam and Emma roar like a lion.
What's that?
It's a very tall giraffe.
It has a long neck.
Oh, look! Zebras!
What sound do zebras make?
That's funny!
What are they?
They're sea lions.
Shhh. They're all sleeping.
Here is a monkey.
The zookeeper can hear a monkey.
Oh no, zookeeper! He's not a monkey!
They all laugh.
The zoo is fun!

Unit 9: Places

Narrator: Dad, Mom, and Chris are going out today.
Hurry up, Dad!
Oh no! The car is broken.
What can they do now?
They can ride a bike.
No. The bike is no good.
They can go by bus.
They're too late!
They start to run.
They are in the city.
Grandma is waiting.
Stop! The ambulance is going to the hospital.
They cross the street.
Grandma is still waiting.
She is tired.
Stop! The traffic light is red.
Now it's green. Go!
Hurry up!
Grandma is waiting.
Run!
"Come on," says Dad.
Wait! Where's Chris?
Stop! Chris, where are you?
There he is!
He's talking to a firefighter.
Grandma is waiting, Chris.
"Let's go in the fire truck," says the firefighter.
They drive past tall buildings.
Hello, Grandma!
Grandma is happy.

Games

Throughout the lessons in *My Little Island*, there are many varied activities, including games. The following additional games are provided to use whenever they fit in with classroom needs. Let the games, language learning, and fun begin!

PICTURE CARD GAMES

Correct Order

Invite eight children to front of the classroom and give each a unit Picture Card. Then call out the names of the cards in a certain order and have children, in turn, arrange the cards on the chalk tray (or other suitable place) in the order you called them. Repeat with other groups of eight children.

Guess the Card

Cut out a small square hole in the middle of a sheet of paper about the same size as a Picture Card. Hold the paper in front of a Picture Card, allowing children to see only a little bit of the picture through the hole. Have children guess what it is. Repeat with other Picture Cards.

Echo

Model for children what an echo is with Sammy the Squirrel. Say a unit vocabulary word and then have Sammy repeat the word, gradually fading out. Then tell children you will say a word and they will be your echo. Show them a Picture Card and say the word. Cue children to echo it by repeating it several times, becoming quieter and quieter. Vary the game by having volunteers choose a Picture Card and saying the word for the class to echo.

Collect the Cards

Hold up Picture Cards that children know. Ask for a show of hands for children to identify a card by naming the item. Let the first child to correctly identify the card keep it. Announce the winner as the child who has the most cards at the end.

Memory

Tape six to eight Picture Cards in a row on the board. Encourage children to memorize the cards. Then place sheets of paper the same size as the cards over them and invite children to name the items. For a more challenging game, ask children to name the items in the order they appeared on the board. Remove the sheets of paper to confirm.

Snap!

Write a word on the board or say one from a unit's Picture Cards. Show the Picture Card for the word along with several others, one by one. Have children call out: *Snap!* when they see the Picture Card you named. Continue with other unit Picture Cards.

Who's the Fastest?

Arrange the class in two teams and have them line up in two rows, facing the board. Put a group of familiar Picture Cards on the board. Call out the name of one Picture Card and have the first child in each line race to touch the right card. Give a point to the fastest child's team. Continue in this way until all cards are used.

Name It

Arrange the class in two teams and have them line up in two rows. Have the first child in each row come up to the front and have all of them turn their backs to you. Hold up a Picture Card, and count to three and say: *Turn around*. Give a point to the team of the first child to turn around and correctly name the card. Continue with the rest of the cards.

Pass the Picture Cards

Choose a group of eight Picture Cards and pass them facedown around the room. Cue children to guess who has the card when you say: *Stop* and ask: *Who has the [taxi] card?* Give a point to the child who correctly guesses which child has the *[taxi]* card. Continue with the rest of the cards.

Games

"Basket" Ball

Arrange the class in two teams. Show a child from one team a Picture Card. If he/she can correctly identify the card, allow that child to "shoot" a small, safe ball or other object at a target (a wastebasket or small box). If the "ball" goes into it, award the child two points. If the "ball" just hits the target without going in, give one point. Continue until each child has played.

Countdown

Arrange the class in small groups. Mix Picture Cards from different units together and divide them into piles, one for each group. Have groups arrange the cards into categories (feelings, food, rooms at school). Announce the first group to finish arranging the cards in correct categories as the winner.

What's Missing?

Place several Picture Cards facing upwards on the floor or on a large table. Allow children a few minutes to study them. Tell children to close their eyes while you remove a Picture Card. Have children try to identify the missing card. Continue with other cards.

*X*s and *O*s

Arrange the class in two teams: one is *X* and one is *O*. Draw a large grid on the board with nine spaces. Put one Picture Card facing the board (so children can't see the picture) in each space. Have a child from each team, in turn, turn one over and identify it. If correct, remove the card and write an *X* or an *O* for the team. The first team to get three in a row wins. Repeat and continue until all children have had a turn.

Picture Card Fun

Show a unit's Picture Cards (such as the ones for clothes) and have children each draw a simple picture of one item. As they draw, write the words on small slips of paper and put them into a bag. Ask children to all stand up. Pull out the slips of paper and read the words, one at a time. Have children who drew that word sit down. Continue until all children are seated.

At the Zoo

Call a child to the front of the class and secretly show him/her a Picture Card of an animal (a lion). Blindfold the child. Give out several Picture Cards of animals, including the lion, to children around the room. Have children make the sound associated with the animal on their Picture Card. Have the child remove the blindfold and walk around room and listen to find the animal he/she was shown (*roar* for a lion). Continue the game until each child has had a turn. Be prepared for lots of noise!

Who Has It?

Invite several children to the board and give each one a different Picture Card. Have children show the class their cards. Ask: *Who has the [fire station]?* Have children answer: *[Kim] has the fire station*—correctly identifying the child with the Picture Card of the fire station. Continue until all children have had a turn.

Sponge Toss

Place the unit or other group of Picture Cards facedown on the floor. Have children take turns tossing a sponge or other soft object and identifying the card it lands on by turning it over and naming it.

Easy or Difficult

Divide twenty Picture Cards into two stacks: an easy stack (cards from earlier units that have been reviewed and recycled) and a difficult stack (cards from more recent units). Divide the class into two teams. Award five points for each correctly named Picture Card from the difficult stack and one point for each correctly named one from the easy stack.

Picture-Card Mime

Invite a child to the front of the class. Show him/her a Picture Card that can be acted out (for example, feelings, animals, actions at school) while hiding it from the rest of the class. Have the child pantomime the word. Have the child who correctly guesses the word pantomime the next card, and so on.

Spin the Spinner

Arrange the class in several teams and have a game spinner available. Put the Picture Cards on the board and number them from 1-5. Call out a word and have a designated team say the corresponding number. If it's correct, have that team spin the spinner and award that team that number of points. Continue with the other teams in turn.

Where Is It?

Display familiar Picture Cards in different places around the classroom. Call out the name of one and have children find it and point to it. Or say a sentence with the word *I have a [carrot]* and have children point to or retrieve the card with a picture of a [carrot]. Continue with the rest of the cards.

Hit the Card

Display all of the Picture Cards of one vocabulary category on the board. Have two children come up to the board and stand a few yards away. Call out a word. Announce the winner as the first child to run to the board and "hit" the correct Picture Card. Play the game in teams and award points for each correct "hit."

✓ or ✗

Gather Picture Cards that begin with initial sounds children know. Then write a checkmark (✓) and an ✗ on the board for children. Hand out two large sheets of white paper to each child. Tell children to draw an ✗ on one card and a checkmark (✓) on the other. Tell children you will show them a Picture Card and then say a beginning sound. If the Picture Card begins with the sound, they should hold up the checkmark card. If it doesn't, they should hold up the ✗ card. Make intentional mistakes. Stick the card on the board when you and the children make a match and say: *Yes, [socks] starts with [/s/].*

Bluff

Invite several children to the board and have them stand in a row. Give them each a Picture Card and tell them not to let the class know which it is. Cue the first child in the row to say a word that might or might not correspond with the Picture Card he/she is holding. Have the class guess whether or not the child is bluffing. Have children say: *Bluff* if they think the child is bluffing. Have the class play the game in teams and award points when teams guess correctly.

Picture Card Race

Play the game with three or more teams. Give each child a number between 1 and 5. Display a group of Picture Cards on the board. Say: *Number 2. [mountain].* Cue all children with the number 2 to race to the board and touch the [mountain] Picture Card. Award the first child to touch the card a point for his/her team.

Same Sounds

Choose a beginning consonant sound that children know. Display a Picture Card of a word that begins with that sound (*dentist* for /d/). Now say a group of familiar words, one of which has that sound: *doctor, post office, taxi, bus, school.* Have children say the word with the same sound as dentist (doctor). Continue with other words and initial sounds that children know.

Games

TPR AND OTHER KINESTHETIC GAMES

Number Groups

Play some lively music and ask children to perform a specific action (jump, march, flap arms) around the room to the music. Stop the music and call out a number from 2–5. Cue children to quickly get together in groups of that number. Have any children leftover sit out until the next round.

Guess the Object

Put a familiar object into a bag for children to guess by feeling it and not looking at it. Continue with other objects until each child has had a turn.

Teacher Says

Give children instructions but tell them to follow them only if you say "Teacher says" first. Give this example: if you say *Hold up three fingers*, children should do nothing but if you say *Teacher says hold up three fingers*, children should hold up three fingers. Explain to children that if they do an action when they shouldn't they are "out." Play a few times until children get the idea. To make the game more interesting, say the instructions faster or have more proficient children take turns giving the instructions.

Pass the Ball

Have children sit in a circle. Make a paper ball out of tissue paper. Choose a category and have children pass the ball around. Explain that children must say a word from that category when they get the ball and leave the circle if they can't. Alternatively, play music while children pass the ball and say words. Then stop the music and have the child who is holding the ball leave the game.

Drawing Game

Have children take turns drawing pictures on the board of target vocabulary. Tell them to draw slowly, line by line. Have the class try to guess what a child is drawing before he/she finishes the picture. Have the first child to guess draw the next picture.

Grab It

Have children sit in a circle with their hands behind their backs. Place some classroom objects (no scissors) or Picture Cards in the middle of the circle. Call out an object and have children race to find and touch it. Arrange children in teams and award points to winners.

TEAM GAMES

Drawing Race

Arrange the class in two teams and invite a child from each team to the front of the class. Whisper a vocabulary word to each and have them draw a picture of it. Explain that the first team to correctly identify the picture wins a point.

Phonics Race

Divide the class into several groups. Copy familiar Picture Cards and provide each group with a set. Call out a consonant sound that children know. For a given amount of time, have children put into a pile Picture Cards that begin with that sound. Award groups one point for each correct word.

Chair Race

Arrange the class in two teams. Have each team line up behind a chair with another one facing it across the room, a few yards away. Have one child from each team sit in the chair at the front of their team's line. Call out an action (jump). Cue children on each team to jump across to the other chair. Explain that the first child to reach his/her team's chair after doing the right action should sit in it. Award a point to that team. Continue with other actions.

Board Game

Draw a large race track on the board with "Start" and "Finish" labeled. Arrange the class in two teams. Use small colored circles as markers for each team (children on one team have red markers and children on the other have blue). Show Picture Cards, other pictures, or real objects children know and ask: *What's this?* Alternatively, show classroom objects in different numbers and ask: *How many?* Cue children to move ahead one space if they guess correctly. Announce the winner (the team to reach the finish first).

Stop!

Arrange the class in two teams. Put sets of familiar Picture Cards into a large bag along with a few others on which you have taped a sheet of paper with a *Stop* sign drawn on it. Have children reach in and take a card without looking and identify it. Explain that if he/she correctly says the word, his/her team wins a point but that if he/she draws a card with a *Stop* sign, the team loses all of its points.

Spinner Game

Arrange the class in two teams. Tell a child from each team to draw an item you name from the target vocabulary. Explain that if the item is the one you named, he/she spins the spinner and wins that number of points for his/her team. Continue until each child has had a turn.

Whoops!

Arrange the class in two teams. Put familiar Picture Cards into a large bag. Tape a sheet of paper onto several other cards with the word *Whoops!* written on each (write the word on the board). Add the cards to the bag. Have children from each team, one at a time, come up to the front of the class and take a card from the bag. Tell them to identify the picture by saying the word. Explain that if they correctly identify the picture, they keep the card and receive one point for their team and that if they incorrectly identify the picture, that you will keep the card. Tell them that if they take a card with the word *Whoops!* on it, they sit down and don't receive any points. Or to add some suspense, take away all points when a *Whoops!* card is drawn.

Name the Shape

Cut out several familiar shapes from colored paper (colors children know). Stick or carefully pin a shape to the back of a child's shirt without letting the child see which one. Have the child turn around to show the class the shape and color. Then have the child try to guess which shape and color it is. Elicit *a blue star? a red rectangle?* For more proficient classes, suggest that, when the child guesses the right shape but the wrong color, the class call out: *Shape!* Cue children to do the same for the correct color but incorrect shape by calling out: *Color!* Continue with the other shapes and other children until everyone has had a turn.

Number Spin

Arrange the class in teams and have a number spinner available. Invite a child from each team to the front of the classroom. Put several Picture Cards on the board. Ask him/her to choose one of the Picture Cards on the board. Then spin the spinner and have the child say the word that number of times. Explain that if the child does this correctly, he/she wins that number of points for his/her team.

Yes or No?

Bring in several toys, classroom objects, or stuffed or toy animals in different colors and sizes or use Picture Cards of them. Put them on a table where the class can see them. Explain that you will think of one of the items and the children must guess which one you are thinking of but you can only answer "Yes" or "No" to their guesses. For example, children might ask: *Is it big? Is it red? Is it a monkey?*

Graphic Organizers: T-Chart

Use this graphic organizer to help children list and relate items.

Graphic Organizers: Word Web

Use this graphic organizer to help children group items.

Graphic Organizers: Venn Diagram

Use this graphic organizer to help children compare items.

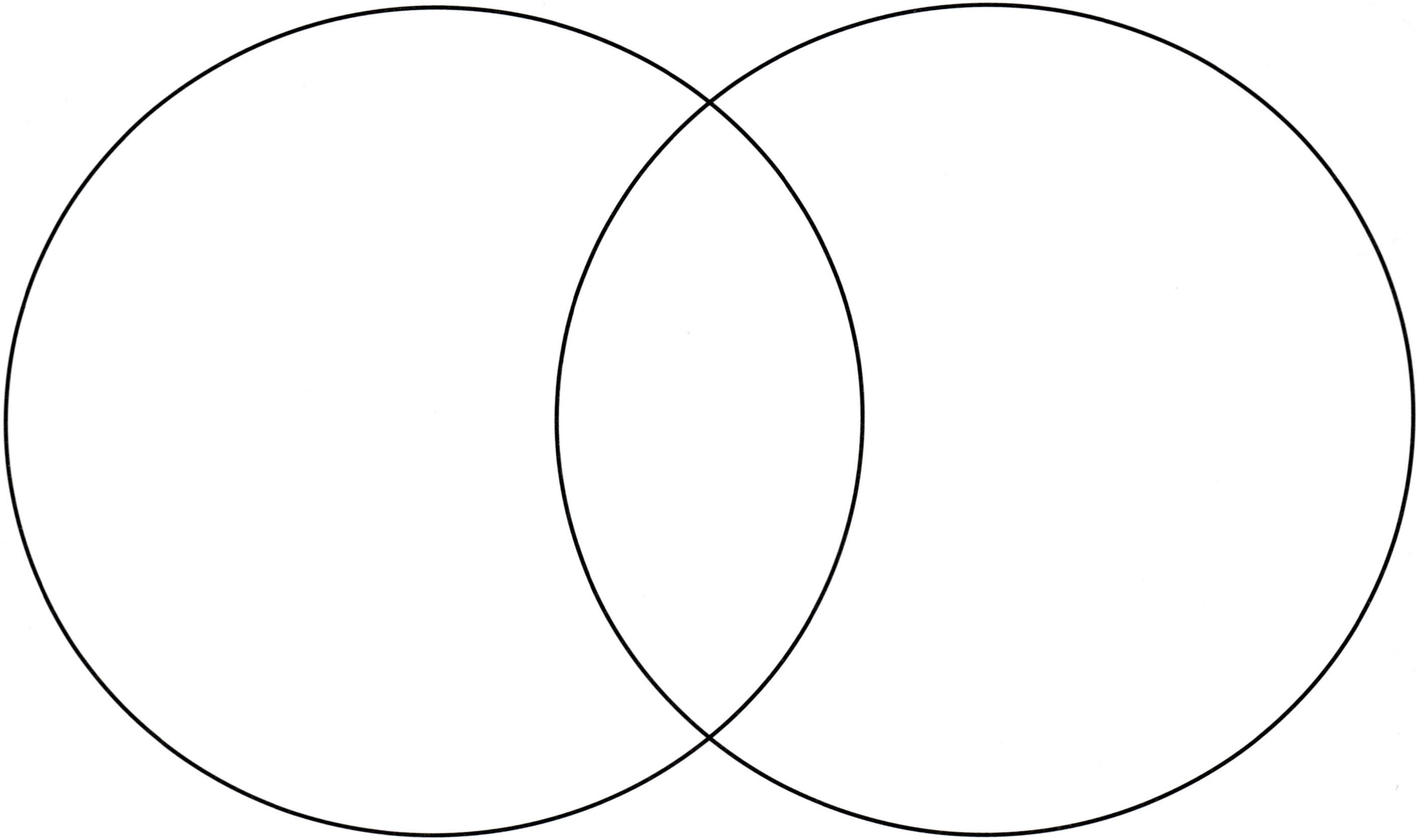